# FORCED LABOR

# FORCED
# LABOR

## Coercion and Exploitation in the Private Economy

EDITED BY
### Beate Andrees
### Patrick Belser

LYNNE RIENNER PUBLISHERS

Published in the United States of America in 2009 by
Lynne Rienner Publishers, Inc.
1800 30th Street, Boulder, Colorado 80301
www.rienner.com
ISBN 978-1-58826-664-4 (hardcover : alk. paper)
ISBN 978-1-58826-689-7 (pbk. : alk. paper)

and in the United Kingdom by
Lynne Rienner Publishers, Inc.
3 Henrietta Street, Covent Garden, London WC2E 8LU

Paperback edition published in Switzerland in 2009 by the
International Labour Office
CH-1211 Geneva-22, Switzerland
www.ilo.org/publns
ISBN 978-92-2-120164-9 (ILO paperback : alk. paper)

**Library of Congress Cataloging-in-Publication Data**
Forced labor : coercion and exploitation in the private economy /
    Beate Andrees and Patrick Belser, editors.
    Includes bibliographical references and index.
    1. Forced labor.  2. Forced labor—Government policy.  3. Slave labor.
4. Human trafficking.  5. Crimes against humanity.  I. Andrees, Beate.
II. Belser, Patrick.
        HD4871.F67 2009
        331.11'73—dc22

                                                    2009009737


**British Cataloguing in Publication Data**
A Cataloguing in Publication record for this book
is available from the British Library.

Printed and bound in the United States of America

∞  The paper used in this publication meets the requirements
    of the American National Standard for Permanence of
    Paper for Printed Library Materials Z39.48-1992.

    5  4  3  2  1

# Contents

*Foreword,* Roger Plant                                                    vii

*Acknowledgments*                                                           xv

Introduction, *Patrick Belser and Beate Andrees*                            1

1   "Slave Labor" in Brazil, *Leonardo Sakamoto*                           15

2   Debt Bondage and Ethnic Discrimination in Latin America,
    *Eduardo Bedoya, Alvaro Bedoya, and Patrick Belser*                    35

3   Bonded Labor in Pakistan, *Ali Khan*                                   51

4   The Legacy of Slavery in Niger, *Ali R. Sékou and
    Saidou Abdoulkarimou*                                                  71

5   Trafficking for Forced Labor in Europe, *Beate Andrees*               89

6   Strengthening Labor Market Governance Against Forced Labor,
    *Beate Andrees and Patrick Belser*                                    109

7   Criminalizing Human Trafficking and Protecting the Victims,
    *Rohit Malpani*                                                       129

8   Empowering Communities: Lessons from Tamil Nadu, India,
    *Isabelle Guérin, Caroline O'Reilly, Marc Roesch,
    Maria Sathya, and G. Venkatasubramanian*                              151

9    Improving Forced Labor Statistics, *Patrick Belser and
     Michaelle de Cock*                                        173

*References*                                                   195
*The Contributors*                                            207
*Index*                                                       211
*About the Book*                                               229

# Foreword

*Roger Plant*

In early 2000, I was asked by the International Labour Organization (ILO) to draft a global report on modern forced labor and the means to tackle it. It seemed like a millennial challenge, but coming at the right time. In 1998 the ILO had adopted its Declaration on Fundamental Principles and Rights at Work, calling on all its member states to respect and promote core labor standards relating to freedom of association and collective bargaining, the elimination of forced and child labor, and the elimination of discrimination in respect to employment and occupation. Also at that time, drafters were putting the final touches to a new United Convention Against Transnational Organized Crime, including a protocol on human trafficking for both sexual and labor exploitation, finally adopted in December 2000 in Palermo.

The ILO's first global report on forced labor, *Stopping Forced Labour,* was published in 2001. It examined the multiple forms of forced labor in the world today, including those that result from human trafficking. Lamenting that the subject was insufficiently on the radar screens of policymakers worldwide, it called for a specific research program to identify the local, social, cultural, and economic factors that give rise to or sustain forced labor. It also proposed a specific ILO program to ensure a holistic approach to eliminating this terrible practice.

The suggestion was heeded by the Governing Body of the ILO later that year, and a Special Action Programme to Combat Forced Labour (SAP-FL) was created in early 2002. From the outset it attached importance to improving the knowledge base on forced labor in practice, through both research on thematic concerns and country surveys as a base for awareness-raising activities and a policy dialogue on the means to combat it. Moreover, sensing that forced labor and trafficking affected in some way almost every country of the world, rather than being confined to pockets in a few developing countries, we aimed to give significant coverage also to the industrialized countries. This was a political as well as technical decision, mandated by the Governing Body. Forced labor is an incredibly sensitive issue, even more so than child labor, and developing countries were hardly likely to cooperate with a systematic program of research and surveys if they felt singled out, perhaps even facing diplomatic and trade reprisals if knowledge of forced labor in practice were to come out in the public domain.

The results of a first round of studies, both quantitative and qualitative, were summarized in a second global report, *A Global Alliance Against Forced Labour*, published in 2005. This appears to have had immense impact around the world, not least by doing what no other international organization had previously attempted, putting global and regional figures on the incidence of forced labor. The global estimate of 12.3 million persons in forced labor at any one time is a sharp reminder that there are more women and men in forced labor today than the total number of Africans transported during the height of the transatlantic slave trade. A further figure, of almost US$32 billion of total illicit profits raised from trafficking in forced labor, also helped galvanize public opinion as to the immensity of the problem and the urgency of tackling it. The report also showed that 80 percent of all forced labor today is in the private economy, mainly in the rural and informal sectors in developing countries, but also penetrating the supply chain of major companies in the developing and industrialized world alike.

Together with the figures, the qualitative studies improved understanding of the main forms of forced labor and their causes. The first report contained a broad typology of different forms and manifestations of forced labor today, such as slavery and abductions, compulsory participation in public works, forced labor in agriculture and remote rural areas, domestic workers in forced labor situations, bonded labor in South Asia, forced labor exacted by the military, prison-linked forced labor, and forced labor related to trafficking. The second report, assisted by the global and regional estimates, chose to break all this down into the three main categories of forced labor: forced labor imposed by the state for economic, political, or other purposes; forced labor linked to poverty and discrimination; and the forced labor that arises from trafficking and unprotected migration across the world, often linked to globalization. We accepted that such categorizations can only be approximate, that there can be an overlap between the last two categories, and that the more "traditional" forms of forced labor are transmuting into new ones. The fundamental message was a vitally important one, that there is systematic evidence that forced labor exists in all types of economies, with some 360,000 persons affected in the major industrial countries.

The chapters in this book contain original research, either by country or by theme. The country-based chapters present a number of case studies using primary research underpinned by solid research methodologies. These are all innovative, given that the largely hidden nature of modern forced labor does not lend itself to conventional research and survey techniques. The case studies covering African, Asian, European, and Latin American countries provide exemplary models of action-oriented research, designed to improve the law and policy framework.

The later chapters of the book draw on both commissioned research and the work of our core SAP-FL program, addressing the policy response and the means by which forced labor can be prevented, punished, and eliminated. The policy responses discussed in the book include the enforcement of appropriate regulations to govern labor markets, a combined emphasis on the criminalization of human trafficking and the protection of victims, the empowerment of local communities, and also statistical tools to identify the problem and monitor the situation. One major challenge identified in different ways in several chapters is indeed the problem of identifying persons in forced labor. With few exceptions, forced labor is rarely recognized by labor inspection services or the police, recorded in official databases, or prosecuted. In the case of cross-border trafficking, victims are, despite recent policies designed to afford them more support, as often deported to their countries of origin as protected. It is therefore urgent that law enforcement agencies worldwide improve their ability to recognize forced labor situations and take appropriate action.

This leads on to the critically important questions of the definition of forced labor (and related abuses including slavery and slavery-like practices, bonded labor, involuntary servitude, debt bondage, and human trafficking) and of suitable indicators to identify these abuses in practice. *The Economist* observed (August 14, 2008) that "coercing hapless human beings into sex or servitude is obviously evil, but defining the problem (let alone solving it) is very hard." Reasons for this can include ambiguities over concepts of unfree labor and coercion and some differences of opinion as to whether or not the offense of trafficking, for labor or sexual exploitation, actually requires the existence of coercion rather than extremely poor conditions of work.

The ILO definition of forced labor is contained in its first standard-setting instrument on the subject, the Forced Labour Convention, No. 29, adopted in 1930. Paraphrased, men and women are in a forced labor situation when they enter work or service against their free choice and cannot leave it without punishment or the threat of punishment ("menace of a penalty"). The same convention specifies that forced labor is a serious criminal offense and that adequate penalties should be laid down by national law to treat it as such. A further convention on the abolition of forced labor, No. 105, was adopted in 1957 at the height of the Cold War period. It calls for the immediate abolition of forced labor for a range of political, ideological, and other purposes. Thus while specifically addressing forced labor imposed by the state, and calling for urgent measures against it, it in no way changes the earlier definition of what constitutes forced labor.

The ILO has supervisory mechanisms, the main one being an independent Committee of Experts, to monitor the application of these conventions.

On forced labor, its jurisprudence over some 80 years provides indications of what practices are considered to be in breach of the ILO instruments. In 2007 this committee produced a general survey on the eradication of forced labor, the first since 1979, which dwelled inter alia on present-day problems in the private economy, including slavery and slavery-like practices, trafficking in persons for the purpose of exploitation, privatization of prisons and prison labor, and forced overtime. It was generally confirmed that abusive practices such as slavery and human trafficking fall within the scope of the ILO's forced labor conventions.

This is important from a legal standpoint, clarifying the scope of forced labor under international law. In the meantime, governments and other actors, including the business community and the trade union movement, have been coming to the ILO and its SAP-FL program for practical support and guidance. How can they identify a forced labor situation? What is a suitable mechanism to coordinate the policy response? How can labor market actors, particularly labor inspectorates, complement the activities of other law enforcement, including the police? What are effective means of rehabilitation? How can business keep forced labor out of its supply chains? How can trade unions get their own members more actively involved on behalf of forced laborers, usually reaching out beyond their normal constituents?

Definitions and indicators of human trafficking remain the subject of often heated debates. What makes up the process or offense of human trafficking, for either sexual or other forms of economic exploitation? Who can be the victims, and for what purpose? Many interest groups, and also some national law and policy instruments, still consider that the offense of *trafficking* refers only to the sexual exploitation of women and children. Yet there has now been a clear shift of thinking, leading to a general acceptance that trafficking is an abusive process, through which a range of exploiting agents abuse the vulnerability of individuals in order to make unfair profits at their expense. In international law, the most widely accepted definition of human trafficking is that in the Palermo Trafficking Protocol to the United Nations Convention Against Transnational Organized Crime, adopted in 2000 and followed since then by other international instruments. Although particularly concerned with the plight of women and children, this protocol indicates that trafficking is an abusive process that can also affect men and that its purpose is *exploitation,* which includes as a minimum "the exploitation of the prostitution of others or other forms of sexual exploitation, forced labour or services, slavery or practices similar to slavery, servitude or the removal of organs."

In 2003, a report by the European Union identified forced labor as the "crucial element" of a trafficking situation, as it is the presence of coercion that makes it possible to separate it from smuggling. Otherwise put, smugglers, however much they charge, can be seen as providing a service for the persons they move clandestinely across borders. Traffickers by contrast deliberately set out to ex-

ploit their victims. And the employers at the end of the chain also exploit the
trafficked persons in a very deliberate way.

There has still been much debate since then as to the linkages between
forced labor and trafficking. As the Palermo Protocol has entered into force in
more and more countries, they have had to amend their criminal laws to recognize the offenses of trafficking for labor as well as sexual exploitation. They
have also needed benchmarks and indicators to guide their response: how they
can identify cases of labor trafficking in practice, how they can prosecute them
and what kind of penalties should be provided, as well as what kind of compensation should be provided for the wrongs suffered and by whom. One issue
of contention is whether the offense of trafficking requires movement, either
within or across borders. A more serious one, for law enforcement purposes,
is whether or not it requires coercion in the sense of the ILO's conventions on
forced labor.

In conducting its 2005 global estimate on forced labor, in which trafficking is seen to account for about one-fifth of all forced labor worldwide, the
ILO took the position that the offense of trafficking has the three elements of
deceptive or coercive recruitment, movement, and forced labor exploitation at
the place of destination. Others have taken a different stance, arguing that
movement is not a necessary criterion for identifying a trafficked person. In
the words of the US government's 2007 *Trafficking in Persons Report,* "to define trafficking in persons on the basis of movement is to create an artificial
and unfounded distinction between victims who are exploited without being
moved and those who are moved prior to and during their exploitation." These
can be largely semantic and perhaps trivial concerns. What matters is that there
be strong laws against coercive exploitation, vigorously enforced, covering all
human beings including nationals and migrant workers. It does not make much
difference whether the letter of these laws is against forced labor or trafficking, as long as they capture the elements of coercion and as long as they can
be applied against contemporary manifestations of forced labor.

The second concern is a more complex one. The fight against forced labor
is only one part—and in statistical terms quite a small part—of the fight against
exploitative labor practices in today's global economy. At the bottom end of
the labor market, vulnerable workers, including migrants, can work for excessively long hours in difficult and dangerous circumstances for scarce remuneration, and the media often refers to such practices as modern slavery or slave
labor. But it is not unfree labor, in that extraeconomic forms of coercion are
applied. There has been growing concern at what is sometimes dubbed "consensual exploitation," through which workers without any viable alternative
can subject themselves through rational choice to conditions that most people
used to the enjoyment of labor standards and rights would consider inhumane.
They can do this, sometimes incurring huge debts to recruiting agents, in the
hope that they can work off these debts through laboring twice a normal work-

day or more, often seven days a week, and eventually making the savings or re-mittances to which they aspire.

Certain countries have in their antitrafficking laws or elsewhere in their criminal codes the legal concept of working conditions "incompatible with human dignity." Others are now grappling with the concept of exploitation, for which there is almost no precedent in international law, seeking to identify which kind or degree of abusive practice should be pursued through criminal courts and what practices might better be addressed through labor justice and administration. Other countries have laws against forced labor, including within its scope such criteria as late payment of wages that—while perhaps a useful indicator of forced labor—is not based specifically on coercion. India's Supreme Court in the early 1980s passed a judgment presuming that all persons not paid the legal minimum wage were in forced labor conditions and placing the onus on their employers to prove that this was not the case.

Some analysts now argue that there is a continuum from the most flagrant forms of coercive exploitation, through to the "lesser" forms of abuse, and up to what the ILO has termed the "decent work" conditions to which all workers would naturally aspire. This is one of the challenges that this book tries to address, by examining the policy response to different kinds of coercive situations, arguably displaying different degrees of gravity. When these are systemic patterns of labor market abuse, affecting millions of workers worldwide, what is a suitable blend of criminal law enforcement, awareness-raising and prevention, protection of workers against abuse, and also pressing for the law and policy reforms needed to address the root causes?

Most forced labor is not officially identified, prosecuted, or punished. In a very small number of countries, there has been a slow but steady rise in efforts to prosecute labor trafficking over the past few years. In its 2007 *Trafficking in Persons Report,* the US government indicated for the first time the number of total prosecutions and convictions that relate to labor trafficking (490 prosecutions and 326 convictions, out of a total of 5,682 prosecutions and 3,427 convictions for all cases of trafficking).

Criminal prosecutions are certainly necessary in the most extreme cases, an example being a scandalous incident of July 2006, involving cooperation between the Italian and Polish police in response to extensive allegations of slavery-like practices against Polish and other migrant workers in farms of southern Italy. But the main objective of any policy response should be to assist those who have suffered from labor trafficking, not only through medical and social care where necessary, but in particular to help them to secure compensation for lost earnings. If the single motive of labor traffickers has been to make large and unfair profits at the expense of the vulnerable, then the response should be self-evident. Confiscate the profits and assets of the traffickers, perhaps also imposing prison terms in severe cases. And make sure that the trafficked persons are duly compensated for loss of earnings, receiving at least the equivalent of a minimum wage payment for all the hours they have worked.

In most cases, the primary concern of workers is the protection of their wages. In 2007 the Supreme Court of Greece passed an important judgment, that irregular migrants have a right to receive unpaid wages from unscrupulous employers, who also have to pay a fine. As more and more countries crack down on illegal employment, it is important that the workers themselves not suffer from these measures. They are only responding to demand, usually doing the work rejected by the nationals of the countries in which they work.

The ILO is a tripartite organization of governments, workers, and employers. On complex issues such as modern forced labor and trafficking, we believe strongly in dialogue among the social partners. Important issues are the licensing or registration of recruitment agencies, controls over fee charging in order to avoid debt bondage situations, and also monitoring of their activities. An important convention was adopted in 1997 on private employment agencies, establishing the principle that employment agencies shall not charge any fees or costs to workers, save in exceptional circumstances after the government has consulted with employers' and workers' organizations. The convention also calls for safeguards against the abuse of migrant workers and for prohibition of the agencies that engage in fraudulent practices and abuse.

Our recent third global report on forced labor has served to indicate why modern forced labor must be seen as a labor market concern, rather than one of criminal justice alone. This is not to downplay the gravity of the forced labor offense, because criminal and labor justice must complement and reinforce each other. Rather, it is to show that the policy response, including law enforcement and prevention, must address the systemic and underlying problems in the global economy, rather than focusing only on a small number of high-profile cases. Since our second global report in 2005, which brought the issues into the open, the ILO and its program on forced labor have increasingly concentrated on developing the training and guidance tools needed by different actors, so they can all play their part in fighting forced labor today. Some have been prepared for labor inspectors, others for legislators, yet others for judges and prosecutors. A handbook was launched in 2008 for business actors, showing how companies with the support of employers' organizations can address forced labor in their own supply chains and business operations. Headway has also been made with trade unions, supporting international efforts to promote a workers' alliance against forced labor and trafficking.

None of this could have been done without the thematic and country research that identifies the basic facts and causes of forced labor today. This book provides the opportunity to share the findings of our earlier research with a broad audience and also to highlight some of the major policy concerns that are now engaging attention. We hope that it will contribute to and enhance the knowledge base on a human rights concern of immense global importance, on which better knowledge and understanding will be a prerequisite for more effective action.

# Acknowledgments

This book is dedicated to the memory of the three labor inspectors and their driver who were murdered in Unaí (MG), Brazil, on January 28, 2004, while investigating cases of slave labor: Erastótenes de Almeida Gonçalves, Nelson José da Silva, João Batista Soares Lages, and Aílton Pereira de Oliveira.

\* \* \*

We would like to thank Charlotte Beauchamp, Roger Plant, and Zafar Shaheed for their support, as well as Coralie Thompson for her excellent and very generous assistance.

—*The Editors*

# Introduction

## Patrick Belser and
## Beate Andrees

Two centuries after the abolition of the transatlantic slave trade, at least 12.3 million people continue to work under coercion in the underground and illegal economy (ILO 2005a). These workers are violated in their dignity and in their fundamental labor rights. Most of them are forced to work in abusive conditions and subjected to serious health and safety hazards, with little or no pay. When recruited, they are deceived about the nature of their jobs, about the wages they can earn, and sometimes also about the destination of their employment. Not part of a trade union, they have little bargaining power and no voice.

The purpose of this book is to present an overview of the contemporary manifestations of forced labor and to improve our understanding of why it survives in the twenty-first century and how it can be eliminated. The book focuses on forced labor in the private economy, which now represents an estimated 80 percent of all forced labor. More precisely, the book looks at the private underground economy, which is defined by statisticians as economic activities that are concealed from public authorities to avoid complying with regulations (OECD, IMF, ILO, and CIS STAT 2002).

Consequently, this book does not cover forced labor imposed by public authorities, which has become less relevant today in numerical terms. Even though prison or convict labor used to be a prominent example of unfree labor systems in the past, it has become less of a concern today. Of course, prison labor outside the orbit of public supervision and for private profit remains a sensitive issue and merits substantive research that this book does not cover. The same is true of some forms of state-imposed forced labor that are not covered, such as the use of compulsory labor by the military in Myanmar (see Bollé 1998).

## Forced Labor as a Labor Market Issue

Forced labor in the private underground economy can be looked at from various perspectives. First and foremost, forced labor involves the loss of a person's freedom and represents a violation of human rights. The Universal Declaration of Human Rights, proclaimed by the General Assembly of the United Nations in 1948, establishes that "all human beings are born free" (Article 1) and that "no one shall be held in slavery or servitude" (Article 4). This principle is also established in the International Covenant on Civil and Political Rights adopted at the United Nations in 1966.

Unfortunately, coerced labor continues to exist, usually in violation of the law. Hence, the book addresses the issue of law enforcement and seeks to understand forced labor through the sociology and economics of crime. It is worth remembering that according to Cohen and Felson (1979), crime can be seen as the result of three main factors: a suitable target, a motivated offender, and the lack of a capable guardian. These factors can relatively easily be linked to the specific problem of forced labor.

A supply of vulnerable workers provides the "suitable target." It is possible to distinguish at least two types of forced labor in the private economy: first, the forced and bonded labor related to poverty and discrimination toward minority groups; second, the global problem of transnational human trafficking, which features migrant workers coerced into labor exploitation or mainly young women deceived into forced prostitution. Both types of forced labor have in common the fact that they involve particularly vulnerable workers. In the case of bonded labor, vulnerability is often linked to poverty and the discriminated status of specific social groups, such as people from lower castes in South Asia or people of slave descent in West Africa. In the case of human trafficking, key factors of vulnerability include poverty, migration status, and discrimination on the basis of gender or ethnicity. For sex trafficking, young unemployed women are often the most vulnerable to be trafficked across borders (see, for example, Andrees 2008; Danailova-Trainor and Belser 2006).

Unscrupulous employers are the "motivated offenders." Profits are the main motivating factor in situations of forced labor. In practice, most forced labor occurs in low-technology, labor-intensive activities or industries such as domestic work, agriculture, construction, or prostitution. There is an economic rationale to this. First, low-skilled activities often place more emphasis on work intensity than on the quality of work, which typically requires more educated and less exploitable workers. Second, it is in the labor-intensive sectors that savings on labor costs have a relatively higher impact on production costs and on profits (since a given reduction in labor costs tends to increase profits in proportion to the ratio of costs to profits). In general, the larger the ratio of total labor costs to profits, the bigger the growth in profit that results from reduced labor costs. As a result, employers in labor-intensive sectors may be more tempted to exploit workers.

Weak state capacity contributes to the absence of a "capable guardian." Better implementation of labor standards has been a major theme of publications by the International Labour Organization (ILO). The weak capacity of the state to enact and to enforce laws—and the resulting culture of impunity—has been repeatedly identified as the main cause of forced labor, including, for example, the case of so-called slave labor in the Brazilian Amazon provinces of Matto Grosso and Pará. Weak law enforcement has also consistently been identified as a major determinant of human trafficking. In general, exploitative practices appear to thrive mostly in places that lie outside the reach of labor inspection services or other government enforcement bodies.

This being said, the problem of forced labor should not be approached as a narrow law enforcement issue. Indeed, we believe that forced labor needs to be understood from a broad labor market perspective. The book illustrates in particular how forced labor situations arise as a result of a series of labor market failures. The term *labor market failure* is used here as meaning the failure of unregulated labor markets—or of markets in which existing regulations are weakly enforced—to produce socially acceptable outcomes, in terms of both equity and efficiency. The argument about market failures calls for governments not only to punish forced labor as a penal offense but also to step in and effectively regulate the economy.

Two labor market deficiencies are particularly pertinent to understanding why forced labor continues to flourish. First, labor markets are characterized by asymmetric information. Information is particularly relevant in the process of labor recruitment. In the absence of regulations that address the imbalance of access to information, recruiters will find it easy to deceive workers and to conceal their real intentions. Second, labor markets are made up of agents with unequal bargaining power, namely workers and employers. When labor regulation and labor institutions are weak, limited to certain sectors or categories of workers, some employers will be able either to impose unfavorable conditions of work or to violate existing labor agreements to their advantage. Our empirical evidence suggests that, if circumstances permit, some employers will ultimately turn to the use of coercion and treat the payment of wages as discretionary.

As this book aims to demonstrate, these labor market failures reinforce each other. They are widespread in labor-intensive economic sectors with a high labor turnover and seasonal shifts, such as agriculture, construction, mining, textiles and garments, restaurants, and others. We find these problems in developing countries with traditional bonded labor systems as well as in industrialized countries that are exposed to contemporary forms of human trafficking.

Analyzing recruitment systems is crucial in understanding how workers enter forced labor. Recruitment is the first step in an employment relationship. In principle, it can be defined as a free act of contractual agreement whereby one party commits itself to pay predetermined wages in exchange for which the other party commits itself to perform predetermined tasks in a predetermined time. The most efficient way of recruitment is the direct recruitment of workers by employers. In practice, however, recruitment agents—whether private or public—play an important role in the labor market. They are the link between labor supply and demand in a situation of imperfect information. In economic sectors with a fluctuating demand for labor as well as in highly specialized economic sectors, recruiters are often the necessary intermediary between workers and employers.

In our research, we have identified several recruitment mechanisms that either lead directly to forced labor or contribute to an increased vulnerability of workers to be subjected to forced labor at the employment stage. Abduction and kidnapping are obviously forms of "recruitment" that are a direct expression of force. In quantitative terms, they are not the most widespread forms, but they are certainly the most radical deviation from a free contractual agreement between workers and employers. Abduction and kidnapping occur in countries or regions where legal systems, including labor market regulations, have broken down completely.

More frequently, however, recruitment or labor contract systems in the world today are maintained by a range of legal, semilegal, or illegal private recruiters. Often, these recruiters operate in a legal vacuum or in an environment of impunity, where abuses are not investigated and prosecuted. This makes it relatively easy to deceive workers about the nature of the jobs, the wages, and the living conditions that are proposed in a distant place of employment or about the fees that have to be paid. Deception is the most commonly used means of recruiting workers into situations of forced labor. The true nature and characteristics of jobs can be concealed because recruiters often have a monopoly over employment-related information.

Credits are also used, together with deception, to recruit workers into forced labor. They can take the form of private loans or wage advances and are often proposed to migrants to fund travel costs and upfront fees. Credits generate a debt for the workers, which can be manipulated for the purpose of extracting forced labor. Typically, creditors suddenly inform debtors about some unexpectedly high interest rates and require that both the loan and usury interests be repaid through long hours of work or personal services. Such mechanisms of "debt-bondage" play a particularly important role in areas where poverty is widespread, such as in rural South Asia or Latin America, or when relatively poor migrant workers seek employment abroad. It is also used to force young women against their will into prostitution.

The ultimate purpose of forced labor—into which workers enter through failed systems of recruitment—is almost always economic exploitation through payments to workers below the level that appeared to have been mutually agreed upon and negotiated. In an efficient and well-functioning labor market, employers are expected to pay mutually agreed-upon wages to employed persons in exchange for their work or services.[1] But, as will be seen throughout the book, in practice there exists a whole series of manipulations by employers—such as wage deductions, debt manipulations, payment in kind, or simply the nonpayment of wages—that lead to the economic exploitation of workers and that are facilitated by weaknesses in the protection of wage payments. In the best of cases, forced laborers obtain reduced payments for their work or services; in the worst of cases, they receive no payments at all. The duration of these exploitative practices can vary from a few months to a lifetime. Whatever their duration, these practices represent a serious failure in the area of wage payments.

Of course, from an employer's perspective, wage manipulations push down labor costs and increase profits. Nowhere is this more evident than in the sex industry, where young women maintained in prostitution can generate an annual turnover in the hundreds of thousands of dollars. But it is also becoming increasingly clear that large profits can arise from the nonpayment of wages in more traditional economic sectors. In total, the annual profits from forced labor have been estimated at more than US\$44 billion, with \$32 billion alone arising from the exploitation of trafficked victims (Belser 2005). The more inefficient employers also use forced labor to shift economic risk onto workers: if sales are low, they simply withhold wages.

Means of coercion can be used all along the chain of recruitment and exploitation to create a situation of subjection. Recruiters use various forms of threats or even violence to intimidate workers and to make sure that they are not already trying to leave at this early stage. Later, employers also use coercion to prevent workers from leaving their exploitative employment situations. Typical forms of coercion include threats to the workers or their families, confiscation of identity documents, or menaces of denunciation to immigration authorities. It is worth noting that all these aspects of forced labor—the recruitment, the exploitation, and the coercion—tend to involve collusion between recruiters and employers. Such a triangular employment relationship makes it easier to conceal abuses and more difficult for workers to claim their rights.

### Historical Perspectives and Debates—A Brief Overview

Even though they adjust to global changes, none of the contemporary forms of forced labor are really new. They are part of a historical pattern that started with the slavery that emerged at the dawn of civilization. It is therefore not surprising that historians have greatly contributed to the academic literature and debates. But the rise and fall of forced labor systems has also puzzled economists, sociologists, anthropologists, and jurists alike. In the following, we provide a brief overview of these historical perspectives and debates without claiming to be comprehensive. It would remain a separate task to analyze how the ILO itself contributed to these debates as well as how it was shaped by them in the past.

Slavery was practiced in Ancient Egypt and Greece and became widespread during the Roman Empire, where there were perhaps up to 1.5 million slaves in Italy, representing 25 percent of the total population (Scheidel forthcoming).

In the seventh century a large slave trade fed the expansion of the Islamic world in Africa and the Middle East (Chebel 2007; Lovejoy 2000). From the sixteenth to the nineteenth century, an estimated 11 million slaves left Africa, and 9.6 million arrived on the American continents (Eltis 2001). These practices were only abolished in the relatively recent past. The last country on the American continents to abolish slavery was Brazil in 1888.

There are, of course, major differences between past slavery and modern forced labor. One such difference lies in the definition of these two practices. Slavery has been defined in the League of Nations Slavery Convention of 1926 as "the status or condition of a person over whom any or all of the powers attaching to the right of ownership are exercised" (Article I). Hence, slavery was a legal institution. This contrasts with the ILO definition of forced labor as being an illegal practice. One of the earliest ILO conventions (No. 29, adopted in 1930) defines forced or compulsory labor as "all work or service that is exacted from any person under the menace of any penalty and for which the said person has not offered himself or herself voluntarily" (Article 2.1).

Despite the differences between slavery and forced labor, there are also important similarities. As in the case of modern forced labor, slavery can also be characterized by two elements discussed above: abusive recruitment and economic exploitation. On the recruitment side most slaves sold in the "New World" were bought from traders who had bought them from African intermediaries who had, in turn, obtained them from a wider network of captors. There are strong echoes of this past method in the long and intricate systems of modern subcontracting in the recruitment of trafficked labor.

Economic exploitation also characterized slavery. Eric Williams famously observed in his book *Capitalism and Slavery* (1944) that slavery was an economic institution that cheapened the cost of production and contributed to the rise of capitalism in the colonial metropolis. The profitability of slave labor was also a major theme of Fogel and Engerman in *Time on the Cross* (1974), which triggered a passionate debate (see debates in the *American Economic Review* in 1977 and 1980). The authors argued that southern slave farms were more efficient than farms with free labor, demonstrating that the unit cost of slave labor was below that of free labor. They thus challenged the thesis that economic factors led to a natural demise of the slave system and, instead, emphasized the deeply moral nature of the antislavery movement.

Indentured labor was another form of unfree labor that has many parallels with contemporary forms of human trafficking. It has received particular attention from migration researchers. Potts (1990) calculated that indentured workers were used in 40 countries by all the major colonial powers. It involved between 12 and 37 million workers from 1834 up to 1941. Indentured laborers were mainly recruited in India and China and to a lesser extent in Japan, Oceania, and Java.[2] Although sheer economic pressure was usually enough to force people into migration, violent recruitment methods were also used, particularly in China. Recruitment agents deceived workers about working conditions and tricked them into contracts that established many years of servitude in the colonies to which they were transported under appalling conditions. Even after the end of their contracts, workers were often compelled to stay with their employers and to sign another exploitative contract. The system of indentured labor was made possible through a conflation of interests between powerful plantation owners (as well as mining or infrastructure companies), colonial administrations, or governments of former colonies (Cohen 1987; Kloosterboer 1960; Potts 1990; Tinker 1974).

One academic debate focuses on the reasons behind the continuity of compulsory labor after slavery. An early contribution was made by Kloosterboer (1960), who argued that other forms of compulsion evolved out of economic necessity after the abolition of slavery. Looking at contract labor systems, penal laws (especially laws against "vagrancy"), and policies to deny former slaves access to land, she argued that employers and colonial administrators used compulsion to respond to acute labor shortages. Brass (Brass and van der Linden 1997; Brass 1999) argues that various forms of unfree labor have been developed by ruling classes with the objective of preventing the "proletarization" of workers (for example, forming unions, migrating for better jobs). He argues that bonded labor systems survived agrarian capitalist restructuring in Latin America and India owing to a variety of factors, including class struggle, kinship (actual and fictive), and reciprocity under bonded labor. He emphasizes that bonded labor is not the result of choice or free agency on behalf of the peasant, as argued, for example, by Srinivasan (1980, 1989).

The persistence of bonded labor or debt bondage, particularly in India, has given rise to a relatively large literature. Debt bondage was defined by the UN 1956 Supplementary Convention of the Abolition of Slavery, the Slave Trade, and Institutions and Practices Similar to Slavery as "the status or condition arising from a pledge by a debtor of his personal services or of those of a person under his control as security for a debt, if the value of those services as reasonably assessed is not applied towards the liquidation of the debt or the length and nature of those services are not respectively limited and defined" (Article I[a]). The same convention considers that all persons subjected to debt bondage are persons "of servile status."

Economists such as Bhaduri (1973) explain the existence of debt bondage or bonded labor by the underdevelopment of credit markets. In his view, bonded labor and exploitation result from the interlinking of transactions in credit, land, and labor markets between the same landlord and tenant. In particular, when landowners derive their income both from sharecropping and from usury linked to the perpetual indebtedness of tenants, technological improvements that raise labor productivity end up being undesirable to landowners. This perverse incentive occurs when better technology increases landowners' produce from the land less than it diminishes income derived from the usury of loans to the sharecropper.

But bonded labor can also be the result of an employer's power to constrain workers' alternative opportunities or, in economic language, to reduce labor's opportunity cost (on this, see also Taylor [1977] and Sevilla-Siero [1991] for the related literature on "contrived dependence"). Basu (1986), for example, argues that when a powerful landlord makes an apparently unattractive job offer to a worker and at the same time threatens that refusal will mean no one else will trade with him or her, it will be in the interest of a rational worker to accept the job offer. Although this looks like free choice, the worker is pushed into an exchange from which he or she does not benefit, which is precisely one of the key characteristics of coercion. Indeed, according to Naqvi and Wemhöner (1995), the definition of coercion is the use of power for the purpose of "compelling an agent to engage in transactions which, given the agent's feasible set of actions, he would unilaterally not have chosen to engage in" (p. 191). From the perspective of the employer, such a use of coercion allows—according to Basu—"maximum extortion."

The manipulation of wage advances or loans to migrant labor features more prominently in the literature on the new forms of debt bondage, sometimes called "neobondage" (Bales 2000; Lerche 2007), as well as in the literature on human trafficking. Recent studies on human trafficking display broad consensus that economic exploitation is the main—and often unique—objective of contemporary traffickers. Human trafficking has been defined by the United Nations Protocol to Prevent, Suppress, and Punish Trafficking in Persons (the so-called Palermo Protocol), supplementing the United Nations Convention Against Transnational Organized Crime, adopted by the UN General Assembly in 2000. The slightly convoluted definition of trafficking in the Palermo Protocol defines human trafficking as the recruitment or receipt of persons for the purpose of sexual exploitation, forced labor, slavery, or the removal of organs.[3] This definition provides for an important distinction between "trafficking in persons," which is characterized by the intent to exploit, and the act of "smuggling of migrants," which refers to the procurement of the illegal entry of a person into a state of which the person is not a national or a permanent resident. An expert group of the European Commission concluded that "the key element to the Trafficking Protocol is the forced labour or slavery like outcomes" (European Commission 2004, p. 52).

The European police organization Europol (2003) found that trafficking inevitably results in the financial exploitation of the victim, which often continues long after the movement from a source country to a destination country, and characterized trafficking as a "low risk–high reward" enterprise for organized crime. Shelley (2003) also believes that what makes human trafficking attractive to criminal groups is the combination of high profits, low risk of detection, and minor penalties involved.

The sex industry stands out and remains the primary focus of trafficking studies in many countries. Although there are many stories of girls and young women who are forced into prostitution, there is still much disagreement about the exact meaning of "coercion" in this industry. Some feminist and religiously inspired abolitionist groups are emphatic that "all prostitution is sexual slavery," whereas other feminist groups disagree with this view. Abolitionist groups typically propose to address the "demand-side" of trafficking through the criminalization of all prostitution. Other feminist groups would like to see prostitution legitimized so that sex workers are "afforded the civil and labour rights enjoyed by other citizens and workers" (for a discussion of these positions, see O'Connell Davidson 2006, p. 17).

Domestic service also features prominently in the area of trafficking for labor exploitation in industrialized countries (Free the Slaves and Human Rights Center 2004) as well as in the Middle East, where temporary workers from South Asia sometimes live in the households of their employers in conditions "based on violence, exploitation and denial of fundamental freedoms" (Jureidini and Mourkarbel 2004, p. 582; see also Anggraeni 2006). In poor developing countries, studies have also described how poor families sometimes place their children with wealthier families, who use them as little "slaves" (see, for example, the autobiography of Cadet [1998] on Haiti).

Much of the academic literature on human trafficking has been stimulated by current political debates and is highly critical of some of the underlying assumptions. The critique has focused on the overemphasis of supply-side factors, the blurred boundaries between exploited trafficked "victims" and irregular migrants who are often criminalized, the denial of agency to those defined as trafficked victims, the lack of data, and—last but not least—the lack of clarity of the concepts (see, for example, Breman 2007; International Organization for Migration 2006). This book is intended as a modest contribution to this growing literature, proposing a new analytical framework for the understanding of forced labor that uses a clear set of definitions and suggests improved methods of data collection. We hope that the case studies, detailed below, will also be a useful empirical addition to the critique of the criminalization and victimization of those trafficked or in forced labor, which is also addressed in our proposed policy responses.

## Structure of the Book

The book focuses on case studies, all based on primary research. These case studies are in no way exhaustive. Many forms of forced labor are not covered, but this does not mean that they are less important or that they deserve less attention. The present collection only provides a sample of studies, highlighting some useful areas of research and possible methodological approaches that could be extended into other areas in the future. The second part presents policy responses and discusses their strengths and weaknesses. Impact research on forced labor and trafficking is still in its infancy, and the chapters presented here should only be seen as a first attempt to analyze the consequences of policies, laws, and community-based measures. More work is clearly needed to develop indicators to measure progress over time and to correct action if necessary.

In the first chapters of the book, the emphasis of our empirical case studies is on understanding *what* forced labor is and *how* it is linked to abusive recruitment and wage payment systems in different economic, social, and cultural contexts. To be sure, there are many underlying factors in the persistence of bonded labor in Asia, rural debt bondage in Latin America, slavery-like practices in Africa, or human trafficking to developed countries. By comparing these different cases, however, we find that abusive or deceptive recruitment and various forms of wage manipulations are the key mechanisms in depriving workers of their freedom to leave or change their employer. The nonenforcement of ethical recruitment practices and fair wages has repercussions well beyond the informal economy, but most of all it affects workers who are not associated with and covered by labor law.

The first of the empirical chapters, a case study written by Leonardo Sakamoto, discusses forced labor in Brazil. It mainly takes place in the remote Amazon regions of the country to which people from poorer provinces are transported and then held in situations of debt bondage. This case study can also be discussed as "internal trafficking" of labor, although in Brazil it is defined as "slave labor." The chapter analyzes recent data on forced labor from labor inspection services and nongovernmental organization (NGO) sources, thereby focusing on recruitment patterns, types of economic activities, and forms of coercion. It also provides an overall context of approaches against slave labor in Brazil that are further discussed in the second part of the book.

The following case study, also from Latin America, is written by Eduardo Bedoya, Alvaro Bedoya, and Patrick Belser. It presents empirical findings of anthropological research carried out on the nature of debt bondage in Peru, Bolivia, and Paraguay. Labor intermediaries recruit workers and induce them into an artificial debt through wage advances and other manipulations that they cannot repay, thus keeping the workers in poverty. Such practices are always accompanied by very poor working conditions. The chapter discusses these practices as used in the Amazon region of Peru for illegal logging, in Bolivia for nut collection and on cattle farms and sugar plantations, and in Paraguay on the traditional cattle farms in the Chaco region.

A study of debt bondage, rooted in traditional practices, is then presented by Ali Khan, who summarizes research carried out in nine different sectors covering various provinces in Pakistan. This provides a comprehensive overview of bonded labor in that country. The study is based on a qualitative analysis of labor arrangements in these sectors where bonded labor is still recurrent. Particular emphasis is put on the *peshgi* system of wage advances that was prohibited by the Bonded Labour Act in 1992 but continues to play a key role in the relationship among employers, workers, and sometimes also intermediaries. The empirical research provides evidence of bonded labor practices having spread from agriculture to other economic sectors. It is argued that this is closely linked to the recent changes in economic production in which traditional obligations between employers and workers have been weakened while the bargaining position of workers has not been strengthened. This is particularly evident in the unequal debtor-creditor relationship that underpins bonded labor.

The next empirical case study, from Niger, looks into the legacy of slavery in West Africa. The authors, Ali R. Sékou and Saidou Abdoulkarimou, discuss forced labor and discrimination against people of slave descent. The research focuses on the nomadic northern part of the country where forced labor practices continue to exist. As for the rest of the country, traditional practices of slavery have largely transformed into more or less severe forms of discrimination against people of slave descent. The case study highlights the difficulty of clearly distinguishing between forced labor and exploitation that is deeply rooted in traditional beliefs and mechanisms of social exclusion. In areas where people are discriminated against on the basis of their origin and where extreme poverty is the norm, coercion may not be needed to recruit and retain workers.

The next chapter, on human trafficking, is by Beate Andrees. Human trafficking is a form of forced labor that has received much global attention in recent years. In this chapter, particular emphasis is placed on Europe, with information gathered from various countries. Although the coercion of migrant women in the sex industry has been well documented, less is known about the situation of migrant workers in labor-intensive sectors such as construction, garment, agriculture, or food processing. As in sex trafficking, workers are typically recruited under false pretenses in their country of origin and forced to work in the country of destination under the threat of dismissal, violence, or other coercive methods. The chapter discusses the modus operandi of trafficking by focusing particularly on the recruitment process, the occurrence of debt bondage among migrant workers, extortion, and wage manipulations.

The second part of the book looks at ways that governments and their partners can reduce the incidence of forced labor and ultimately eliminate it. This aspect of the present book is of course closely linked to the previous section. Consistent with the focus of the book on forced labor as a labor market issue, the chapter by Beate Andrees and Patrick Belser discusses the role of labor market institutions in national policies against forced labor. Case studies in this book shed light on the mechanisms of recruitment and economic exploitation that are largely linked to the nonpayment of wages or illegal wage deductions leading into debt bondage. The chapter therefore discusses strategies toward a stronger role of labor inspectors, trade unions, and employment tribunals in the fight against forced labor. It also highlights the importance of regulating and monitoring labor recruitment.

The following chapter, by Rohit Malpani, focuses on attempts to criminalize human trafficking through national law as well as to enforce these new provisions across different countries in Europe as well as in the United States. It takes a closer look at laws and penal code revisions and asks whether these new criminal laws have been effective tools to use to prosecute trafficking-related offenses. The chapter argues that unless antitrafficking provisions clearly elaborate the concept of vulnerability and forms of coercion, they will fall short of effectively prosecuting traffickers. Furthermore, it is argued that many states have not yet sufficiently implemented human rights standards aimed at the protection of victims.

The chapter by Isabelle Guérin, Caroline O'Reilly, Marc Roesch, Maria Sathya, and G. Venkatasubramanian discusses the impact of models for the prevention of bonded labor and for the rehabilitation of bonded laborers through community-based and microfinance-led interventions. It draws on empirical research carried out in India. The main purpose of these interventions is to alter the unequal debtor-creditor relationship. The chapter discusses the overall socioeconomic context in which bonded labor occurs and raises questions about the roles and responsibilities of different actors in shaping these interventions and about what the overall purpose of these interventions should be.

The final chapter by Patrick Belser and Michaelle de Cock presents strategies to improve national statistics on forced labor. When the ILO published its global estimate on forced labor in 2005, it was based on a double counting method (capture and recapture), using available reports on forced labor across different regions of the world. The next logical step is to develop better national statistics from which aggregate global data can be generated. Statistics are not a purpose in themselves—they are the necessary compass for good policy formulation. This chapter first discusses national experiences in data collection and ways to replicate these experiences. It further reviews existing global estimates and proposes ways to produce statistically robust national estimates.

The different contributions to this book suggest that effective measures against forced labor will always require strong labor market institutions, political will, precise information, good legislation, effective law enforcement, and the empowerment of victims as well as viable economic alternatives for the victims and the potential victims. The mix of policy responses and the relative weight that should be given to different approaches in different circumstances, however, remain open to debate.

There are still many unknowns in the forced labor equation. First, the chapters in this book inevitably suffer from the fact that the combination of factors that cause forced labor remains imperfectly understood. Second, the experience accumulated so far on what works and what does not work is still rather scarce. Finally, the impact of globalization also remains open to more detailed investigation. On the one hand, globalization seems to be accompanied by new forms of forced labor such as human trafficking and exploitation in global subcontracting systems. On the other hand, globalization has also led to new demands from governments, social partners, civil society, and consumers for stronger mechanisms to promote shared moral values and universal labor rights. The present book is itself part of the ILO's overall response to these demands. We hope that it will contribute, if only modestly, to a future free of forced labor.

## Notes

1. ILO Convention No. 95 defines wages in Article 1 as "remuneration or earnings, however designated or calculated, capable of being expressed in terms of money and fixed by mutual agreement or by national laws or regulations, which are payable in virtue of a written or unwritten contract of employment by an employer to an employed person for work done or to be done or for services rendered or to be rendered."

2. Though less developed as a system, indentured labor was also used during the great European migration to the New World.

3. More precisely, the Palermo Protocol defines trafficking in persons as "the recruitment, transportation, transfer, harbouring or receipt of persons, by means of the threat or use of force or other forms of coercion, of abduction, of fraud, of deception, of the abuse of power or of a position of vulnerability or of the giving or receiving of payments or benefits to achieve the consent of a person having control over another person for the purpose of exploitation" (Article 3[a]). The protocol further specifies that "exploitation shall include, at a minimum, the exploitation of the prostitution of others or other forms of sexual exploitation, forced labor or services, slavery or practices similar to slavery, or the removal of organs" (Article 3[a]).

# 1

## "Slave Labor" in Brazil

### Leonardo Sakamoto

In the twenty-first century, Brazil has demonstrated global leadership in the struggle against modern forced labor. This was internationally acknowledged in the ILO's 2005 global report, *A Global Alliance Against Forced Labour* (2005a). Unfortunately, all the efforts have so far remained insufficient to solve the problem. "Slave labor" continues to be used to deforest the Amazon and prepare the land for cattle breeding or agriculture.

Victims are recruited in poor regions of Brazil by labor contractors, who promise good jobs and transport voluntary workers in buses over long distances. Upon arrival, workers are surprised to find that the reality differs from the promises. Workers are informed that they already have a debt for the cost of transportation and for the food they received. They are also told that they will be charged for the tools, boots, hats, and clothes that are necessary to carry out the job, as well as for the rental of their beds. The cost of their food is also retained from their salaries. Workers who complain are told that they cannot leave until they have paid their debt. Those who still do not submit are retained by violence.

This chapter provides an overview of this internal trafficking of workers into rural slave labor. The first section offers some important background information on the definition of *slave labor* and on the existing legislation and the policies adopted in Brazil to combat this problem. This section also includes a presentation of the Mobile Inspection Unit, which has provided much of the information used in this study. The second section presents the methodology, which relies heavily on the quantitative and qualitative analysis of the administrative databases maintained by the Mobile Inspection Group within the Ministry of Labour and Employment. In the third section, I discuss the results. I show that most slave labor occurs in places that are affected by violence and deforestation. I also construct a profile of the enslaved laborers and identify the areas where they are recruited, which appear to be the states characterized by high levels of poverty and illiteracy. Finally, I document how "slave workers" are exploited through the manipulation of debts and the nonpayment of wages and show in which economic sectors this occurs most frequently. I also describe the extremely poor working and living conditions of these workers, often sleeping under a roof of leaves, with no health and safety measures. The last section concludes with some recommendations on how the fight against slave labor can be strengthened even further in the future.

## From Official Recognition to the Development of a National Policy

Brazil is a large and diverse country, with an economically active population of about 83 million people. In the early 1990s, Brazil's development model changed from an inward-looking model to a more open and liberalized economy. There have also been some relatively minor reforms that have made the labor market more flexible (Berg, Ernst, and Auer 2006). Despite these changes, the Brazilian labor market remains characterized by large inequalities that are typical of countries with dual economies and dual labor markets: on the one hand a modern economy employing a relatively small number of highly skilled workers, and on the other hand a large informal economy with many low-paid workers striving to lead a decent life (see Ernst 2007). It is in the latter type of economy that forced labor has flourished.

In Brazil, the offense of forced labor is known as "slave labor" and is covered under Article 149 of the Penal Code, which since 2003 has provided sanctions for the crime of subjecting a person to a condition "analogous to that of a slave." This is defined as subjecting a person to forced labor, to arduous working days, or to degrading working conditions or as restricting the person's mobility by reason of a debt contracted in respect of the employer or representative. Any person who retains workers at the workplace by preventing them from using means of transportation, by retaining their personal documents or property, or by maintaining manifest surveillance is also liable to the same prison sentence. In practice, the term *slave labor* refers to a situation of degrading work combined with some deprivation of freedom.

The first denunciations of slave labor in Brazil were made in 1971 by the Catholic bishop in Amazonia, Pedro Casaldáliga. A few years later, the Pastoral Land Commission (CPT), an NGO linked to the Catholic Church, started to denounce estates linked to multinationals that were committing such crimes. The CPT collected testimonies from farmworkers who managed to escape on foot from these properties and gave international exposure to the problem. Denunciations of slavery started being sent to the ILO as of 1985.

The federal government of Brazil acknowledged the existence of slave labor before the Brazilian public and to the ILO in 1995, via a declaration by the then president of the republic, Fernando Henrique Cardoso. In doing so, Brazil became one of the first nations in the world to officially recognize modern slavery. On June 27 of that year, decree number 11538 was issued, creating the first government structures to combat this crime, in particular the Executive Group for the Suppression of Forced Labour (GERTRAF) and the Mobile Inspection Group, coordinated by the Ministry of Labour and Employment. Almost one decade later, in March 2003, the president, Luiz Inácio Lula da Silva, launched the National Plan for the Eradication of Slavery.

New institutions were created, such as the National Commission for the Eradication of Slavery (CONATRAE), in replacement of previous institutions, and the Mobile Inspection Group was kept in place and strengthened. Altogether, the National Plan comprises a total of 76 measures. These measures revolve around several general objectives: the improvement of statistical data, the enactment of legal reforms, the implementation of prevention and repression projects, and the consistent involvement of all main stakeholders. But perhaps most important is the political priority given to the combat against forced labor. The introduction to the National Plan expresses this commitment in unambiguous terms: "Conscious that the elimination of slave labor is a basic prerequisite to ensure a democratic state of law, the new Government has chosen as one of its main priorities the elimination of all forms of contemporary slavery." One of the key institutions that had been created in 1995 was a Mobile Inspection Unit (MIU) composed of labor inspectors, labor attorneys, and the federal police. The MIU investigates allegations of forced labor and inspects workplaces in remote rural areas—often under extremely dangerous conditions. It has greatly contributed to the increase in the numbers of released workers and the conviction of offenders (see Chapter 6).

In addition, since the end of 2003, the government has published a so-called Dirty List, which is a list of employers who were found to have maintained workers in conditions of slave labor. This list is updated every six months and includes employers who are barred for a period of two years from public procurement, public subsidies and credits, or fiscal benefits. The name of an offender is included in the list after the procedures activated by the labor inspection services are concluded. In turn, removal of a name is dependent upon monitoring the violator for a period of two years. If the crime is not committed again during this time, and all of the penalties arising from the inspection and all workers and welfare benefit debts have been paid, the name will be removed.

As a result of this mechanism, the Bank of Brazil, the Bank of Northeast Brazil, the Bank of the Amazon, and the National Bank for Economic and Social Development (BNDES) have all suspended their credits to those named on the Dirty List. Since 2003, the National Institute for Colonization and Agrarian

Reform (INCRA) has also investigated whether listed employers have been engaged in any illegal land grabbing. According to the Ministry of Agrarian Development, to whom INCRA is responsible, in cases where the irregular occupation of public lands is identified, the property will be reclaimed by the federal government and given priority for agrarian reform.

In addition to the Dirty List, there exist some positive initiatives by the business sector itself. In the first half of 2005, socially responsible enterprises—coordinated by the Ethos Institute for Corporate Social Responsibility—launched a National Pact for the Eradication of Forced Labour. This pact was signed by more than 80 national retailers, wholesalers, exporters, and other companies that committed to terminating subcontracting arrangements with enterprises that were on the Dirty List. In a letter to the president of Brazil in June 2005, the Ethos Institute recognized that slave labor begins on the rural estates named on the Dirty List, but then it passes through their direct and intermediate buyers and ends in the final consumer market. Following the publication of a study on the slave labor supply chains, representatives of large retail enterprises, exporters, industry, and professional associations became aware that they had unwittingly been buying products from estates that were using slave labor. Disturbed by the existence of this problem, the private sector established this broad National Pact as a further incentive against the use of slave labor.

## Methodology

The main part of this chapter, however, focuses on the analysis of the information and data stored in administrative databases, including mainly the database updated by labor inspection services after each operation of the Mobile Inspection Unit as well as the records held by the CPT and the Dirty List updated by the Ministry of Labour and Employment. The quantitative analysis and some key summary statistics presented in this chapter are always accompanied by a qualitative interpretation based on extensive discussion with key informants. This means that the statistical analysis of the database from labor inspection services was always complemented with a qualitative analysis of the reports filed by Mobile Inspection Units as well as open interviews with the inspectors themselves. Interviews were also held with the most informed individuals within different institutions engaged in the combat against slave labor, such as the Pastoral Land Commission, Regional Labour Offices, or the Human Rights Commission.

When labor inspectors return from a mobile inspection—investigating denunciations, imposing fines, rescuing people found in slave labor, and initiating legal actions against rural landowners—they also provide information necessary to update the Ministry of Labour and Employment's database on slave labor. Whereas in the past not all of the information on rescued workers was systematically recorded by the inspection teams, the quality of this database has improved over time. Columns 2 and 3 of Table 1.1 use this database. Column 2 shows the total number of rescued workers from 1995, when the Mobile Inspection Group was created, to mid-2007. We see that the group rescued 25,064 workers. Column 3 indicates that, overall, these workers were rescued as a result of inspections carried out in no less than 1,789 farms. Column 4 in Table 1.1 shows the total number of complaints related to slave labor as collected in CPT offices and included in their database. These can be complaints made to the CPT directly or to any other institution. We can see that the number of complaints systematically exceeds the number of rescues.

Of course, the figures in Table 1.1 represent only a fraction of all cases of slave labor. How large is this fraction? This is difficult to answer at the present stage and would require further statistical work. In 2004, when Brazil recognized before the United Nations the existence of slave labor, it estimated that at least 25,000 people were held in slavelike conditions in the country each year. The statement was based on an estimate by the Pastoral Land Commission and represents about 10 times the number of persons rescued by Mobile Inspection Units during that same year and about five times more than the highest annual number of rescued victims.

Also, we do not claim that these databases are significant statistical samples. Indeed, the databases only include available information collected from

**Table 1.1 Summary Statistics**

| Year | Number of Rescued Workers | Number of Farms Inspected | Total Number of Complaints |
|---|---|---|---|
| 2007[a] | 3,296 | 112 | 4,325 |
| 2006 | 3,417 | 209 | 7,120 |
| 2005 | 4,348 | 189 | 7,612 |
| 2004 | 2,887 | 275 | 5,812 |
| 2003 | 5,223 | 188 | 8,306 |
| 2002 | 2,285 | 85 | 5,840 |
| 2001 | 1,305 | 149 | 1,823 |
| 2000 | 516 | 88 | 799 |
| 1999 | 725 | 56 | 966 |
| 1998 | 159 | 47 | n.a. |
| 1997 | 394 | 95 | n.a. |
| 1996 | 425 | 219 | n.a. |
| 1995 | 84 | 77 | n.a. |
| Total | 25,064 | 1,789 | 31,158 |

*Sources:* Columns 2 and 3: Secretariat of Labour Inspections and Ministry of Labour and Employment; Column 4: Pastoral Land Commission.
*Note:* a. First six months.

rescued workers or from workers who made complaints. This may induce some statistical bias, with less data coming from places where the Mobile Inspection Group lacks representatives of civil society to both collect denunciations and direct them to the proper channels. Furthermore, the Mobile Inspection Units and the CPT are essentially engaged in the combat against rural slave labor and do not really deal with urban slave labor. There now exist indications of this type of exploitation in the municipality of São Paulo, involving illegal immigrants from neighboring countries in Latin America. Hence, the databases are not representative of all the forms of slave labor that may exist in Brazil. Despite these shortcomings, these databases remain the principal and most reliable source of information to understand the trafficking of people into rural slave labor.

## Findings

### The Geography of Slave Labor, Violence, and Deforestation

Both the labor inspections and the CPT databases indicate that slave labor occurs most frequently in the state of Pará. Figure 1.1 uses the statistics from the CPT on the total number of complaints. We see that almost half of all complaints

**Figure 1.1  Slave Labor by State**

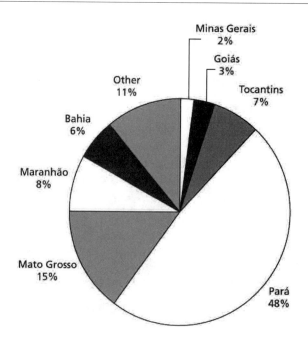

originate from the state of Pará. According to other CPT data (not shown here), the state of Pará is also the state with the highest number of rescued slave laborers: 6,000 people were rescued between 1995 and December 2005, representing 37.5 percent of the total persons rescued during that period. Other states with high incidence of complaints include Mato Grosso, Maranhão, Tocantins, and Bahia.

This observation suggests that regions with a high incidence of slave labor are the same regions that also have a high incidence of overall violence as well as a high incidence of deforestation. This can be verified in Table 1.2, in which Brazil is divided into 21 macroregions (which do not necessarily correspond to any existing administrative or political territorial divisions). The table provides data for the regional share of all successful mobile inspections, the regional share of all murders related to land conflict, and the regional share of

**Table 1.2  Slave Labor, Violence, and Deforestation (in percentage)**

| Macroregion | Share of Successful Inspections | Share of Total Murders in Brazil | Share of Amazon Deforestation |
|---|---|---|---|
| Southern/Southeastern Pará | 35.29 | 16.67 | 29.34 |
| Agricultural frontier/Pará | 13.6 | 27.45 | 9.17 |
| Araguaína/Bico-do-Papagaio | 10.29 | 0 | 1.2 |
| Southern Maranhão | 9.93 | 0 | 3.48 |
| Northern Mato Grosso | 6.25 | 1.96 | 15.54 |
| Araguaina/Mato Grosso | 4.04 | 1.96 | 9.06 |
| Southern Rondônia | 3.31 | 0 | 2.19 |
| Southern Mato Grosso | 2.94 | 6.86 | 5.05 |
| Western Bahia | 2.57 | 0 | 0 |
| Rio de Janeiro and Espirito Santo | 1.84 | 4.9 | 0 |
| Guaraí/Tocantins | 1.84 | 0 | 0 |
| Goiás | 1.47 | 0 | 0 |
| Flatlands of Maranhão | 1.47 | 1.96 | 3.86 |
| Minas Gerais | 1.47 | 0 | 0 |
| Northeastern Pará | 1.1 | 3.92 | 8.07 |
| Gurguéia/Piauí | 0.74 | 0 | 0 |
| Northwestern Maranhão | 0.37 | 0 | 0 |
| Mato Grosso do Sul | 0.37 | 0 | 0 |
| Marajó/Pará | 0.37 | 2.94 | 0 |
| Rio Grande do Norte | 0.37 | 0 | 0 |
| Interior of São Paulo | 0.37 | 1.96 | 0 |
| Share of national total | 100 | 70.6 | 87.0 |

*Sources:* Author compilation of data from labor inspection services, Pastoral Land Commission, and the INPE.
*Note:* Some totals have been rounded.

all Amazonian deforestation. The data on the number of rescued slave laborers were provided by the labor inspection services for the period between January 2002 and November 2004. Numbers of murders in the context of land conflicts include the period between 2001 and July 2004 and were provided by the Pastoral Land Commission (only those municipalities with two or more murders are included). The data on deforestation take into account the 60 municipalities with the highest rates of deforestation in the Legal Amazon according to the National Institute for Space Research (INPE). We see clearly that the two macroregions with the highest levels of slave labor (southern and southeastern Pará and the agricultural frontier in Pará, which together account for 48.89 percent of the total number of rescue operations) are also those with the highest numbers of murders related to land conflicts (44.12 percent) and the highest contribution to deforestation (38.51 percent).

The correlation between slave labor and the number of land-related murders does not mean that the deaths are necessarily related to slave labor, but rather that these areas are dangerous for workers and have been the arenas for rural conflicts. Violence in these areas has a historical origin. During the military dictatorship, the federal government granted a series of subsidies to companies to establish themselves in the Amazon region, in order to open the area to agricultural, extractive, and industrial development. This was done, however, without ordinances regulating land demarcation or the establishment of services necessary to guarantee an effective state presence and security for small tenant farmers and settlers. As a result, many places in the Amazon became lawless, and conflicts over landownership were settled by the individual use of force. This gave rise to what we may call a "culture of violence," which continues to this day. The sad state of affairs is that leaders of workers' unions continue to be murdered at regular intervals. One recent casualty, in February 2005, was the former president of the Parauapebas rural workers union, Daniel Soares da Costa Filho.

The relationship between identified cases of slavery and deforestation has been observed during inspections carried out by the mobile groups. As discussed in more detail below, much of the slave labor is used to increase agricultural activity in the Amazonian region. A refined analysis of the available data shows that the municipalities where cultivation is expanding most rapidly are the same ones where most slave workers have been freed. In fact, the rural properties that use slave labor are concentrated exactly in the arched strip of land clearances that goes from Rondônia to Maranhão.

According to a report by the World Bank, *Causas do desmatamento na Amazônia Brasileira* (Causes of Deforestation in the Brazilian Amazon) (Margulis 2003), the expansion of cattle ranching is the principal reason for the deforestation of the Amazon, occupying around 75 percent of the cleared areas. This deforestation and growth in cattle herds are concentrated in the so-called

Deforestation Arc located in southern and southeastern regions of Amazonia, mostly in the states of Pará, Mato Grosso, and Rondônia. Cattle ranchers are attracted by the rate of return on investment, up to four times greater than in the south-central area of the country. These high profits are due to favorable geoecological conditions, as the region experiences shorter dry periods than in the southeast and has high levels of rainfall, high temperatures, and high humidity relative to the climate, all of which reduce the costs of the dry period.

This attractiveness has resulted in a number of problems, including the constant opening of new forest areas, carried out at low cost by landless peasants and sometimes slave workers, who prepare the land for more profitable investment. This is often done illegally. Since the rights to the property are best ensured through the physical occupation of the land rather than through any legal ownership documents, lumber and land concerns often recruit landless peasants to occupy lands and ensure that they are held until their possession is eventually legalized. It is not surprising, therefore, that it is the large and medium-sized owners who are principally responsible for deforestation. According to the INPE, in 1997, 10.1 percent of the area deforested in the Legal Amazon was occupied by properties of less than 15 hectares, and 38.8 percent was occupied by properties larger than 200 hectares.

## Recruitment into Slave Labor

Workers in slave labor are usually contracted by so-called *gatos* (or cats), who act as labor contractors for estate owners. They come looking for workers in buses or trucks, or, in order to escape inspection by the Highway Patrol, they may travel on regular buses or trains. These contractors "hook" the workers with duplicitous promises. They offer work on rural plantations and ranches, with guaranteed salaries, lodging, and food. To seduce the worker, they offer "advance payments" for the family and free transport to the work site. Some migrant workers are also recruited by *gatos* from "farm workers' hostels" by the sides of the road, where they are put up while they wait for work. The *gatos* then "buy" their unpaid bills and take them off to the estates. At that point, the workers become indebted. It is only upon arrival that workers realize that they have been deceived and trapped into a situation of slave labor.

Who is recruited into slave labor? This section provides a profile of the people who were trapped into situations of slave labor. The places of origin of these people are taken from the forms filled out for the payment of unemployment benefits—a right that has been extended to all rescued workers. Instituted in 2003, this scheme began to fully cover rescued workers in 2004, owing to difficulties in institutionalizing the procedure. In 2005, it covered almost all rescued workers, and coverage has continued to increase since then. This means that in a few years' time, the database on unemployment benefits will become an even more effective tool for identifying trends in the profile of the groups affected.

Figure 1.2 shows where rescued workers were born. During the period between 2003 and April 2007, 9,762 persons were registered to receive unemployment allowances. This represents about 59 percent of the 16,431 workers who were rescued during the same period. The data indicate that victims are born far away from the Amazon, in states located in the agricultural frontier zones of the Amazon and the Cerrado, such as Maranhão, Pará, Tocantins, Bahia, and Piuaí. According to the available data, Maranhão is the main state of birth of slave workers, accounting for 34 percent of the total, and its municipalities also head the list as regards towns where freed slaves were born. These areas in the northeast region of Brazil are characterized by high levels of poverty, high unemployment, and low indexes of human development. These conditions trigger large flows of people who have to leave their homes and go elsewhere in search of work, rendering them vulnerable to the dirty tricks of labor contractors.

The overwhelming majority of slave labor concerns young adult male workers with low levels of education. Indeed, the same data source on unemployment

**Figure 1.2  State of Origin of Victims Rescued from Slave Labor**

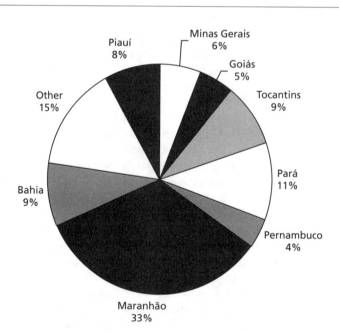

*Source:* Ministry of Labour and Employment, slave labor database.
*Note:* Percentages do not add to 100 due to rounding.

benefits shows that 95 percent of rescued workers are male, a majority of whom are between the ages of 18 and 34. This can be explained by the stamina and physical strength required for the work. Children under 18 years of age represent less than 4 percent of the victims. The few women who were found in situations of slave labor worked as cooks, responsible for preparing the food for the farmworkers, and were normally wives of the workers or the contractors. Sometimes they brought young children with them who helped prepare and distribute food and water to the workers. In terms of education, the data show that no less than 75 percent of slave laborers are either illiterate or have not completed primary school. Hence, slave labor seems to affect a vulnerable workforce with few alternatives and few qualifications beyond their own physical labor capacity.

### A Case Study on Recruitment in Pará

Where are people recruited? This is a fundamental question, for one of the biggest challenges for policymakers is the lack of systematic data on the places from which the workers were recruited. Such data have been dependent upon the information collected by the Mobile Inspection Group—which only recently initiated procedures aimed at standardizing the collection of information during operations. I use the state of Pará, which has the highest number of rescued workers, to illustrate.

The places of recruitment were obtained from all 16 available reports from mobile inspections operations carried out between 1997 and 2002 in the south and southeast of the state of Pará. It was not possible to have access to all reports of operations carried out in the area, and some reports were excluded as they did not include demographic data on the workers. Whenever information on the area of recruitment was available, it was entered into a database. Overall, this information was available in 763 cases.

Figure 1.3 shows that a majority of rescued workers (51 percent) were recruited outside the state of Pará. Of the workers that came from other states, almost half (42.5 percent) were from Maranhão. The others were from Piauí, Tocantins, or other northeastern states. These workers typically are contracted in their place of origin by *gatos*. These workers are preferred, as the estate owners and contractors consider them to be "harder working" and "less demanding." Some groups are especially "ordered" and go directly to a specific estate. Generally, these workers are acting on vague impressions from relatives or friends who have already been to Pará and who, upon returning home, tell them that "Pará is a good place to earn money." Often these workers are poor. They become easy prey to the estate owners and *gatos* offering work along the roads or in the hostels. The fact that they do not know the area leaves these workers vulnerable, as they have trouble orienting themselves. Often they do not even know where they are, having been taken directly to the estate.

**Figure 1.3  Rescued Workers by Area of Recruitment, 1997–2002**

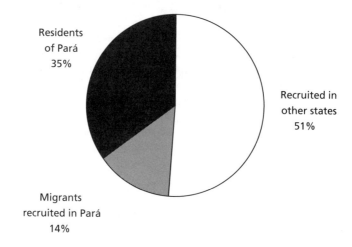

Residents
of Pará
35%

Recruited in
other states
51%

Migrants
recruited in Pará
14%

*Source:* Ministry of Labour and Employment, slave labor database.

Neither do they know whom to turn to if they have problems, and the *gato* himself is in some cases the only person they know in the area.

Another group, making up 14 percent, is migrant workers recruited in the state of Pará. These people often live by migration and roam back and forth between cities, estates, and states. They constitute a very vulnerable group that does not aim to settle and has no place to which to return. They live on their own, putting up in hostels, with no permanent social contact group. They have casual friends but go their separate ways after a time. Those who eventually do earn some money from working end up spending it for immediate gratification. The majority left their places of origin many years before and no longer have contact with their families.

Among the young people who have not been on the road for very long, two types can be identified. The first are those who decided to "go out into the world," in order to escape the limitations of their place of origin and their family, and normally maintain some kind of links with their family. The second type is those that definitively cut off any ties with their origin. They have nowhere to which to return. The sole asset of the migrant worker is his *cachorra,* the pouch in which he carries his personal belongings. This, with its contents of new clothing and any valuable possessions, is what he has to leave as security at a hostel when he owes money for his lodgings. The debt to the hostel is often paid by the *gato* who contracts him and who brings him, already in debt, to the estate where he is going to work.

As can be seen in Figure 1.3, only a minority (35 percent) of the rescued workers actually had residence in Pará when they were recruited. Among those who lived in Pará, a large majority (73.6 percent) lived on the outskirts of the region's largest cities. In fact, among these people only some 8.5 percent were born in Pará, most of them young people born in the region to families who had migrated to Pará during the 1970s and 1980s. The others were recent migrants, who had come to work on an estate and then bring their families. In the majority of cases, the situation of such people in the area is precarious. Most live with their families but own no land and live in the city. Dependency on work on the estates for their daily survival is, however, common to all. Even though they know the area better than workers who arrive from other states to do temporary work (and therefore are in a better position to assess the methods used by local estates and contractors), local workers do not always manage to avoid exploitation. It is striking, also, that 80.7 percent of local workers in the state are working in municipalities other than those in which they live—often in remote areas where agricultural exploitation is currently expanding. Thus, many are migrant workers within their own state.

## Coercion and Economic Exploitation

*Debt and the nonpayment of wages.* Once workers are recruited (or "hooked"), the labor contractors transport workers via buses in very poor states of repair or in makeshift and unsafe trucks. Arriving at the work site, many workers are surprised to find situations completely different from those promised. First, the *gatos* inform them that they already owe the *gatos* money. The advance, the transportation, and the meal expenses during the trip have already been listed in a "debts notebook" that remains in the possession of the *gato*. In addition, the worker finds that the costs of all of the tools or implements needed for the work—scythes, knives, power saws, among others—are also noted in the debts notebook, along with boots, protective gloves, hats, and other clothing. Finally, expenses for the accommodations (lacking basic hygiene facilities) and the unreliable food are also noted down, all at prices much higher than their normal sale prices.[1] Often, the *gato* does not tell the worker how much he owes but just notes it down.

This debt contracted on the estates is understood by the majority of workers as an obligation that must be cleared. To pay it is seen as a question of honor. If the worker nonetheless thinks about leaving, he will be prevented from doing so on the pretext that he is in debt and cannot leave as long as he has not paid what he owes. Many times, those that complain about their conditions or try to escape are subjected to beatings. Rescued workers emphasize the public humiliation and threats, which maintain workers in a state of fear. When laborers complain about their situations or want to leave the estate, armed overseers make them change their minds. Armed people sometimes watch the workers. It is not rare that Mobile Inspection Units come across revolvers, rifles, and a great deal of ammunition. Psychological threats, physical force, and arms are also used to keep victims working.

In extreme cases, workers in slave labor may be killed. In fact, it was one such extreme case that led to a series of policy responses in Brazil. José Pereira Ferreira had been held in slavery-like conditions on the Espírito Santo estate, city of Sapucaia, in southern Pará. In September 1989, at the age of 17, he fled the maltreatment and was ambushed by armed employees from the property, who shot him in the face. José Pereira Ferreira miraculously survived, but his case was ignored by the executive branch of government and hence was later taken to the Organization of American States (OAS). This then triggered a policy response in which Brazil assumed a series of obligations to combat slave labor.

Nonpayment or reduced payment of wages is also characteristic of slave labor. In some cases, workers are simply told that their debt exceeds the pay that they were promised or are paid much less than the sum initially agreed upon. In other instances, estate owners simply discount the cost of food and other items bought by workers from the estate's company store at inflated prices. In still other instances, the economic exploitation of workers occurs through a number of more creative ways. In one case, workers received their payments by check, which the workers were unable to cash (because the bank used by the owner was not located in the same municipality as the estate) and which could be used in the company store only at a discounted rate. These more creative ways seem to arise sometimes as a strategy to hide their practices from labor inspectors.

Overall, data from Mobile Inspection Units indicate that the amount of the wages and labor benefits due to the rescued people between the year 2000 and mid-2007 was 32.7 million Brazilian reals, equivalent to almost US$18 million. This represents on average of more than US$400 for each of the 43,277 rescued workers during this period. This may not seem like much, but it represents almost four months of the 2003 minimum wage.

*Economic activities.* Figure 1.4 identifies the principal areas of activity of the rural properties appearing on the register compiled by the Ministry of Labour and Employment, known as the Dirty List, which records those employers found using slave workers. The list referred to is that updated on January 25, 2007. To develop the chart below, I took into account the primary activities of farms using slave workers that appeared on the Ministry of Labour and Employment's register. Of course, in reality some properties use slave labor for more than one activity at the same time, for example, both for raising livestock and for producing charcoal.

### Figure 1.4 Main Products of Farms on the Dirty List

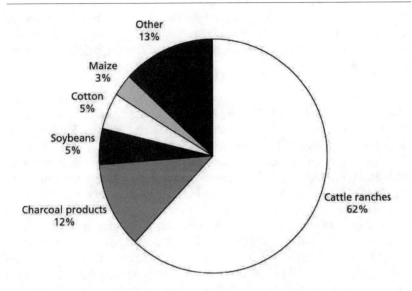

Other
13%

Maize
3%

Cotton
5%

Soybeans
5%

Charcoal products
12%

Cattle ranches
62%

*Source:* Ministry of Labour and Employment, slave labor database.

Cattle farms are the main offenders. Of the employers listed on the government's Dirty List, about 62 percent of the estates raise cattle, 12 percent produce coal for the iron and steel industry, 5.2 percent soybeans, 4.7 percent cotton, and 3.1 percent maize. Production of sugarcane, a raw material for the production of sugar and ethanol, does not appear among the primary economic activities if we consider the number of properties where this crime occurs. If the number of workers is the point of reference, cultivation of this crop would become one of the leading activities, as a lot of manpower is required to harvest sugarcane. Overall, however, only a few sugarcane plantations are involved in cases of slave labor. The incidence has been higher as regards cases of labor overexploitation and degrading work—which are also serious problems.

Additional statistics show that on the farms, the majority of freed rural workers had been working either to clear land or look after pastures. In the case of cattle ranching, workers are often used for opening tracks through virgin forests (to clear the way to bring in electric saws), felling trees, then using the timber to enclose the land, and pulling out tree stumps and roots in order to prepare the land intended for use as pastures. Soybean and cotton farms also clear lands, but the more frequent pattern is the purchase of already existing pasture lands and their conversion to crop cultivation.

It must be emphasized here that only a small number of rural Brazilian properties were found using slave labor—about 1,800 from a total of more than four million enterprises. Estates found using slave labor tend not to be small properties, however, but rather large landholdings, producing only one crop on thousands of acres, often for the needs of national industry or the external market.

*Living and working conditions.*  In all these activities, workers in situations of slave labor suffer not only from coercion and economic exploitation but also from substandard living and working conditions. This section highlights the areas of lodging, health, sanitation, and nutrition.

The type of lodging depends upon the type of work for which the workers were contracted. The worst conditions are normally associated with clearing lands of native vegetation, owing to the inaccessibility of the areas and the long distances separating them from urban centers. As there is a complete absence of infrastructure, and the landowner offers no lodging, much less transport to enable the worker to sleep near the estate headquarters, the solution is usually to put up tents made of tarpaulin or palm leaves in the middle of the forest, jungle, or other vegetation that is to be cut down. Rural workers are left exposed to the sun and the rain. Rescued workers emphasize how they suffered the cold, drenched by the Amazonian thunderstorms beneath tents made of yellow tarpaulin. Workers on cattle farms have also been found living in a corral, sleeping with the cattle at night.

Rescued workers are often found in poor health. In areas newly put under cultivation, tropical diseases such as malaria and yellow fever are endemic, and these areas also have a high incidence of diseases such as tuberculosis that are disappearing in other areas. When they are ill, the slave laborers are often abandoned to their fate by the *gatos* and the estate owners. Those that can walk will travel for kilometers until they arrive at a health post. There, in the most serious cases, they remain for months, in ill health, until they either recover, someone comes who can take them to the city, or in the worst-case scenarios, they end up dying. It is not unusual to hear stories of people who were simply sent away immediately after suffering an accident at work.

There are also important occupational risks. As we have seen, cattle rearing is one of the main enterprises that use slave labor, for tasks such as cutting down native growth to create or enlarge pasturelands and pulling up bushes, noxious weeds, and other undesirable plants. For the latter, as well as manual labor, poison is also used. But those applying the poison are not provided with the safety equipment recommended by legislation, such as face masks, goggles, protective gloves, and special clothing. After a few weeks, the workers' skin may be eaten away by the chemicals, leaving sores that never heal, and the workers also suffer dizziness, nausea, and other symptoms of poisoning. Furthermore, there are generally no wells to ensure provision of good-quality drinking water, much less toilet facilities for the workers. The stream from which they draw water for cooking or drinking is often also the same one where they bathe and where they wash their clothing, cooking utensils, and work implements. It should also be remembered that runoff from the rains carries the poison used on the fields to these same streams.

The quality of the food is also deplorable. Food is usually limited to beans and rice. *Mistura* (meat) is rarely provided by the owners. On one estate in Goianésia, Pará, people freed in November 2003 were obliged to hunt armadillos, paca (a guinea pig–like rodent), and monkeys if they wanted meat. Meanwhile, more than 3,000 head of cattle were grazing on the estate, which extended over some 7.5 million hectares. "There were times when people would go more than a month without meat," remembers Gonçalves, a peasant who worked on the estate (interview with author). On many estates, the only time that workers eat meat is when a steer dies. At the estate from which Luís was freed in February 2004, the only *mistura* available to the workers was rotten meat, riddled with worms.

## Future Challenges

The impressive progress made in the fight against slave labor has contributed to an increase in Brazilian awareness about the existence of such slave labor in Brazil. According to an unpublished survey carried out by the ILO, the number of articles in the printed media about modern slavery leaped from 77 in 2001, to 260 in 2002, and reached 1,541 in 2003, maintaining nearly the same level in 2004: 1,518. The increase in the number of actions carried out by the government and civil society to combat slavery and the awareness-raising campaigns on the issue were reflected in the media, which for their part, became important partners in the conscious-raising campaigns. Slavery became a topic for public discussion and an item on the agenda of national concerns. Despite the impressive progress made in the fight against slave labor, however, many challenges remain.

First, despite all the labor inspections, there are still very few convictions under Article 149 of the Penal Code, which provides for two to eight years' imprisonment. None of those convicted have actually served a prison term. There were a larger number of court decisions that found against the defendants. Nevertheless, given the lengthy period taken by the courts to handle proceedings, the period during which they can be punished lapses, the sentences are annulled, and the rural landowner remains the prime culprit. So, for example, if the proceedings take four years and the judge imposes a minimum penalty of two years, the crime and punishment are "prescribed" and are no longer legally actionable. Of course, increasing the minimum penalty of sentences for slavery would lessen the chances of sentences of slave labor being prescribed.

Many jurists who are arguing for a change in Article 149 of the Penal Code, which deals with the crime of holding people in slavery-like conditions, consider that four years would be an appropriate term.

Second, there is the issue of the seizure of lands and expropriation. In 2004, a court decision calling for the seizure of an estate for having used slave labor set an important precedent in terms of rendering effective the social function of property in Brazil and as regards the agrarian reform itself. According to the Ministry for Agrarian Development, for the first time in history, the failure by the owner to fulfill the social, environmental, and labor functions of property was invoked for the purposes of dispossession. Article 186 of the federal constitution states that the social function of property is fulfilled when the rural owner simultaneously complies with the following requirements: (1) rational and appropriate use, (2) appropriate use of available natural resources and conservation of the environment, (3) observation of regulations governing labor relations, and (4) production processes that contribute to the well-being of owners and workers. The landowner, however, filed an appeal and obtained a temporary restraining order on implementation of the decision.[2] Now, government and nongovernmental entities that work for the eradication of slavery support approval of a proposed constitutional amendment to allow the expropriation (confiscation without indemnity) of lands on which slave labor is found. This proposed amendment has come to be considered a key symbol of the struggle against modern slavery.

Finally, there is a need for implementing preventive policies. Repression alone is insufficient. It is also necessary to institute effective prevention policies in the municipalities where the workers are recruited. As will be clear from this chapter, most victims of slave labor originate in the municipalities of the north and northeast of Brazil, where poverty is highest and where human development indices are lowest. Agrarian reform in particular can be considered as one of the most effective means to prevent this modern slavery. In May 2005, based on consultations with the Ministry of Labour and Employment and the Federal Department of Justice, the Ministry of Agrarian Development and INCRA launched the Plan for the Eradication of Slave Labour, which is oriented toward two major themes: the prevention of illegal practices and the reintegration of rescued workers into society. At the same time, there is a need to encourage alternative employment opportunities for poor workers. All these measures will be fundamental for the success of eradicating forced labor in Brazil.

## Notes

Research assistance for this chapter was provided by Camila Rossi, Iberé Tenório, and Ivan Paganotti. Research on the profile of the enslaved workers in the state of Pará was conducted by Ana de Souza Pinto and Maria Antonieta da Costa Vieira.

1. It should also be remembered that the plantations and ranches are far from commercial centers, making it impossible for the worker to avoid becoming completely dependent on this "company store" system imposed by the *gato* at the estate owner's orders or directly by the estate owner.

2. As of this writing, the federal Supreme Court had not issued a decision on the matter.

# 2

## Debt Bondage
## and Ethnic Discrimination
## in Latin America

*Eduardo Bedoya, Alvaro Bedoya,*
*and Patrick Belser*

This chapter describes the findings of a multiple-case study conducted in rural areas of Bolivia, Paraguay, and Peru over a period of nearly two years. The study documents and describes the modalities of a particular form of forced labor called debt bondage. Under this system, intermediaries recruit agricultural workers through wage advances, and workers agree to pay back these advances with their labor or the produce of their labor. Once at the workplace, however, some workers find out that they have been deceived by the intermediaries and discover that the value of their labor is not properly accounted toward the reimbursement of the advance.

Coercion is used to prevent workers from leaving. Because they are being paid very little or nothing at all during the initial "reimbursement period," workers enter into further debt to buy their food and other essential goods at inflated prices from their employers or recruiters. Under this system, workers sometimes work a whole season without receiving any cash payment. In worst cases, workers end the season with a debt and remain bonded to their employer or intermediary for more than one season.

The existence of such practices illustrates how the absence of effective government regulation and labor standards can sometimes lead to dramatic labor market failures instead of the efficient outcome predicted by some economic models. It illustrates that, when left to itself, the market can be so much pervaded by problems of asymmetric information and unequal bargaining power that it can lead to gross forms of labor exploitation that involve deception and coercion.

The individual studies that comprise this multiple-case study were initially published separately in all three countries and targeted at policymakers in government, trade unions, employer associations, and civil society.[1] They have become part of a process of policy dialogue among national governments, social partners, and the ILO and have also been used as inputs for the development of national policies against forced labor. This has led to some significant policy changes. President Alan Garcia launched Peru's national action plan against forced labor on May 1, 2007, and President Evo Morales of Bolivia has pledged the government's support for the implementation of a comprehensive development plan for indigenous peoples in the Chaco region. Paraguay has also started—albeit more slowly—to identify measures for the elimination of debt bondage in its rural areas.

The chapter is organized into four sections. The first section describes the objective and the methodology of the study. The second section presents the main results of our multiple-case study. This includes a detailed discussion of the recruitment through wage advances and the manipulation of the debts that results from the advances, as well as the failures in the payment of wages. We include a discussion of the possible number of workers involved in forced labor in the third section. The concluding section deals with some policy options.

## Methodology

Our case study tests the hypothesis that debt bondage exists in geographical areas characterized by a weak capacity of the state to implement labor legislation, a supply of highly vulnerable workers, and a demand for low-skilled workers in labor-intensive sectors.

### The Choice of the Countries

Our individual case studies in Latin America were carried out in five locations, most of which are remote and difficult to access: (1) The departments of Madre de Dios and Ucayali in the eastern part of Peru, close to the border with Brazil; (2) the departments of Santa Cruz and Tarija in rural Bolivia; (3) the departments of Beni and Pando in Bolivia's remote northern Amazon region, which borders Brazil; (4) the Chaco region of Bolivia; and (5) the departments of Boqueron and President Hayes in the Chaco region of Paraguay. We believe that these five regions cumulate the three characteristics identified above as possible determinants of forced labor. In addition to a weak state capacity, all these regions are characterized by a supply of vulnerable workers as well as by the existence of low-technology, labor-intensive economic sectors.

Regarding labor supply, the high incidence of poverty certainly contributes to the large stock of vulnerable workers. The element that differentiates these five regions from much of the rest of Latin America, however, is their high proportion of indigenous people. Whereas indigenous peoples represent 10 percent of Latin America's population (Hall and Patrinos 2006), census data indicate that indigenous people represent 62 percent of the population in Bolivia and 25 percent in Peru. In Paraguay, although the overall proportion of indigenous people is low (about 2 percent of the population), indigenous people represent 30 percent of the Chaco region, a sparsely populated region that covers more than half the country's territory.

In all three countries, indigenous peoples are subjected to a considerable amount of discrimination in the labor market. In a recent study, Hall and Patrinos (2006, p. 3) calculated that the proportion of earnings inequality between indigenous and nonindigenous people that can be attributed to labor market discrimination is very high.[2] Furthermore, a study by Trivelli and Morales in Peru (forthcoming) indicates that discrimination is a more powerful explanatory variable of differences in wages and conditions of work in the rural areas— where we have focused our study—than in the urban areas.

There exists also a literature that shows how, in the past, people of indigenous origin were held in debt bondage in rural areas. Brass (1986), for example, has described the existence of debt bondage in the semitropical eastern lowlands of Peru in the 1970s. Similar practices were documented in other parts of Peru, including the Amazon basin during the rubber boom (Chevalier 1982); in the coca, tea, and coffee plantations of the Alto Huallaga (Bedoya 1993); and in the indigenous communities of the upper Ucayali (Gray 1997). In Paraguay, a small literature describes how indigenous people have suffered from poor working conditions and sometimes forced labor (Chase-Sardi, Brun, and Enciso 1990; Kidd 1994; Renshaw 1996; and Zanardini and Biedermann 2001). Kidd, in particular, has documented the existence of debt bondage among the ethnic Enxet in the isolated and distant region of the Chaco. Several sources have also documented the persistence of debt bondage in Bolivia, particularly among workers who collect nuts in the northern Amazon region, but also among ethnic Guarani workers in the sugar plantations of Santa Cruz (see Assies 2002 and Henkemans 2001). This literature also reveals some controversies. According to some authors, the *castaña* (Brazil nuts) boom has led to an improvement of labor conditions and the suppression of traditional forms of debt bondage (Stoian 2000; Bojanic Helbingen 2001).

## Objectives

Our study aims to be both descriptive ("does forced labor occur and, if yes, what is the modus operandi?") and explanatory ("why, in which circumstances, does it happen?"). The primary motivation for the study was policy oriented. The methodology that we have used is the so-called multiple-case study, which consists of five individual case studies conducted in three different countries. In Peru, the study focuses on the logging industry in the Amazon region. In Bolivia, research was carried out in the nut collection sector of the northern Amazon, the sugar plantations around Santa Cruz, and the cattle farms in the Chaco region. The last study was carried out in the remote Paraguayan Chaco, covering traditional types of cattle ranches. Since all studies were published separately, this chapter does not dwell on individual cases.[3] Instead, we provide a cross-case analysis focused on the modus operandi of rural debt bondage, highlighting similarities but also differences across the five cases.

Like most case studies, all our individual studies have relied on a variety of sources: documents, interviews, and—whenever possible—direct observation. This approach allows for some triangulation and corroboration strategy, whereby facts can be supported by more than a single source. For each country we started with a thorough review of documentary evidence, starting at the ILO.[4] We then conducted open-ended and semistructured interviews in all five regions as well as in the capital cities of all three countries, namely Lima, La Paz, and Asunción. The overall strategy in each country was to start with key informants in the capitals and to follow the trail of information, which determined or confirmed our choice of the five specific locations. When concrete cases of debt bondage were mentioned, we sought additional information (written or oral) to corroborate the cases.

In total we interviewed more than 300 people: government officials, judges, labor inspectors, police officers, trade unionists, indigenous leaders, representatives of NGOs, international civil servants, members of the church, labor contractors, and, of course, workers and employers. Interviews with workers were conducted either individually or in the format of focus groups with the number of participants varying between 5 and 20 people. These interviews were semistructured and always geared toward obtaining information about forms of recruitment and the existence of debts, working conditions, the level and frequency of wage payments, whether the whole family worked for the same employer and in what conditions, and the liberty of movement, as well as the existence of company stores and their prices. Given the sensitivity of the requested information, anonymity was always guaranteed to all interviewed people.

During the fieldwork, we were able to augment evidence from written sources, such as copies of labor contracts or copies of the accounts where labor intermediaries recorded the wage advances and wage deductions. On one occasion we were able to access and photocopy the notebook of an *enganchador* (contractor) who recruited workers for the sugar harvest in Santa Cruz, Bolivia. The notebook registered the individual debts of the workers. Whenever we could, we also checked the prices of the subsistence goods that company stores sell to the workers. This evidence allowed us to verify some of the information obtained through the open interviews.

Probably the single most revelatory document that we found was a previously confidential report from a high-level commission in Bolivia that provides evidence of families held in debt bondage in the Chaco region. With the support of the new authorities, we published this report as an appendix to the individual studies in Bolivia (see Bedoya Garland and Bedoya Silva-Santisteban

2005b). Other important documents included a report by the Senate Commission of Bolivia on the situation of workers in the nut collection sector in the northern Amazon region as well as registered denunciations in the Office of the Human Rights Ombudsperson (Defensoría del Pueblo) in La Paz.

In addition to using multiple sources of evidence to obtain a convergent line of inquiry, we verified the validity of our findings by submitting our individual studies to a procedure of validation. A total of nine validation meetings were held with representatives of government, trade unions, and employers' organizations in all three countries. Although some individual reviewers disagreed with the findings or with the estimated extent of the problem, the meetings largely corroborated the facts contained in this chapter. The most substantial comments were taken into account in the final versions of the individual case studies.

Finally it must be pointed out that all five individual cases were conducted and implemented by the same research team. This usually increases the reliability of multiple case studies by avoiding complications related to the guiding and training of different investigators in carrying out data collection and interpreting and recording the findings. It certainly made direct comparison among the five individual cases much easier.

## Results and Findings

The individual case studies reveal that debt bondage still exists in all five regions of Peru, Bolivia, and Paraguay, with varying degrees of intensity and duration. Indigenous people represent a large share of all the bonded workers, but they are not the only victims. *Mestizos* (individuals of mixed colonial and indigenous descent) are also affected.

In Peru, we found that debt bondage is being used against mixed-blood workers and indigenous people—Shipibos and Ashaninkas—in the Amazon basin for the purpose of illegal logging and wood extraction. Most illicit logging operations take place within national indigenous community reserves, usually for the extraction of mahogany and cedar wood. These operations occur through the falsification of the documents provided for wood extraction or concessions—a practice known as *blanqueo de Madera* (or wood laundering). Other indigenous workers are bonded through wage advances within their own communities rather than in logging camps.

In Bolivia, debt bondage is used against indigenous Guaranies in the Chaco region and against *mestizos* and indigenous workers in both the sugar plantations near Santa Cruz and the nut collection activities (*castaña,* or Brazil nuts) of the northern Amazon. The Bolivian Chaco is possibly the most severe case of forced labor among our individual studies. Our evidence shows the existence in some farms of unfree labor relationships, where indigenous people work in condition of servitude, raising cattle or producing corn, peanuts, and chili peppers in traditional farms. They are sometimes paid with an old pair of trousers at the end of the year. These workers can be part of a whole community held in bondage by traditional landowners, who sometimes use open violence. Information from interviews was corroborated by a hereto confidential report of a high-level commission comprising various ministries, which describes concrete cases of debt bondage and unpaid labor in the two communities of Casa Alta and Laurel.

We also found debt bondage in Bolivia's northern Amazon, where the rubber industry of the previous centuries has been replaced by the collection and processing of *castaña*. Although 30 percent of the *castaña* is collected by independent communities who own their land, most of the remaining 70 percent of nut production takes place in about 300 jungle estates called *barracas* (cabins) where rural migrant workers and their families are employed during the harvest from January to March. Our interviews indicate that employers continue to recruit workers through intermediaries who provide wage advances to workers before the start of the harvest. This system of recruitment, called *habilito,* is still used in many parts of the Bolivian and Peruvian Amazon. Workers complain about their high level of indebtedness and the use of debt to retain them in the *barracas.*

Debt bondage also exists in the sugar plantations in the departments of Santa Cruz and Tarija. Every year, from March/April to September/October, about 30,000 workers and their families temporarily migrate from other regions (such as Chuquisaca or Potosí) to these plantations to make a living. These workers complement the local labor supply and fulfill the large overall seasonal demand. One widespread form of recruitment is the system of *enganche* (hooking), whereby workers receive wage advances from intermediaries. On the plantations, this system can turn into debt bondage. Most workers are of indigenous origin, from the Quechua and Guarani groups. Here again, this has led to a series of social conflicts among employers, intermediaries, and workers and to some complaints from the local trade union,[5] asking for a prohibition of this system of recruitment.

In Paraguay, we have observed debt bondage against members of the indigenous ethnic group Enxet Sur in the rural communities of the Chaco, but only in the more traditional and remote cattle farms. Permanent male workers are typically employed as *playeros* (ranch hands) to perform a variety of tasks such as gathering and cutting wood or milking the cows. Women perform domestic services such as cooking and cleaning. Casual workers are hired for completing *changas*—short-term assignments such as clearing fields or repairing walls. It is also not unusual for indigenous workers to be remunerated for a few months of work with a shirt, a pair of trousers, and a pair of boots. Women are sometimes not remunerated at all.

In the following sections we look in more detail at the modus operandi and sequence of events that lead ultimately to debt bondage and forced labor. We emphasize both similarities and some differences across the cases.

### The Recruitment Through Wage Advances

Workers in debt bondage are generally recruited through wage advances by labor contractors or middlemen, who promise them good pay and decent working conditions. Unfortunately, "talk is cheap" (Stiglitz 2002, p. 471). The problem of adverse selection is that intermediaries do not have any incentive to tell workers the truth at the moment of recruitment and hence deceive them about future working conditions. This illustrates the general problem that the "free market" does not provide appropriate incentives for information disclosure.

The wage advances mark the start of a spiral of indebtedness, which later can lead to situations of debt bondage. Employers provide a sum of money to these intermediaries who, in turn, use this money to provide wage advances to workers. In some instances the chain of intermediaries can be relatively long. In Peru, for example, it was observed that some employers pay an advance to so-called *habilitadores,* who then make smaller advances to local *patrones* (bosses), who in turn recruit workers through wage advances. In Bolivia, some employers advance money to *contratistas* (contractors), who in turn hire *sub-contratistas* to recruit workers through advances.

As a result of these subcontracting chains, employers rarely sign any contracts with workers directly. Labor contracts are usually concluded orally between the workers and the middlemen. Employers expect middlemen to deal with all labor issues and therefore may not always be aware of the conditions agreed upon between workers and middlemen. In Bolivia the term used to indicate this method of recruiting labor is called *habilitación* (facilitation) in the case of Brazil nuts and *enganche* in the case of sugar. Both cases refer to money advances through intermediaries. In practice, the differences between both systems are not significant.

In the few cases where written contracts could be found, they have confirmed the suspicions of debt bondage. In the sugar plantations of Santa Cruz (Bolivia), for example, standard written contracts were signed by employers, workers, and a "guarantor." The contracts stipulate that all transactions between the employer and the worker be channeled through the "guarantor," who is considered to represent the workers' interests. This guarantor is in fact a middleman whom the contract designates as responsible for paying back any of the workers' "pending accounts" (debts, for example) to the employer. Thus, for all labor issues, workers have to deal with the middlemen, not with the final employer. Through this system, employers try to elude legal responsibility with respect to the hiring of labor and the conditions of work.

The amount of the wage advance made to individual workers varies considerably. Interviews as well as accounts of middlemen in Bolivia suggest that employers advance to each middleman a sum that varies between US$3,500 and US$4,500. This advance is then used by middlemen to provide many smaller wage advances to workers that range from US$20 to US$150, with an average of about US$65. This average represents about one month of the minimum wage, or about 10 to 15 percent of the total wage payments that workers may expect for one season of temporary agricultural work. In Peru, workers similarly receive wage advances that represent between 10 and 20 percent of the total expected payments. This may not seem like a high amount, but it often only represents the first step in the cycle of indebtedness.

Although the wage advance is generally made to the workers—usually migrant workers in their communities of origin or in nearby cities—some middlemen were also found to make advances to indigenous leaders in exchange for a commitment to provide the necessary amount of wood at a given date. In Peru, for example, *patrones* have been reported to make initial advances of up to US$1,400 to the leaders of an indigenous community. In other cases, *patrones* have made advances not in the form of cash but in the form of food and goods (such as salt, rice, pairs of boots, or sewing machines) in exchange for a commitment by indigenous leaders to provide a predetermined quantity of logged wood at an agreed-upon moment in the future. It is then the indigenous leaders who order community members to cut the wood. This explains why the *enganchador,* who is essentially a contractor of labor, is sometimes perceived by indigenous communities as simply proposing an exchange of goods (see Dean 1995).

Although it is always the men who receive the original wage advance and who contract the debts, the entire family is often expected to provide labor. In the majority of cases, the women and children of the workers do not have any contractual relation with the employer. They are considered as "helpers." In the Bolivian sugar plantations, women cook for their families and peel and store the canes that are cut by men and their older sons. In Peru's logging camps, women also prepare the food. And in all three countries, women and their daughters often provide free domestic services to the landlord. In the cases where women are actually paid, their remuneration is usually added to that of the husband or father and paid to the latter. This practice reflects the stereotypical image of women as "secondary" earners, which legitimates low pay or no pay at all.

## The Manipulation of the Debt

One common feature of debt bondage—and indeed one key aspect of its definition—is that the work provided by the debtor is not properly accounted toward the reimbursement of his or her debt. In practice, this means that the debt or the implicit interest rate is fraudulently increased in order to extract more than the legitimate amount of work from the debtor. Through such manipulations, the value of the labor provided ultimately exceeds the true value of the debt. This extra work is what allows the creditor to reduce average labor costs and to extract an illegitimate economic rent.

In practice, intermediaries manipulate workers' debts in several complementary ways. As we have already seen, workers are usually indebted through a wage advance from a labor intermediary before the beginning of the work. As a result, workers are generally unpaid for their work during some initial period of time (the reimbursement phase). During this time, debts often continue to increase because workers have no alternative other than to buy food and subsistence goods by taking up credit at the company store. This is all the more inevitable when the workplace is geographically isolated or when employers prevent any exchange between workers and outside traders.

This new debt has itself a fraudulent dimension because prices in the supply stores are often artificially inflated. Cash-strapped, debt-ridden workers are made to face a monopoly supplier of basic goods, who charges prices that—according to our study—have a 50 to 400 percent markup compared to prices in the nearest towns. In Peru, members of the antilogging police estimate that prices of basic goods in company stores are three to four times higher than in the nearest city. Thus, instead of diminishing as a result of their work, the debts of the workers continue to increase as a result of their consumption. In Peru, for example, many workers claim to be unpaid during the first two or three months of their work. During this time, the debts owed to company stores accumulate to sometimes very high levels.

Typically, the "patron" tries to be, as much as possible, the only supplier of goods in the communities where he works. This monopolistic control is easiest to establish in the most remote zones of major rivers, in high river basins, and in more traditional communities. This allows the patron to manipulate the debts with greater ease. Since there are no alternative sources of supply, the workers have no choice but to accept the conditions that are imposed. This, however, does not always happen. In the zones closer to the main rivers or more important urban centers, workers have more alternatives, and by the same token, they have a greater capacity to negotiate.

Intermediaries not only manipulate the books by inflating prices at the company stores. They also deflate the value of the work provided by the workers. This can happen through unexplained (virtual) wage deductions. In Bolivia, for example, we found the books of a middleman, who made deductions he could not explain under an apparently arbitrary heading called "savings" (*ahorro*). In a complementary manipulation, intermediaries sometimes provide a large share of workers' salaries in kind (with a pair of overvalued trousers, for example). Such practices contribute to further slowing down the rate at which workers can repay their debts. In Peru, the undervaluation of work can also be done in a more systematic and methodical way. As we have already pointed out, *patrones* sometimes make initial advances to indigenous communities in the form of food or goods in exchange for a certain quantity of wood to be delivered later. In the mildest form of deception, *patrones* take advantage of the community's unfamiliarity with the value of the goods to overprice these goods. In a more serious form of deception, *patrones* turn to a practice known as *castigo de madera* (wood punishment), which is the faulty measuring of the wood: when the communities provide the agreed-upon amount of wood, the patron undervalues the wood he is given, and—though he usually takes all of the trunks he is provided—also declares some of the wood unusable. The *patrones* then explain that the indigenous community has a pending debt that it can cover either by providing more wood or by sending workers to nearby logging camps.

According to Alvarez (2003), one community in Peru signed an agreement or "contract" agreeing to extract an amount of wood estimated by the author to have a market value of almost 500,000 soles (US$150,000) in return for an electric generator worth less than 5,000 soles (US$1,500). In another case, one indigenous worker thought he had done good business when he agreed to extract 40 trunks of mahogany (worth 370,000 soles on the market [US$115,000]) in exchange for a motor engine worth exactly 1,270 soles or US$396. Worse still, the contractor rebalanced his accounts and informed the indigenous man that he still owed him money. These are plausible stories.

Most of the time the two mechanisms of debt bondage—inflation of the debt and deflation of the value of work—occur simultaneously. One farm that we visited showed us their account books: we saw that the intermediary paid indigenous workers about 10 percent less than the minimum wage and that he paid out 25 to 50 percent of wages in kind instead of cash. At the same time, the prices in the company stores were on average 50 percent above the price of the same products in the nearest town. Thus, overall, workers remained indebted until the end of the season. Note that neither the wage advance nor the intermediary is absolutely necessary for debt bondage to arise. In the Chaco of Paraguay, for example, we found no evidence of wage advances or labor contractors. Debt bondage there is essentially the result of inflated prices in company stores and of the undervaluation of the work that is provided by the workers.

Although all these economic rents are obtained through the manipulation of debts, the arrangements are often enforced through threats, including physical violence. In Peru, key informants report that armed guards are almost always present in the illegal logging camps, and the documents of the Defensoría del Pueblo also confirm that *patrones* possess guns. These guns are used to intimidate workers. Informants report the existence of death threats against workers, who are not allowed to leave the logging camps until all debts are settled. When informants refer to workers' decisions to abandon the logging camps, they generally use the words "escape" or "flee." Workers often do not dare to protest and after several weeks—because of their low literacy and numeracy—they lose track of the amount of their supposed debt. Workers are told that they "owe" the intermediary or the employer—but they are not told how much.

## The Duration of Debt Bondage and the Nonpayment of Wages

In general terms, the result of the aforementioned practices is that the system of wage advance (*habilitación* or *enganche*) progressively transforms itself into a system of debt bondage, where workers are retained without being paid. The workers subjected to these debts cannot resort to other mechanisms to pay their debts, such as working for another employer or soliciting a loan from someone else. The indebted worker has no choice but to pay the debt by working for the *enganchador* to whom he or she is indebted, entering into a circle of advances, deceit, more advances, and more debt.

Most of the bonded labor documented in our study is of a short-term nature, lasting generally no more than one harvest. Indeed, most workers terminate the harvest season with no debt or with a small positive balance. This positive balance often remains unpaid. Those workers in Bolivia's northern Amazon who end the harvest season with a small positive balance are usually told by the labor contractors that their balance will be settled once they have gone back to their hometowns. The Defensoría del Pueblo (the human rights ombudspersons) and regional labor inspectors indicate, however, that many workers complain about unpaid wage balances. Hence, for many workers, debt bondage means that they receive little or no money for several months of work. In effect, they work only in exchange for food and for paying off debts.

This short-term debt bondage has some similarities to so-called neobondage relations in South Asia (see, for example, Srivastava 2005, Breman 2007, or Lerche 2007). The short-term nature of debt bondage also supports the hypothesis that the purpose of the system, from the point of view of the intermediary or the employer, is not so much to ensure a long-term labor supply as it is to push down labor costs as much as possible. Inflated prices at food stores, arbitrary wage retentions, and exaggerated implicit interest rates on workers' debts all contribute to reducing workers' final take-home pay.

There remains, nevertheless, a small minority of workers who remain trapped with their employers after the harvest. In some cases, employers confiscate workers' belongings until they pay off the manipulated debt with cash. In most cases, employers force workers to pay off the debt through additional labor, either by returning to the same employer for the next harvest or by staying on after the harvest. In Bolivia's northern Amazon, for example, some workers remain in the *barracas* after the harvest to perform maintenance work—sometimes until the next harvest.[6] In some rare instances, especially in the smaller *barracas,* the workers' debt further increases during this additional period. It is thus not impossible that short-term debt bondage ultimately results in long-term bonded labor.

Some debts can last for many years and even for whole generations. Such is the case of the debts acquired in the illegal logging of wood in Peru, especially in the case of indigenous communities. The pending debts can be used to keep indigenous workers in debt bondage for decades or generations. The existence of long-term servitude was also confirmed from other sources in the Chaco region of Bolivia. A 1999 investigation by the Vice-Ministry of Justice and the Office of the Human Rights of Indigenous People confirmed in particular that some Guarani indigenous communities were held captive on the land of wealthy farmers. The final report of the investigation concluded that in one community "the debt represents a means to retain and force [workers] to continue working for the same employer as long as the debt is not repaid, but it happens in many cases that the debt can never be repaid, and hence that workers can never stop working for the same employer" (see Bedoya Garland and Bedoya Silva-Santisteban 2005b, p. 104).

### Numbers of Workers

In the absence of specific survey instruments, it remains extremely difficult to estimate with any degree of precision the number of persons involved in debt bondage. According to the ILO, there are 12.3 million people in forced labor worldwide, of which 80 percent are in the private economy. In Latin America, the ILO (2005) estimates that more than one million workers are trapped in forced labor. This includes a large number of workers in debt bondage but also domestic workers and women in forced prostitution (including child prostitution). The problems that we have documented in this chapter thus only represent a small share of the global problem. Our back-of-the-envelope calculations are shown in Table 2.1. We estimate that in the five rural regions covered in the present study, there are probably between 80,000 and 113,000 people in bonded labor.

**Table 2.1  The Magnitude of Forced Labor**

| Country | Estimated Numbers in Rural Forced Labor |
| --- | --- |
| Peru | 20,000–45,000 |
| Bolivia | 52,000–58,000 |
| Paraguay | 8,000–10,000 |
| Total | 80,000–113,000 |

In Peru, debt bondage occurs with two separate groups: the first is workers recruited in the closest urban centers to work in logging camps; the second is whole indigenous communities who live in the Amazon forest. We provide an estimate of both groups. Regarding the first group, the environmental police estimate informally that there are at least 1,500 logging camps. Based on our observations and on the available literature, we estimate that each camp employs an average of 10 to 20 workers, of which two-thirds are low-skilled debt-bonded workers (the other third are more skilled workers who are less likely to be bonded by debts). This represents an estimate of 10,000–20,000 people.

Regarding the second group, the only available data are from the 1993 Indigenous Census, which found that indigenous communities in the Amazon represent approximately 300,000 people, of which 75,000 are males in the 15–39 age category. We assume—based on our observations—that the number of people within indigenous communities who work in conditions of debt bondage ranges from 10,000 to 25,000. Summing up the figures of the two groups, we find a total of 20,000 to 45,000 exploited people in Peru.

In Bolivia, the most severe forms of forced labor are in the sparsely populated Chaco region of Chuquisaca, where an estimated 10,000 indigenous people work on farms. Our rough estimate is that 7,000 of them are in conditions of forced labor. More workers are engaged in the nut collection sector of the northern Amazon and the sugar plantations of Santa Cruz. Although estimates of the number of temporary workers involved in the collection of nuts are very variable, one of the more reliable figures is that there are 12,500 male workers, many of whom are accompanied by their families (Henkemans 2001). If half of the workers are accompanied by their wives and an average of two children, then we obtain a total of about 30,000 workers—all recruited through the system of wage advances. Of course, only a small proportion of these workers remain bonded for more than one harvest.

On the sugar plantations, the total number of temporary workers (including families) is estimated informally at 33,000 people, about two-thirds of which work on the large plantations where—in turn—an estimated 63 percent are recruited through the system of wage advances called *enganche* (Pacheco 1994). This represents about 15,000 people in debt bondage. It is possible, however, that—even in the smaller farms where wage advances do not take place during the recruitment phase—debt can arise as a result of inflated prices in company stores. We assume that this affects at most one-third of the workers in such smaller farms, representing 6,000 workers. Hence, in sugar plantations our estimate is of 15,000 to 21,000 people in short-term debt bondage. Adding up the estimates for the three regions of Bolivia, we find 52,000 to 58,000 people working in mostly short-term debt bondage.

Finally, in Paraguay, the 2002 national census on indigenous peoples showed that about 1,800 heads of household out of Paraguay's total 16,000 indigenous families receive their payments "in kind" instead of cash or buy their food and essential goods with credit in company stores. If we assume that these people are precisely those in debt bondage and that half of all male workers are accompanied by their families (the size of which varies by ethnic group), this represents an estimated 8,000 people. In addition, we estimate that there may be up to 2,000 nonindigenous workers in similar conditions, bringing the total for the Chaco region of Paraguay to anywhere between 8,000 and 10,000 people in debt bondage.

## Conclusions and Policy Discussions

This chapter has described how some of these cases of debt bondage can occur as a result of market failures in rural areas where there is a supply of particularly vulnerable workers, a demand for low-technology labor-intensive work, and a very weak capacity of the state to enforce fundamental provisions of its legislation. The modus operandi shows that debt bondage in rural Latin America starts with deceptive recruitment through intermediaries who provide wage advances to workers. This generates a debt that can be manipulated by intermediaries or employers for the purpose of reducing workers' pay and exploiting them economically. At the end of the season, many workers have little or no wage to take home. Some are paid with used pieces of clothing.

What can be done? We suggest actions consistent with the three main causes of forced labor that are identified in this chapter. First and most urgent is the need to strengthen the capacity of the state by updating the relevant legislation and increasing means of enforcement. Forms of unpaid compulsory labor to which indigenous peoples were subjected during colonial times were generally abolished in the nineteenth century, and the current constitutions of all three countries now prohibit all forms of slavery, servitude, and human trafficking. The constitution of Peru specifies that nobody should be forced to work without consent or without a fair and decent wage. These general principles, however, are not enough. Labor codes and penal codes generally lack adequate provisions to prevent and combat forced labor. Specific norms are needed, in particular, to regulate private recruitment and wage advances or to extend the coverage of the labor code to rural wage workers.

Although better legislation is a necessary element, it must be complemented by more resources for labor inspection services. The few existing inspectors in rural areas often lack sufficient training and information on forced labor practices and are sometimes subjected to strong pressure on the part of local employers. When inspectors are isolated and poorly remunerated, corruption also becomes an issue. At the time of this study, there was not a single labor inspection office in the Chaco region of Paraguay. Much could be learned in Peru, Bolivia, and Paraguay from the experience of Brazil's Mobile Inspection Units that are centralized in the capital, Brasilia, and that, together with protection from the federal police, undertake inspections in remote farms that are suspected to use "slave labor."

But law enforcement alone is unlikely to succeed in eradicating forced labor. Additional measures should focus on reducing the supply of vulnerable workers. In the long term, this will require the development of alternative employment opportunities and poverty reduction. In the shorter term, vulnerability can be reduced through awareness-raising campaigns to inform workers of their rights and by promoting freedom of association and the unionization of indigenous and rural workers. One major challenge in the area is for established trade unions to step out of their traditional sphere of urban influence and reach out to workers in the informal sector and the rural economy. Such measures to promote unionization and social dialogue could be accompanied by major programs to promote the literacy, education, and professional skills of indigenous peoples.

The demand side too should be addressed. It makes, of course, no sense to advocate the prohibition of low-skilled, employment-generating economic activities. Employers can be made more aware of the economic risks linked to the violation of fundamental labor rights, however. Indeed, the large majority of employers do not use forced labor and know that in the global economy reputational risks can be very expensive. The practices of a few employers or farmers—when exposed on the front pages of global newspapers—can lead to consumer boycotts that in turn can affect whole economic sectors or even bring entire countries into disrepute. It would be useful to transfer the good practices from employers who respect workers' rights and their own codes of conduct to those employers who are less up-to-date. Of course, one important challenge here is that most employers who use forced labor remain outside of mainstream employers' associations and, thus, can be difficult to reach. The sharing of good practices could also be coupled with subsidized business services or other public services.

Ultimately, however, all these and other measures will only be implemented if governments themselves can muster the political will to eliminate forced labor practices and confront the vested interests that lobby for impunity. A free media and public information campaigns can play a key role in this, insofar as they can lead to public opprobrium and democratic pressure. The linkage between trade policy and core labor standards—although hotly debated and rejected as protectionist by most economists—may also promote this noble objective.

### Notes

1. See Bedoya Garland and Bedoya Silva-Santisteban (2005a, 2005b, and 2005c)
2. The study shows that in Bolivia and Peru, 26 percent and 58 percent respectively of the differences in labor earnings between indigenous and nonindigenous peoples

cannot be explained by differences in education levels and hence may be attributed to discrimination in the labor market.

3. We have also excluded from this chapter much of the discussion on the context that prevails in the five regions that we have studied, as they are covered at length in the individual reports.

4. Peru and Paraguay ratified the ILO Forced Labour Convention, 1930 (No. 29), in 1960 and 1967, respectively (Bolivia ratified it in 2005). Both countries have had an extended dialogue on the existence of forced labor problems with the ILO's Committee of Experts of Application of Conventions and Recommendations, which reviews the implementation of ratified ILO conventions. In 1998, the Committee of Experts expressed concerns in relation to information that it received from the World Confederation of Labour (WCL) about cases of forced labor against indigenous peoples, especially in the Amazon regions of Atalaya and Ucayali. Similar concerns were raised in 1997 about Paraguay and the situation of indigenous peoples in the farms of the Chaco region. These concerns were expressed again in 2003, this time in the context of the discussion on implementation of the Indigenous and Tribal People's Convention, 1989 (No. 169).

5. The Federación Sindical de Trabajadores Zafreros de la Caña de Azúcar de Bolivia (Filial Santa Cruz y Filial Bermejo).

6. In 2000, the Federación Sindical Unica de Gomeros y Castãneros de Bolivia complained about this practice, and the Comisión de Trabajo del Senado received similar information.

# 3

## Bonded Labor in Pakistan

### *Ali Khan*

Bonded labor in Pakistan and India almost certainly accounts for the largest number of forced labor in the world today. As a response, the government of Pakistan adopted a National Policy and Plan of Action for the Abolition of Bonded Labour and the Rehabilitation of Freed Bonded Labourers in September 2001. In Pakistan the term *bonded labor* is defined in the 1992 Bonded Labour System (Abolition) Act (BLSA). The definition is cast rather broadly, embracing situations in which a debtor who has received an advance (or *peshgi*) in cash or in kind has to work for the creditor for no or nominal wages; one who does not do so forfeits freedom of employment, movement, or the right to sell labor at the market rate. Pakistan's National Policy and Plan of Action provides for an integrated range of measures to combat the problem. It also identifies the inadequacy of existing statistical and qualitative information on the extent and nature of bonded labor as one of the major constraints to effective action against it.

In an attempt to address the limited economic or social research on the issue and to provide a balanced, holistic picture of the ground realities, the ILO and the government of Pakistan instituted a number of research studies. Surveys have been undertaken on bonded labor in brick kilns in Punjab and among Haris (sharecroppers) in Sindh.[1] This chapter, in contrast to such reports, draws on material from a range of qualitative studies that have been undertaken since 2003 and that are anchored firmly on intensive fieldwork. Preconceived notions and perspectives were set aside so that an issue that has been prone to widely differing accounts in the past could be revisited with a clean slate. It was hoped that this would allow the research to move beyond the stereotype of bonded labor and would highlight a much wider range of labor arrangements, thereby shedding a fresh perspective on the issue.

This chapter uses the information obtained from the studies to analyze two major issues—recruitment systems and wage systems across the sectors surveyed in Pakistan. Essentially it is these two areas that are key to understanding how an individual falls into a bonded labor relationship (recruitment) and how she or he remains bonded (wage systems). The studies show that older forms of coercion and bonded labor are mutating into new ones. Although bonded labor continues to exist in agriculture, often rooted in traditional agrarian systems, the problem has now also been detected in other economic sectors, where intermediaries recruit workers through wage advances that can lead to significant indebtedness and, ultimately, debt bondage.

The first section of the chapter describes the methodology of the research. The second section discusses recruitment mechanisms in various segments of the agricultural sector as well as in some selected industries. Although the modalities differ, wage advances are common both in agriculture and in selected industries. The third section discusses wage systems as well as the causes and possible consequences of wage advances and how they can lead to bonded labor. The final section provides a brief summary of the debate about numbers and conclusions of this qualitative research.

## Methodology

The research process, at the outset, was overseen and guided by a Bonded Labour Research Forum that comprised senior representatives of the Pakistan government and chosen researchers with an interest and expertise relevant to the issue of bonded labor. The role of the forum was to ensure the quality of the research process and its outputs, such that the results would be credible and useful in terms of guiding practical and effective action by government and its partners. I was part of the forum as the appointed research coordinator. The research coordinator was nominated to help the researchers chosen to undertake the field studies on questions of design and methodology for fieldwork, to facilitate contact and exchange of information and lessons learned between the researchers, and to ensure the quality and uniformity of the final output. The research coordinator also undertook fieldwork with the separate researchers.

### Sector and Site Selection

The most fundamental decision made prior to the start of fieldwork was which sectors were to be selected for investigation. The sectors finally chosen by the Research Forum were those suspected of having the highest incidence of bonded labor. The sectors or economic activities selected were the following: agriculture, brick making, marine fisheries, mining, carpet weaving, hazardous industries (tanneries, construction, and glass bangle manufacturing), begging, and domestic service.

In the case of agriculture, brick making, mining, and carpet weaving, the widespread nature of these sectors and the potentially significant regional variations meant that the assessments would have to be undertaken in all four provinces.[2] The countrywide coverage would also assist in confirming or refuting assumptions that in certain sectors problems were limited only to particular provinces. This was particularly the case for agriculture, where it is often assumed that Sindh is the only province in which bonded labor is widespread. This is not the case, and some of the worst abuses that researchers encountered were found in the areas of northern Punjab. The inclusion of hazardous sectors was driven by the hypothesis that the nature of working conditions was such that coercive recruitment and wage systems could explain why workers continued to remain in employment in these sectors, particularly considering the low wages on offer.

In the case of the hazardous industries, two of the three subsectors are largely concentrated in a few main locations.[3] Therefore it was decided that these major concentrations be geographically targeted and focused on rather than spreading the survey to locations where the sector is too small for meaningful information to be gathered. In contrast, the construction, begging, and domestic work sectors are so widely spread out that it was decided that research would be best served by concentrating on three types of population centers: large cities, small cities/towns, and rural areas. The rapid assessment on marine fisheries was confined to Sindh and Balochistan, as those are the only two provinces with a coastline.

Overall, it was decided that the rapid assessments should be undertaken on a sectoral rather than provincial basis. Researchers felt more comfortable working on their sector of expertise rather than being assigned a particular province and multisectors. Moreover, as most had experience in working throughout Pakistan, provincial differences were not seen as being an obstacle. In addition, the rapid assessments were undertaken by teams that often utilized the services of local researchers. This was particularly advantageous where key local information or expertise was required or where informants were reluctant to speak openly to outsiders. Where a sector was particularly large and conditions were likely to vary considerably between regions, the research was undertaken by two separate researchers—as in the case of agriculture.

Keeping in mind the sensitive nature of the research and the short time period allocated, the choice of sites within each sector was made on the basis of detailed interviews with key resource persons as well as the past experience of the researchers. Furthermore, rather than concentrate on selecting random sites from a wider list of sites where the incidence of bonded labor was suspected, it was felt that the quality of the information would benefit from selecting sites with which researchers were familiar and in which they had personal contacts. The final selection of sites in the different sectors nevertheless represents a balanced provincial cross section.

## Fieldwork

The actual fieldwork for the rapid assessments was conducted over a period of 12 weeks. The appointed researchers worked with and supervised field teams. The use of teams allowed the rapid assessments to cover a greater number of locations and informants. In light of the specific characteristics of each sector, the different field teams adopted slightly different techniques to best suit conditions on the ground. Nevertheless, there were certain common themes that were built upon and used to form the basis for the rapid assessments. These included (1) an analysis of existing secondary information including national surveys and censuses, NGO and international organization reports, demographic and labor force surveys, and newspaper and magazine reports, and (2) the use of ethnographic methods of research to generate qualitative information, rather than focusing on quantitative information. Considering that generating quantitative data would require systematic sampling and administering comprehensive questionnaires, it was felt that these tasks would not be possible within the time period allotted.

The characteristics of rapid assessments—flexibility and adaptability— make this research tool well suited to study bonded labor. Bonded labor represents a sensitive area of research. It remains an illegal activity, and workers are hesitant to speak openly about their experiences for fear of suffering repercussions from their employers. In light of this, informal methods of gathering information—considered the least threatening modes of collecting data—were deemed the most appropriate. As a result, fieldwork focused on qualitative tools revolving around informal interviews, focus group discussions, building on existing contacts in the sectors, case studies, key informant interviews, community and workplace profiles, and observation. The studies covered interviews with employers (mine owners, landowners, small-scale industrialists), intermediaries (contractors, subcontractors), and workers and their families. Meetings were also held with concerned government officials at the federal, provincial, and district levels and with trade union leaders.

Certain sectors proved to be particularly challenging. Research on domestic workers is among the most difficult to gain entry into because it is confined to the private sphere of the home. The begging sector is often associated with criminal elements and drug use. Mining involves exposure to hazardous conditions. A more general difficulty is that employers are often influential people with links to government and police officials. This means that government and police officials are also often unwilling to divulge information on a system in which they may be implicated. The sensitivity surrounding research on bonded labor meant that even the informal techniques used by researchers had to be further adjusted and innovations had to be made during fieldwork.

It was generally found that even a checklist prepared by researchers for their own reference was abandoned as being too restrictive and formal. The use of tape recorders and cameras was considered disruptive and threatening. Although employers did not show an inclination toward threatening researchers in the field, there were some attempts to disrupt interviews with workers. On one occasion an interview with a mine worker was interrupted by the mine owner's repeatedly revving the engine of a truck while the interview was ongoing. On another occasion, carpet weavers in a workshop were warned against speaking to researchers. Despite the cooperation of the federal government, some district government officials also tried to dissuade researchers from visiting certain sites. This being said, in most cases research was undertaken without hindrance. Most employers appeared more concerned that researchers were tax officials rather than individuals working on labor conditions.

Informants were reluctant to speak to researchers in the presence of government officials or employers. Thus, wherever possible, interviews with the different groups involved were undertaken separately and often away from the place of work and after "work hours." This went some way to decreasing the threat felt by some of the informants. It was also found that informants gave very different responses depending on where interviews were conducted.

Overall, the strength of the method—pioneered in anthropology—is that it enables researchers to gather in-depth information on a sensitive area of research. Limitations, however, do need to be noted. The studies did not employ scientific sampling methodologies, and as such the results obtained cannot be quantified or generalized. Furthermore, researchers did not engage in the intensive, long-term participant observation that characterizes anthropological fieldwork and therefore could not provide the level of intricate detail that ethnography does. But the studies did go some way to gaining an understanding of the nature of bonded labor and confirming or refuting its existence in a particular sector. It is on the strength of the in-depth information gathered from the aforementioned studies that this analysis of recruitment and wage systems in sectors where bonded labor was identified is based.

## Recruitment Systems

The starting point for an arrangement that may lead to bonded labor is the recruitment system in place within particular sectors. How do individuals fall into relations of bonded labor, and, more important, why do they? A holistic response to these questions requires an understanding of the sociocultural factors that underpin the institution of bonded labor. Such an analysis will also address the more subtle, noneconomic factors that are sometimes overlooked when examining bonded labor. Recruitment mechanisms differ broadly between the agricultural and industrial sectors, although there is an increasing amount of overlap between the sectors. The two sectors will be analyzed separately, as this will allow both differences and similarities between recruitment in agriculture and industry to be highlighted.

The agricultural sector should not be seen as an undifferentiated mass, however. The sector displays what I shall refer to as "traditional" as well as more "modern" forms of recruitment corresponding respectively to older forms of debt bondage based on traditional hierarchical relations and those of newer forms of bondage or what Kevin Bales (2000) has described as neobondage. This chapter will use the provinces of Sindh (traditional) and Punjab (newer) to highlight the two different kinds of bonded labor within agriculture.[4] There will also be examples that highlight the transition between the two forms. In examining these variants, it becomes clear that different modes of recruitment can lead to different forms of bonded labor.

### Agriculture (1): Sharecropping Areas

The agricultural sector in Pakistan comprises 45.1 percent of the workforce and accounts for some 21.5 percent of the gross domestic product (GDP). It is therefore unsurprising that the majority of bonded laborers are to be found in this sector. But this is not solely because of the number of workers in the sector; it is also owing to factors intrinsic to the agricultural sector and in particular the influence of the caste system and the patron-client relations that underpin this system.

These patron-client arrangements can be viewed as an institution whereby wealthy individuals commit themselves to guaranteeing the subsistence of their laborers in exchange for the latter's ready availability (Platteau 1995, p. 637). Theoretically the patron-client relationship can be a mutually beneficial and reciprocal one, such that this particular kind of system assures poor people against the risk of starvation. For poor people, it is essentially an effort to maximize security in an uncertain environment. The patron secures access to a readily available, trustworthy, and compliant labor force, not only for productive tasks but also for ritual, social, and political activities or duties. Keeping this in mind, it is unsurprising that large landlords will often emphasize that their "contract" with their sharecroppers is to the benefit of both parties. The system is characterized by a simultaneous exchange of resources such as support and loyalty, long-term credit, and obligations.

Beginning in the nineteenth century, a series of legislative measures in the form of Tenancy Acts was instituted to "legalize" these relations and provide the tenants some protection.[5] Therefore, labor arrangements and recruitment in agriculture were mediated not through middlemen or subcontractors but through traditional relations between landowners and tenants and through the relevant

Tenancy Acts that addressed the issues of tenancy rights, duties of tenants and landlords, and the division of produce between them. The patron-client relationship is reinforced, however, through ritual ties and a set of duties and obligations known as the Jajmani system in South Gujrat and the Sepidari system in Punjab. Alavi argues that this system is best described as a form of master-subject relationship (Alavi 1987, p. 352). Essential to this relationship are ritually enacted acts that project the landlord as kindly and humane. Indebted, the recipient of this "kindness" is persuaded to reciprocate with what he can offer, that is, his labor.

In the province of Sindh, such tenancy still remains the most common arrangement for agricultural production. Hence, it is traditional relations between landowners and cultivating castes as described above that determine recruitment patterns. Relations between the two groups are often hereditary and of long standing, sometimes stretching back generations. In such a situation, sharecroppers will often belong to traditional tenant castes such as Meghwars and Kohlis whereas landowners will belong to traditional landowning castes such as Khosas and Talpurs. These traditional relations between landowning and nonlandowning castes provide the link or channel through which recruitment will typically be undertaken in the traditional agricultural sector.

Within this framework, recruitment is sealed through the provision of credit or a *peshgi* to the tenant by the landowner. Most tenants will have little or no collateral and savings. As a result, the *peshgi* is essential for subsistence purposes, and many tenants borrow cash or grain from a landlord at the start of their contract. This lump-sum amount could be interpreted as the "start-up cost" of a tenant and does not relate directly to the agricultural process. So although recruitment will follow lines of relations between groups who have traditionally tilled the land for those who have owned it, it is the offer of the advance that clinches the deal. The *peshgi* therefore becomes the essential element of the recruitment process, and tenants will often decide which landlord to work for on the basis of the initial credit amount that is offered. Moreover, tenants may also instigate a move from one landlord to another based on subsequent loans that landlords offer in order to secure a reliable workforce.

### Agriculture (2): Self-Cultivated Areas

Since 1960 there has been considerable change in land tenure patterns as many landowners have shifted from sharecropping to self-cultivation. From 1980 to 2000, the percentage of workers in sharecropping declined from 45 percent of the total farmers (on 48 percent of all cultivated land) to only 23 percent of the total farming population (on 27 percent of the land). Punjab is the main driver of change, with the tenant population declining from 58 percent in 1972 to only 21 percent of farmers in 2000. In Sindh this process is less advanced, but substantial changes have still occurred, with tenant ratios going down from 78 percent of farmers to 34 percent during the same period (Agricultural Census of Pakistan 1960, 1972, 1980, 1990). It would therefore be correct to state that the increasing trend toward self-cultivation has been at the expense of share-croppers and small farmers.

In response to these changes, the recruitment system has also altered from one dependent on traditional relations to one based on a far less personalized, more market-driven relationship involving two types of workers: casual and permanent. Casual labor refers to labor employed occasionally on a daily wage basis for specific agricultural work. Permanent labor means persons who work on the farm on a full-time basis, are employed for longer periods, and receive wages in cash or kind on a fixed-period basis. In the following paragraphs we describe how recruitment operates for these two types of workers.

Casual laborers, in both Punjab and Sindh, are found most commonly in self-cultivated and large owner-tenant–operated farms. These workers are mobile, tend to be used in the peak season, and usually negotiate wages according to the existing labor supply and demand situation. In both provinces this labor is recruited for the landowner through a labor agent or *jamadar.* These agents charge a finder's fee per laborer from the landlord. Mostly, agents charge the landlord in advance for the labor they provide. Some agents also charge landowners a specific share of their crop in lieu of labor.

The mode of payment is generally on a daily wage or contract basis. Casual workers may take advances or *peshgis,* but this rarely leads to bonded labor, as the amount of the *peshgi* is low and is adjusted as soon as work is completed. The *peshgi* is taken from the labor agent rather than from the landlord. For example, sugarcane cutters in southern Punjab work in groups for about three months. They receive advances that are subsequently adjusted at the time of final payment. Recruitment is for a fixed duration, and casual workers are not bound for further work. This casual labor is used particularly for livestock feeding, application of fertilizer, sowing, and irrigation. The salary for casual laborers ranges between 1,000 and 1,500 rupees (US$16–25) per month.

Permanent labor is found mainly on large farms—owner-operated as well as owner-tenant–operated. In Punjab, 51 percent of owner-operated farms in the 100- to 150-acre size range reported the use of permanent labor in 2000. These laborers perform various farm activities and domestic work. They are paid either on a monthly or yearly basis depending on the initial contract. Most permanent laborers are required to stay at the employer's house and are provided with two meals a day. Unlike sharecroppers, permanent agricultural laborers have no share in produce but are given a monthly salary (usually ranging between 1,200 and 1,800 rupees [US$20–30]). They are known in central Punjab as *seeris* and in southern Punjab as *rahaks.*

As in the case of sharecroppers, the initial advance, or *peshgi,* plays an important role in recruiting this kind of labor. The difference between the recruitment systems of sharecroppers and permanent laborers lies in the fact that the traditional tie between the landowner and his prospective worker has been weakened or severed. As such, the *peshgi* takes on an even more important role, namely that of creating a new relationship of dependence between employer and employee. The patronage and protection that characterized the sharecropper-landlord relation having been replaced by a more market-oriented system of recruitment, workers are left with a situation of open but less personalized "contractual" bondage (Breman 1999, p. 402).

In Punjab, all three kinds of permanent laborers were recruited on the basis of the initial advance offered. Under the arrangements of the *seeri* system, the *seeri* receives a loan from a landlord and in return works as a servant. Landlords often offer large *peshgis* to unemployed workers in return for their becoming *seeris*. Some were highly indebted to their employers as of 2000, to the level of 150,000 rupees (US$2,500). These employees are then expected to work exclusively for their creditor. In return they receive 40 *maunds* of grain each year—equivalent to approximately 1,000 rupees per month.[6] But the quantity of the grain reduces as the loan amount increases. *Peshgis* are also present in other systems of permanent labor found in Punjab. Loans tend to be smaller than is the case with *seeris,* however, and as a result the severity of bondage is also lower.

As a result of these systems, the most severely indebted agricultural laborers in Punjab were not sharecroppers but permanent agricultural workers who did not have a "traditional sharecropping" relationship with the landowners. Hence, it may be argued that in the transition to agrarian capitalism, the bondage of farm laborers has certainly not changed into a free labor system. "Bondage of labour is not a static phenomenon. While debt bondage has always existed, we may expect it to increase rather than decline, given the increasingly desperate economic situation faced by rural labour" (Patnaik 1983, 14). The laborers continue to be indebted to the landowners and are therefore unable to hire out their labor power to other employers, whether in or out of agriculture. Most of the time landowners still continue to immobilize permanent workers through the payment of an advance.

### Recruitment Systems in Industry

As more and more former tenants and small farmers are alienated from the land and from direct cultivation, they join the growing ranks of unemployed rural workers. Some are absorbed back into the modern agricultural sector as permanent or casual farm laborers. Others search for work in possible alternatives such as brick kilns and mines or in the manufacturing and industrial sector. At the same time, the higher landowning castes with historically more wealth and resources have been able to move into industry and now continue to draw on their "dependent" service castes to provide the workforce. Thus, even though the general patron-client relations that underpinned society through the influence of the caste system are more apparent in agriculture, their effects are also visible in the industrial sector, particularly where specific castes have dominated a particular occupation. For example, industries such as construction, tanneries, glass bangles, begging, and brick making are particularly susceptible to ethnic- and caste-based clustering. In these sectors, the patron-client bond is still important and operates against horizontal solidarity in the form of, for example, trade unions.

Apart from the influence of the caste system on industrial relations, the most significant aspect of recent industrialization in Pakistan has been its increasing decentralization and reliance on subcontracting. Initially the impulse for decentralization came in the 1970s, following the coming to power of Zulfiqar Ali Bhutto on the basis of an Islamic socialist manifesto. Bhutto's policies led to a tightening of labor laws, and stronger unions demanded increased representation, higher pay, and better working conditions in factories across Pakistan. As labor laws were not applicable to units employing fewer than 10 full-time workers, however, factory owners simply decentralized their operations, thereby preempting the possibility of further dissent. As a result, work was increasingly done at home. The result was a return to a distributed cottage industry relying not on a fixed labor force but on a casual and cheap pool of workers. This also allowed industrialists to avoid large capital outlays, overheads, and the provision of workers' benefits such as medical coverage, educational benefits, and old age pensions. A decentralized, often home-based labor force meant that trade unions were difficult to establish. Later, the trade union movement was also hampered in Pakistan because of the effects of decades of military rule, which has historically been hostile to any organized opposition to state policies.

The trend toward decentralization is not specific to Pakistan but has been a feature of industrialization in several developing countries that have increasingly seen a move toward dependence on a more flexible workforce (see Knorringa 1996, 1999; Kapadia 1999; Breman 1999; and De Neve 1999). Indeed, the path toward economic development for much of the developing world has seen the expansion of the formal sector outpaced by growth in the labor force. Hence, much of the workforce has been absorbed by what Hart (1973) first termed the "informal sector." Although regular factory employees appear to be relatively well paid and enjoy a range of benefits and rights as guaranteed under the existing labor laws, the much larger number of workers who are not part of the "formal" workforce are subcontracted and are not covered by labor laws.

To separate the economy into tight informal and formal segments would be inaccurate, however, as these two sectors are rarely independent of one another and in fact usually interact closely. For example, the tanneries and glass bangle manufacturing industries clearly have some processes completed in a formal factory environment, but a much larger number of tasks are dependent on a vast informal network. Other sectors such as mining and brick making may have an outwardly formal organization but again depend on a largely informal workforce.

The most important factor for labor relations and critically for recruitment, the decentralization of industry, has led to the reemergence of the subcontractor or labor agent—reemergence because these middlemen also played a role in the early industrialization of Pakistan. Then, subcontractors acted to provide workers from rural areas to industry. But as the industrial sector became increasing formalized in the 1960s and rural-urban migration increased, the role of the subcontractor declined. In their new role, subcontractors have emerged less as leaders of gangs of workers and more as foremen recruiting workers and implementing orders from above and from factory owners to avoid the conditions set by labor laws such as the Factory Act.

Typically, recruitment now starts in the industrial sectors when owners provide a middleman with a sum of money to be offered as advance payment for workers. This, as in the agricultural sectors, is known as a *peshgi*. This middleman then begins the process of recruitment. By giving the lump sum to be used as an advance to the middleman, the employer effectively removes himself from any direct dealings with workers. Once the owner provides the labor agent with a sum of money for a particular "job," the subcontractor becomes responsible for labor arrangements. For a commission, it is the subcontractor who arranges recruitment of a group of workers, supervises their work, mediates on disputed accounts, negotiates and distributes advances, and is responsible for the recovery of debts. This additional pressure on the labor agent means that he, in turn, is likely to give *peshgis* only to those workers he trusts or is confident of "controlling." This normally means workers from his extended kinship network or from his own village.

But even though these middlemen are frequently from the same locality and caste and occasionally from the same extended kinship group as the labor they recruit, these ties do not appear to make the subcontractor favor his laborers past offering them employment and moderating the worst cases of abuse and gross fiddling of accounts. In fact, in order to protect his interests, the subcontractor needs to be able to reduce the chances of nonaccountability of labor, and ensuring compliance is easier when the subcontractor has some previous links with those he recruits. It is also common practice for the middleman to receive the workers' wages from employers and then disburse them at his own convenience. Thus, labor and recruitment arrangements are entirely handled by the subcontractor. The subcontractor may be a co-worker, but his primary role is to enforce the work contract, and he should not be expected to defend workers. In other cases, some subcontractors further contract orders out to smaller subcontractors so that another link is added to the chain and the process is further decentralized.

The tendency to rely on particular caste or kin groups for recruitment often leads to a clustering of workers around ethnicity, caste, and kinship. This is even more pronounced in those sectors where industrial production is broken down into discrete tasks. Decentralization, then, occurs not only at the level of geographic locations but also at the level of tasks and skills. As a result, in those sectors where production consists of a series of related processes, a number of different subcontractors may be involved. For example, in brick making there are often different labor agents for each of the separate processes of molding unbaked bricks, stacking unbaked bricks, baking, and finally removing finished bricks.

Moreover, not only are there multiple subcontractors, but there exist also different levels of autonomy among middlemen—from those with very little autonomy to those who are budding employers themselves. In cases where the subcontractors have established greater autonomy from their owners, they may actually have their own capital at their disposal. In such cases, instead of employers placing orders for items and then providing the raw material and advance for wages to the contractor, it is the contractor himself who is responsible for the entire production process, including the provision of raw material. Once a product is completed, he then sells it to exporters. These contractors provide their own advances to their labor rather than acting as a conduit for the advance. Where the subcontractor has less autonomy, it is the owners who finance the production of goods through providing advances and raw material, but labor arrangements are the responsibility of subcontractors. .

All these subcontractors make use of an informal workforce—usually working at home (carpet weaving, glass bangles) or in small workshops (carpet weaving) and occasionally even in factories, but as the labor agent's subcontracted labor force rather than as employees of the factory (tanneries, mines, and brick kilns). Thus, the role of the subcontractor is to act as the link between capital and workers. Factory owners have little or nothing to do with the recruitment of labor, apart from the few regular employees that make up the formal workforce. Labor and recruitment arrangements are entirely handled by the labor agent rather than the factory owner or manager. In all these arrangements, the wage advance or *peshgi* plays a crucial role, acting as the seal in the recruitment process and enticing workers to accept the conditions of employment offered by the subcontractor along with the advance. As in agriculture, the manipulation of this *peshgi* can become an instrument to ensure that labor remains attached.

## High Debts, Low Wages, and Bonded Labor

We now move to the question of how labor—once recruited—is kept in place or immobilized. So this section progresses from recruitment to wage systems, but the common mechanism remains that of the *peshgi* or the advance on wages. Present in both recruitment and wage systems, it acts as the initial hook for recruitment and also the key element of the wage system. *Peshgi*s or advances, as already discussed, are an essential element in the recruitment process. It was the *peshgi* that acted as the initial hook in recruiting labor in all the sectors surveyed in the urban areas. In the case of agriculture, the *peshgi* is used to "strengthen" a preexisting, often hereditary linkage; where these bonds have been severed, it creates a new link. The *peshgi* initiates and completes the recruitment process. But along with the initial advance, subsequent advances form the dominant element in the wage system—and have important implications for those who become increasingly indebted. Indeed, it is through the increasing indebtedness that the *peshgi* becomes an instrument that ensures that once recruited, labor remains in place.

## Agriculture

In the sharecropping agricultural sector, there are, broadly speaking, two types of credit arrangements that are extended by landlords to tenants. First, many of the tenants borrow cash or grain from a landlord at the start of their contract. This lump-sum amount could be interpreted as the "start-up cost" of a tenant and does not relate directly to the agricultural process. Second, tenants receive agricultural inputs on credit from landlords throughout the crop cycle, against the notional expectation that the amount will be settled at the time of harvest. Debts outstanding at the end of the crop cycle are added by the landlord to the tenant's account. This amount is maintained on the books and would have to be repaid in full if the tenant stopped working for the landlord and sought tenure with a different landlord. The new landlord would then clear the tenant's debt with the old landlord and open a credit account of his own.

In principle, the credit extended by landlords to tenants is supposed to be interest-free. In effect, however, landlords charge interest on credit by overvaluing inputs and undervaluing outputs (Gazdar, Khan, and Khan 2002, p. 35). Moreover, nearly all landowners, in turn, borrow from trader-moneylenders. Thus the *seth* (or moneylender) maintains credit transactions with the landowner, and the landowner, in turn, maintains credit transactions with tenants. Any interest that is charged on the loan to the landowner is usually passed on to the loan given by the landowner to his tenant. Thus, even in those areas where sharecropper families work on a "half-share" tenancy basis, they rarely receive half-shares from the production owing to the deduction of input costs and debts. In some cases, we observed that the landlord was able to recover the entire harvest as repayment of the sharecropper's share of the input costs or as repayment of earlier loans. The end result is that, at the end of the season, the share of the agricultural produce taken by the landlord invariably exceeds the value of the credit he has provided.

For example, in the province of Sindh, the persistent drought, water shortages, and crop failure have meant, as Gazdar, Khan, and Khan (2002) report, that on average, a tenant's credit built up to around 4,000 rupees per acre for just one crop. This was the value of the tenant's share of inputs such as plowing costs, seed fertilizer, and pesticides. The tenant's share of the cost of running the tube well was also added to the total credit extended by the landlord. Once the tenant's share had been accounted for, the final crop shares in the Rabi 2000–2001 wheat crop bore little resemblance to the notional 50-50 division of the crop. The average size of the crop per tenant was 95 *maunds,* and the average amount handed over to the landlord was 82 *maunds* (i.e., more than 85 percent). Only around 10 percent of Haris managed to retain half the crop or more. A large number of tenants reported that they were left with no grain from the harvest at all. These tenants immediately reentered a credit arrangement in which they received a lump-sum advance (Gazdar, Khan, and Khan 2002).

## Nonagricultural Sectors

In a sector related to agriculture, that of domestic work, the wage and recruitment system is similar. Recruitment follows traditional caste divisions, with the majority of domestic workers coming from castes that have historically been associated with this line of work. For example, the Muslim Sheikhs who represent those groups that were part of the Hindu untouchable castes but converted to Islam are still associated with tasks that they undertook as part of their traditional caste obligations, and these include domestic work.

In rural and town settings, a dominant feature of labor arrangements for domestic service is the use of in-kind payment, usually by way of wheat, as a means of compensation. In some villages, there is a tradition of certain families working for the Makhdoom (a landlord caste). Servants who work for them receive the 40 *maunds* of wheat for a year's work. Some family members may also earn an additional 200 rupees and a sack of wheat each for additional work done around the house. This extra income is often used to meet loan repayments. A modified version of in-kind payment is also in evidence in the cities. Domestic servants who work for landlords in their urban homes receive wheat in their villages by way of payment. Men and women domestic servants with other, nonlanded employers also say they receive occasional food and clothing. This is not in lieu of their salaries, however, but in addition to their monthly remuneration.

In nonagricultural sectors, advances are offered at the start of the "contract" and may be offered subsequently as well. These *peshgi*s are taken against the understanding that the worker-borrower will clear his or her account by deducting the advance from the remuneration for his or her labor. Generally, the larger the advance, the more money is deducted from wages. Except for the carpet-weaving sector, there was little evidence of interest being charged on advances. And even in the carpet sector, interest was only charged on large loans. Wages are typically given on a weekly basis.

Workers who were indebted were rarely penalized through a lower wage rate. They may receive lower wages, but that is the result of a fair amount being cut for debt repayment. As such, the wage systems do not appear to have a hidden profitability. It could be argued, however, that the provision of *peshgi* does mean that overall wages are kept low, thereby increasing the employer's profits. Employers as patrons offer workers the "service" of a loan but in return will demand "compensation" through the provision of lower wages across the sector. But to understand fully how the *peshgi* can be manipulated to ensure that labor remains bonded, it is important to examine, briefly, why *peshgi*s are taken and what the implications are of taking them.

### Reasons for Recourse to Peshgis

*Peshgi*s are taken for a number of reasons; the most basic one is the inability of the worker to support his needs through returns in the sector, and it is this chronic and growing debt that the worker incurs while working that is largely responsible for debt bondage. In other words, wages are often below subsistence level, and the ensuing shortfall that the family faces is met by recourse to loans. With a lack of other forms of collateral, the only recourse is to take *peshgi*s and effectively replace collateral with labor (Ray 1998).

Furthermore, work in some sectors, namely glass bangle manufacturing, mining, brick making, fisheries, and agriculture, is characterized by a seasonal demand for labor. In the slack season the worker's income dries up, particularly in areas where options for alternative work are severely limited. For example, our research found that fishermen and agricultural workers found it extremely difficult to find any alternative work off-season. For some, *peshgi*s may instigate migration over large distances for employment in other provinces, as in the case of agricultural workers in certain parts of the North-West Frontier Province who took up mining in Sindh, Balochistan, and Punjab in between cropping seasons at home.

A further reason for taking *peshgi*s and subsequent loans was to try to cover expenditure "spikes" that invariably occur. Even those families that are able to subsist on the meager income of their individual members cannot cope with the costs related to a sudden illness or death. It is important to remember that the majority of employment in the sectors where our studies were undertaken takes place in the unorganized sector of the economy where there are no unemployment benefits, no health allowances, and no social benefits. In the absence of this social security and lack of savings for the segment involved, *peshgi*s are often the only way to make ends meet at times of high expenditure.

Life events such as weddings and funerals similarly demand considerable expenditure. The failure to arrange an "appropriate" wedding leads to an immediate loss of face (*izzat*) for the family in the larger community. It may also result in an unsuitable match for daughters. The expenditure associated with weddings can easily exceed the annual earnings of a family. Some observers have reported this spending to be on average more than 80 percent of the annual income.

### The Degree of Indebtedness and Effective Bondage

The different reasons for taking *peshgis* influence the amount of the advance taken. Small subsistence loans, usually less than 1,000 rupees (US$15), are taken by workers in all sectors. These small loans are taken and returned on a fairly regular basis, although sometimes these small loans do accumulate to larger debts. Those taking (and returning) small loans face far fewer restrictions, however, than those accepting larger loans. Therefore, if we consider all those who at some point in their working lives have taken loans to be bonded laborers, then the incidence of bondage expands to cover almost all labor. But generally small loans do not appear to have the serious implications associated with long-term indebtedness.

Far more problematic are the large *peshgis* that are characteristic of loans taken for marriages or sudden illnesses. Large advances tend to be less common than the smaller loans but were found in all the surveyed sectors. It was these large *peshgis* that typically led to substantive bondage—a condition leading to long-term indebtedness with no real option for debt redemption except to supply labor to the same employer or to transfer the debt to another employer but only at the discretion of the owner. It is here that the *peshgi* becomes an economic instrument of coercion that increases the leverage that the employer has over the indebted worker. In contrast, *peshgi* loses its utility to the creditor when it is returned on a regular basis, as is more common with smaller loans. Repayment decreases the leverage that a creditor has over labor.

Workers take advances ranging from a few hundred rupees to several thousand rupees from their employers. Taking *peshgis* immediately imposes certain conditions on the worker, however, beyond the obligation to return the original amount. At the most basic level, once *peshgi* is taken the worker cannot move from the current employer without repaying the advance in full. This means that better opportunities are forfeited unless another advance is taken from an alternate creditor to pay off the original loan. Again, those with smaller loans will find it far easier either to pay back and move on to better paid employment or to have their (small) loan refinanced by another employer.

But if bondage is to be effective along with being substantive (long-term indebtedness), then the obligation of labor should be accompanied by the threat of noneconomic coercion, that is, it should be seen as enforceable. Noneconomic coercion comes in the form of surveillance, physical confinement of labor, and the threat of violence as well as the actual use of violence. These methods ensure the effectiveness of bondage. They also show that accepting an advance on wages opens up the possibility of severe implications, including being subjected to physical and verbal abuse, the threat of or actual use of violence, the provision of wages below the market level, and the inability to exercise freedom of employment.

In agriculture these implications appear to be more extreme than those evidenced in other sectors. They also impinge on almost every aspect of the indebted individual's or family's life as well as denying the freedom to control the produce of one's labor. The decision on the crops to be sown is made by the landlord, who also handles the sale of the crop and afterwards "settles accounts" with the tenant. Tenants are usually oblivious of production costs and output prices, and how much is received as a share is largely at the owner's discretion. The severity of bondage varies, usually according to the size of the loan (compared to the earning power of the worker) as well as through regional variations. In Sindh province, a household survey[7] specifically asked people whether they could discontinue working for the *zamindar* (landlord) while their debt remained unreturned: in Umerkot and Mirpurkhas, 79 and 76 percent of sharecroppers (Haris) respectively stated that they could not discontinue work without repayment, whereas only 10 percent in Badin reported the same.

In our fieldwork, there was also clear evidence of substantive and effective bondage in the brick-making, mining, carpet weaving, agricultural, and domestic work sectors. For mining and brick making, the owners could insist that some members of an indebted family stay behind as "surety" when others took leave. In more extreme cases guards were hired in order to keep watch over or even lock up "suspect" labor. In one case, the researcher came across a worker who had been kept in chains to prevent his escape. Violence, though rare, was reported in the agriculture, mining, and domestic work sectors.

The increasing burden of *peshgis* coupled with low, piecemeal wages also encourages the inclusion of children and women in the production process. Although child labor is common in all the surveyed sectors, the situation appears most acute in those industries where children are often separated from their families as a result of their being pledged. This occurs in domestic work, where a pledged child can be sent to another employer's home, or in carpet weaving, where in some cases reported in the rapid assessment, children work and live in carpet workshops. The fact that children are paid considerably less than adults simply means that despite the pledging of their labor these unfortunate families are unlikely to ever emerge from their indebtedness. Mention should also be made of the mining sector, where, in order to lessen the burden of debt, parents resort to taking their young sons (usually between 12 and 15) with them to work in the mines.

## The Never-Ending Debt

The initial *peshgi* as a mode of recruitment can be an entrance into what may become a cycle of increasing indebtedness. How that advance and initial debt subsequently grow to unmanageable proportions is linked to the wage system in place. In fact, the most fundamental factor as to why the advance can lead to a continuous cycle of debt is the low level of wages. *Peshgis* on their own reveal only half the story. It is the combination of *peshgi* and low wages that makes for long-term, substantive bondage.

In industry, payment is often made on a piece-rate basis. The piece-rate system is particularly advantageous for the employer when it is used in conjunction with *peshgi* or advances. If advances are combined with wages not based on a piece rate, workers have less incentive to ensure that their output remains high, particularly if they are unsupervised (as is likely in cottage industries and particularly in home-based production). This can lead to a slowdown in worker output once an advance is obtained. If workers are paid on a piece-rate basis, however, the ability to repay a *peshgi* is linked to the worker's output and thereby the production output. Therefore, incentives for workers to maintain a high output are ensured.

In the agricultural and mining sectors, there is also the problem of wages not being paid on time. Interviewed laborers stated that it was common practice for wages to be paid only when material or agricultural produce is sold. This is deeply connected with the continued recourse to advances, as the delay in distributing wages means that workers are forced to meet daily expenses through asking for more *peshgis* from the labor agents. This additional amount is added to their previous balance. In this way even small loans can surreptitiously build up to unmanageable levels.

It must also be remembered that an advance is always part of an unwritten agreement between two "unequal" partners. One party to the contract is often illiterate and has little or no bargaining power and only limited recourse to official or informal enforcement mechanisms. The worker also has little say in maintaining accounts. It is almost without exception the case that the employer or subcontractor maintains the accounts of workers and makes adjustments according to the work performed. It was commonly agreed, however, that account registers did not maintain correct entries. In some cases workers also maintain their own accounts, but these often did not tally with the amounts supposedly owed to employers. Thus, it was not uncommon for workers to complain that their original *peshgi* amount had been inflated by the subcontractor or owner but that due to their illiteracy and powerlessness they could not challenge this. In the event of any disputes, the threat of violence or the use of the police was a strong deterrent for the workers. For example, in both Punjab and Sindh, it was a common complaint by tenants that landlords did not maintain accounts fairly, and payments to tenants were frequently delayed. This simply leads to an increase in the debt of the tenants.

The unequal nature of the relationship means that the negotiating power of the laborer is minimal. In some cases, particularly noted in the construction sector in Balochistan, workers take *peshgis* largely because they are aware of the fact that at the end of a job they may well not be able to enforce the payment of their remaining wages from an existing employer who in all likelihood is also an influential tribal chief and landowner. It is extremely difficult for the weaker partners in a bonded labor relationship to have their part of the deal enforced.

## Conclusion

This research has shown that wage advances (or *peshgi*) remain a key component in both the agricultural and industrial recruitment systems. Larger *peshgis* have more serious implications than smaller advances. These implications include lower wages, increasing indebtedness, and the greater possibility of noneconomic coercion and physical abuse. Ultimately, the advance can lead to an increasing cycle of indebtedness and the immobilization of the worker.

How many workers in Pakistan are subjected to bonded labor? Indebtedness is widespread in rural Pakistan: the 1990 Census of Agriculture showed 2.2 million rural households being indebted, and the 1985 Rural Credit Survey set the figure at 2.9 million households. The great majority of rural credit is noninstitutional, that is, the creditor is a landlord, commission agent, moneylender, or relative or friend. Rural indebtedness varies by region and farm size or tenure. The 1985 Rural Credit Survey, for example, showed that 68 percent of tenant farmers in Sindh were indebted (as compared to 45–50 percent of tenant farmers in other provinces). More detailed case studies show an even higher proportion of indebtedness among tenant farmers in parts of the country, with many casual laborers also reported indebted to their employers. There is less information on the indebtedness of workers in urban areas.

The exact scale of bonded labor in Pakistan remains unknown, however. Indeed, it is the subject of enormous debate and polarized views. At one end of the spectrum, Ercelawn and Nauman (2001) estimated an upper limit of 6.8 million people in the families of debt-bonded sharecroppers; at the other end, certain observers claim that there is effectively no bonded labor in Pakistan.

The situation is not helped by the fact that reporting on bonded labor has been prone to "extremity." Some of this is justifiable, as there have been well-documented cases that represent the worst examples of abuses of human rights. But the tendency to favor extremity at the expense of understanding has promoted a partial understanding of bonded labor, wherein its extreme forms, which are often highlighted in some journalistic and activist reports, have come to color a range of experiences with the same brush. This overwhelmingly negative stereotype may well be part of the story, but it is not the entire story. Moreover, although activists have highlighted shocking incidents, there has been an equally strong denial of these reports by opposed lobbies—resulting in the widely differing accounts of bonded labor in Pakistan.

The present chapter is based on a series of empirically grounded studies that produced substantial qualitative data on the nature and significance of bonded labor in selected sectors of the economy. The information gathered provided an in-depth perspective that had previously been lacking from studies on bonded labor in Pakistan and as such has produced a new understanding of many of the more intricate issues involved in the study of bonded labor.

To design appropriate policy interventions and measure their impact, it would now be useful to obtain a better understanding of the magnitude of bonded labor in the different provinces of Pakistan.

### Notes

1. The surveys have been conducted by the Federal Bureau of Statistics, with the support of the ILO's Social Finance Programme.

2. In fact the survey on brick kilns was confined to three provinces and was not undertaken in Balochistan. This was because the onset of the rainy season meant that kilns in Balochistan shut down for the duration of the survey.

3. Tanneries are concentrated in the district of Kasur (Punjab) and in Karachi (Sindh). Glass bangles are manufactured in Hyderabad (Sindh).

4. The incidence of debt bondage in agriculture in the provinces of the North-West Frontier Province and Balochistan was seen to be negligible and existed only in isolated cases. As a result, the discussion in this chapter is restricted to the provinces of Sindh and Punjab.

5. The First Rent Act of 1859 and the Tenancy Act of 1885 in East Bengal marked the beginning of this policy of protection in favor of the tenants. Some rights were conferred on tenants, and they were secured against arbitrary eviction. This was followed by a series of acts in India beginning in the 1920s aimed at securing the rights of tenants (Hussein et al. 2004).

6. 1 *maund* = 37.32 kilograms.

7. This was the Sindh Rural Development Project, Social Assessment Report, of the Asian Development Bank in March 2000.

# 4

# The Legacy of Slavery in Niger

## Ali R. Sékou and Saidou Abdoulkarimou

The present chapter focuses on forced labor and discrimination against people of slave descent in Niger. Our case study shows that in areas where people are discriminated against on the basis of their social origin and where extreme poverty is the norm, many workers receive no financial wage payments and find that their remuneration is limited to the provision of substandard food and lodging or other payment in kind. In such a context it can be difficult to determine at which point the nonpayment of wages, together with poor terms and conditions of work linked to people's social origin, degenerates into forced labor (International Labour Organization 2005a).

The linkage among past slavery, tradition, and contemporary forced labor is a sensitive issue in West Africa. A number of governments, including those of Niger and Mauritania, have recently implemented important steps to strengthen their legislation and implement policies to bring about change. Niger strengthened its penal code in 2003, and Mauritania revised its legislation and increased penalties against slaveholders in 2007. Niger has now also adopted a national plan of action and implemented some awareness-raising measures. Until then, both countries had been regularly scrutinized by the ILO supervisory body, which verifies the implementation of ratified conventions, and had also received increasing attention from the international press.

The objective of this chapter is to present the findings, gathered through research methods that are widely accepted in social sciences, in a factual and dispassionate manner. The first section discusses the overall context in which debates on the legacy of slavery in Niger are taking place. This section also reviews some historical studies on slavery. The second section describes the methodology of our qualitative study as well as some of the main challenges we faced during the implementation of our research. The third section presents the main findings of our investigation. Results are presented separately for the nomadic North of Niger, where forced labor practices continue to exist, and for the rest of the country, where past slavery has mainly transformed into a form of discrimination against people of slave descent. The last section concludes with some policy recommendations.

## The Context

### Niger and Its Population

Niger is a dry, landlocked country in West Africa. Despite its large size (more than 1.2 million square kilometers), Niger has a total population of only about 13 million people. A large majority of these people (83 percent) live in rural areas, where ethnic identity remains particularly strong. The South, including the capital city, Niamey, is mainly populated by the dark-skinned Hausa and Songhaï-Djerma ethnic groups, which together form about 70 percent of the country's total population. The North includes the lighter-skinned Peul-Fulani pastoralists as well as the nomadic Tuaregs, Toubous, and other Arabic populations. As we will see, these nomadic populations continue to live in very hierarchical societies, dominated by powerful traditional chiefs and small elites.

Unfortunately, the majority of all ethnic groups still live in poverty. Indeed, Niger remains one of the poorest countries on the planet. With more than 80 percent of the population illiterate, a life expectancy of less than 50 years, and a GDP per capita of only about US$800 per year, the country was ranked last on the United Nations' famous Human Development Index in 2006 (United Nations Development Program 2006). The national economy relies mainly on its natural resources, which account for half of the country's total exports. This reflects the fact that Niger is the world's third largest producer of uranium, most of which is used in French nuclear power plants and which has recently also awakened the curiosity of China. Despite the economy's enormous difficulties, there are also positive trends. Since the return of democracy in 1999, a lively and critical media has emerged, and governance has started to improve. According to the National Statistical Office (INS), school enrollment rates and the number of doctors relative to the population are both on the increase. And—apart from some recent Tuareg rebellions in the North—the country has lived in relative peace over the last decades.

### Slavery in the Past

Slavery has existed for as long as historians can remember, in almost all the regions that now belong to Niger. Djibo Hamani (2001) has documented how, in the past, every war generated a new supply of slaves and how slavery was practiced by all the main ethnic groups. No ethnic group had a monopoly over slavery. In the dark-skinned Hausa states, slavery expanded massively between the fifteenth and eighteenth centuries, mostly as a result of the growing political and economic power of some of its cities. The slaves who were captured were used in agriculture and for domestic work. In the North, among the Tuaregs and the Arab populations, slavery also expanded as a result of wars, slave raids, and interethnic conflicts that led to abductions and kidnappings. There, slaves were usually owned by a small group of traditional chiefs and by the members of the aristocracy.

Over the years, as a result, northern kingdoms became segmented into three main classes: the aristocracy, the common people, and the slaves. Masters could also multiply the total number of their slaves by encouraging male slaves to marry female slaves and produce as many children as possible. Of course, masters also used female slaves for their own sexual fantasies and were free to decide whether any resulting children should be treated as slaves or not. Some of the slaves were sold and exchanged in North Africa, Constantinople, and Arabic countries.

In early years of colonialism, the French authorities exploited the existence of this slavery and relied on African chiefs to supply new victims for the transatlantic slave trade. Later, the French colonial authorities attempted to regulate slavery. In 1902, France announced a series of measures to prevent masters from separating slave couples and their children. Henceforth, husbands and wives could no longer belong to different masters, and the master no longer had absolute control over the fate of a child slave. The prohibition to capture new slaves meant that slaves were no longer a renewable resource, so that only biological reproduction could ensure the continued supply of slave labor (Botte 1999).

One problem with such regulations lay with its enforcement. Whereas these prohibitions were more or less enforced in the sedentary regions of the South, the status quo ante was largely maintained in the nomadic regions of the North. In these regions, the colonial authorities continued to rule through alliances with the traditional chiefs and thus found it in their interest to allow the chiefs to keep many of their privileges. Few Tuareg chiefs were ever forced to comply with the new slavery regulations or with compulsory schooling and military service. Therefore, although colonial regulations led to a progressive decline of slavery, they failed to eradicate this institution completely.

## Recent Developments

When Niger became independent in 1960, its new constitution prohibited slavery and declared all humans equal. The country also ratified all of the core ILO conventions related to forced labor as well as to freedom of association and collective bargaining, the elimination of child labor, and discrimination in employment and remuneration. The social reality and customary practices, however, evolved only slowly. Various forms of slavery persisted throughout the second half of the twentieth century, locking some groups into a situation of quasi-permanent poverty and disadvantage.

A number of recent studies have contributed to breaking the remaining social taboo around the legacy of slavery. The continued existence of discrimination and forced labor practices, as a sequel of traditional slavery, has been highlighted in a number of studies (Oumarou 2001; Abdelkader 2004; Kadi Oumani 2005).

The ILO-commissioned study by Oumarou, a former minister of labor, noted that "archaic" forms of slavery continue to exist to this day among the nomadic populations of the North, where chiefs use slaves as if nothing had changed over the past five centuries. There, the study alleged, people are still used as "commodities" that can be given away as presents for weddings and can be used to perform all sorts of work or services whenever required by the master. In other parts of the country—according to the study—people of slave descent continue to suffer from the legacy of slavery: there, they form a kind of social caste of people who are still called "slaves" and who face various forms of discrimination, particularly in terms of marriage and access to land. The author called this "passive slavery."

The legacy of slavery in Niger was also forcefully documented in the study by Gali Abdelkader, commissioned by a local NGO, Timidria, and supported by London-based Anti-Slavery International, which included testimony from people who had escaped situations of slavery. The study also generated a much needed debate about the number of women, men, and children who still suffer from the legacy of slavery in Niger. In its first draft, Timidria estimated that slavery affects more than 870,000 people, of which 600,000 are in Tillabéri and about 60,000 in Tahoua—both of which are located in the South. Overall, such an estimate would represent around 7 percent of the country's current population. Given some debates about the methodology, and the perception that these figures might include some double counting, the final draft of the study also provided a lower bound of 46,382 people still held in slavery or slavery-like situations. This represents 0.3 percent of the population (Abdelkader 2004, p. 88). This figure compares with a rough estimate provided by human rights activist and Tuareg prince Moustapha Kadi Oumani of 8,855 people held in slavery and slavery-like situations (Kadi Oumani 2005, p. 223).

Whatever the exact figure, these studies have established that the legacy of slavery is still a problematic reality in Niger. Despite initial reluctance to discuss this issue, the Association of Traditional Chiefs in Niger (ACTN) also recognized the problem in 2001 and endorsed the ILO Declaration on Fundamental Principles and Rights at Work. By doing so, the chiefs have committed themselves to work toward the eradication of all discrimination, forced labor, and slavery-like practices. A number of awareness-raising activities have since taken place, jointly with the chiefs, in various regions of the country. The government also recognized the problem and has now chosen to address it. In 2003, it modified the penal code so as to increase penalties, to the effect that the crime of slavery is now punished with 10 to 30 years in prison. In 2006 the government also created a national commission—including social partners and civil society—to identify and implement effective measures against forced labor and discrimination, including a wide national campaign. This commission has developed a national plan of action, which was adopted by the commission in November 2007.

The revived debate around the legacy of slavery has also generated some social and political turmoil. During the summer of 2005, Niger caught the attention of the international press, when a Tuareg chief and slave master announced the imminent liberation of 7,000 slaves in his village. The ceremony was to take place in a village in the region of Tillabéri "amid great fanfare" (*The Economist,* March 10, 2005). But it did not go as planned. One week before the release, the government cancelled the special ceremony, arguing that the liberation ceremony was a fraud, and the president of Timidria, who had helped to organize the event, was jailed for a few weeks. As a result, the government of Niger received much unwarranted international attention. Articles on slavery in Niger were published in the French version of the *National Geographic* magazine, the *Smithsonian,* and other papers. These articles sometimes struggled to document and explain the complex realities in Niger and were perceived by many in the country as excessively sensationalist. Ultimately, however, the crisis faded, and both government and civil society continued their march against slavery and slavery-like practices.

## Methodology

This chapter presents the results of a qualitative study whose objective is to better understand and describe the legacy of slavery in Niger, with a view to supporting policymakers and providing some useful material for future research into this important human rights question. In this context, we try to shed some light on the difficult question of when these practices should be seen as forced labor and when they should be understood as a milder (but no less acceptable) form of discrimination. The ILO defines forced labor as "all work or services exacted from any person under the menace of any penalty and for which the said person has not offered himself voluntarily" (Convention No. 29). Discrimination, by contrast, refers to "any distinction, exclusion or preference made on the basis of race, colour, sex, religion, political opinion, national extraction or social origin, which has the effect of nullifying or impairing equality of opportunity or treatment in employment and occupation" (Convention No. 111).

Our study focuses on people of slave descent, who are people whose ancestors were slaves. In practice it is sometimes difficult to distinguish if a person of

slave descent is suffering from discrimination or also from coercion, especially since the two are strongly linked in the case of Niger. In this context, it
is useful to note that the ILO jurisprudence considered that "persons in a relationship resembling a slave-master relationship, lacking freedom to control
their own lives, are, due to these very circumstances, carrying out work for
which they have not offered themselves voluntarily" (International Labour Organization 2003).

Our methodology had three steps: reading literature, undertaking field research, and carrying out direct observations.

First, we started by collecting and reading all the available literature on
the subject; as we have already indicated, this literature tends to be rather
scarce in Niger, given the taboo that has long surrounded and continues to sur-
round this subject. We collected not only academic studies but also official
documents, newspaper articles, and NGO reports. This included, for example,
a letter dated May 10, 2003, from the prime minister to the minister of the interior,[1] in which the head of the government expressed his outrage about these
"practices that are not consistent with a State of Law and which, because of
their immorality, violate the rules of a fair society." Our review also included
a report published in French by the independent National Commission on Human
Rights and Fundamental Liberties (CNDHLF), called *Diagnostic Study on Slavery Practices in Niger;* a study on slavery in Africa by Cissé Souleymane (2002)
at the Institute of Development Studies in Geneva (IUED); and a number of ILO
documents, including individual observations by the Committee of Experts on the
Application of Conventions and Recommendations (CEACR), which verifies
compliance with ratified ILO conventions. Our methodology consisted of study-
ing these documents related to the subject of our research, so as to absorb the
preexisting information and theories. We are aware that any new study is necessarily part of a continuum of research and requires some external validation.

Our second step was to undertake field research. We interviewed key informants in Niamey and throughout the country. This included two different
groups of people. The first group included experts on the topics of slavery and
forced labor, such as sociologists, historians, and other academic researchers.
The second group consisted of key "witnesses," that is, people who, because of
their positions, actions, or responsibilities, had substantial knowledge of the
problem. These included members of NGOs, human rights organizations, labor
inspectors, judges, journalists, schoolteachers, medical doctors, and religious authorities as well as members of the national commission against forced labor and
discrimination created by the Ministry of Labour in 2006. Guidelines were prepared for interviewing key informants at the local, regional, and national levels.

Finally, the third step in our methodology was direct observation. This
consisted of field research with information collected through the administration of previously tested individual questionnaires, the organization of focus

group discussions, and personal observations. This part of the research included all main regions of the country, with particular emphasis on the geographic areas suspected of being more affected by the problem under consideration. We traveled to the departments of Diffa, Zinder, Maradi, Agadez, Tahoua, Dosso, and Tillabéri. Within these regions, we focused on the localities of N'guigmi (in the East of the country), Tanout (in the middle East), Tchintabaraden and Tillia (in the middle North), and Arlit (in the North) as well as Abala and Banki-laré (in the West). Altogether, in these places, we spoke with 396 persons, of which 45 percent were women and girls.

This third step of the research was later complemented with direct observation in three additional villages: the villages of Boukou and Gabou in the region of Tillabéri and the village of Azorori in the region of Tahoua.[2] These villages were chosen as a result of a number of scoping missions undertaken jointly with local authorities and with representatives of the local NGO, Timidria. Ultimately, all three villages were selected because they were thought to epitomize the different forms of what is called "slavery" in Niger. Relevant information was then collected through questionnaires administered to heads of household as well as through participatory methods. Altogether 82 households were interviewed. These included 27 households considered as nonpoor (defined for the purpose of this study as owning cattle, living in decent housing, and dressed in decent clothing). The remaining 55 households were considered as poor (where members do not eat every day of the year and do not own cattle or decent clothes). The research thus provided a voice to some of the usually voiceless people.

Overall, our research project has run into two main difficulties: one related to transportation, the other related to the social hierarchy.

The first difficulty was linked to the *national* character of our study. As pointed out above, Niger is a large country of more than 1.2 million square kilometers. This means that during our research, the different groups of investigators had to travel more than 16,000 kilometers, which required a substantial mobilization of human and material resources. Transportation was particularly difficult in remote places or in places where insecurity exists as a result of sporadic attacks by armed rebel groups. The North is marked by a lingering conflict between the state of Niger and some Tuareg rebels, known as the "road blockers," who call for a better distribution of the revenues from natural resources. Fortunately our fieldwork was conducted in a period of relative calm after the 1995 peace agreement and before the start of a new rebellion in early 2007. Nonetheless, to travel to these regions we had to hire local guides who knew the region and the whereabouts of rebel groups. Although these guides restricted our opportunity to move around freely, we always insisted that interviews and focus group discussions be carried out without the presence of these guides so as to avoid biased answers.

The second main difficulty was to obtain accurate information from chiefs and from people of slave descent. In the villages, chiefs and members of the aristocracy are considered as the only authoritative and valid source of information, and they did not fully understand why we wanted to speak directly to the "common people," or why we were even interested in them. From the point of view of the aristocracy, the information that they themselves provided should be seen as sufficient. Some chiefs tried to prevent us from talking directly to "slaves" or women, sometimes quickly sending them away to some improvised work or domestic chores. We thus tried to use as much diplomacy as possible with the chiefs and also—whenever possible—relied on the assistance of local human rights organizations, in order to gain access to the "slaves." In some instances, "slaves" were difficult to identify, as the social status of people is sometimes difficult to recognize by outsiders; we thus had to rely on resource persons familiar with the local context. When we could identify and speak to the "slaves" in the absence of their masters, we were surprised by their openness and willingness to talk. It must be said, though, that throughout the country, many of the people we interviewed expected some remuneration at the end of our meetings.

### Findings (1): The Nomadic and Pastoral Regions

Our study indicates that "slavery" continues to exist as an institution that involves forced labor in the nomadic Tuareg, Toubou, and Arab regions. We met people of slave descent who did not appear to have their own independent personalities and who remained entirely at the disposal of their masters for any kind of work at any moment in time. Their situations seemed to conform to the ILO's definition of persons who are in relationships analogous to that of master and slave, are unable to dispose freely of themselves, and should therefore be considered as performing work for which they have not offered themselves voluntarily. Hence, we consider that in the nomadic regions of Niger there exist people of slave descent who live and work in conditions of forced labor.

Altogether, in our sample we interviewed eight masters, whose average age was 43 years old. Of these eight masters, three were traditional chiefs, two belonged to the traditional village aristocracy, two were businessmen, and one was a retired public official. The best information we obtained about them and their "slaves," however, came usually not from the masters themselves but from neighbors and other resource persons. For example, in the village of Tchintabaraden we found three masters, all of whom had 10 to 11 persons of slave descent at their service. Only one of them agreed to answer our questions, introducing himself as the "tutor," "protector," and "adviser" of the people who were at his service. We also obtained information directly from people of slave descent at the occasion of two different focus group discussions, which involved an average of 12 people.

## Recruitment and Employment

People of slave descent confirmed that they had never been recruited by their employers, as in a free labor market, but had instead been "inherited" by their employers. Their inferior social status was also "inherited" directly from their own fathers and mothers. In other words, these people were born into slave status: the daughters and sons of slaves, they continued to live like their parents. This implies that the masters did not have to acquire these "slaves"; they simply belonged to families that have traditionally been at the service of the master's family. We also found out that the masters can lend their "slaves" to relatives or friends for a temporary period or even for the long term. Some slaves are also given away or used as compensation if the master has, for example, harmed the slave of another master. In these hierarchical societies, the number of slaves still appears to determine the social status and the power of the masters, which explains why masters are reluctant to let their slaves go. Their credibility and honor seem to be at stake.

The legacy of slavery also explains why differences in the color of the skin of masters and slaves have been largely preserved until this day. So, for example, many Tuareg chiefs are light-skinned, whereas slaves have darker skins. This can be explained by the fact that the masters and aristocracy are individuals with some "berber" blood from North Africa, whereas the people of slave descent are often the descendants of southern people kidnapped from Hausa, Zarma, or other ethnic groups. Among the Arab populations, the white masters (Ouled Souleymane and Chouas) similarly seem to have total control over their slaves, who are usually "black Arabs" (the Chouchane). This is a generalization; clearly not all masters are light-skinned, and not all dark-skinned Tuaregs (the Ballas) or Arabs are people of slave descent.

If people did not choose their employers, why do they not leave? This question is at the source of much ambiguity about whether people of slave descent should be categorized as being in forced labor. Our various focus groups show that few of the "slaves" wish to be "liberated." Their main aspiration, according to their own expressions, is to be allowed to possess their own animals, decide themselves over the marriage and schooling of their children, have more to eat, have a nice master, or have their own domestic workers. This may seem surprising, but key informants explained that slaves generally accept their fate because of cultural attitudes, the lack of economic alternatives, and the fact that they are assured of subsistence and hence consider change as too risky.

This problem may be linked to what Bourdieu (1979) called the *habitus,* which refers to the norms and values that are transmitted to people—in the present case the "slaves"—when they are very young. These values and norms are often the ones formed by the dominant social groups and end up determining the beliefs and attitudes of the dominated groups. Our focus groups show that slaves consider their situations as "normal." We heard statements such as "I belong to my master, I owe him everything," or "Where do you want me to go? What can I say? Such is life for us: we can do nothing against the tradition."

### Occupations, Wage Payments, and Working Conditions

The "slaves" appear to be at the disposal of the master's whole family, whatever the age of the family member. The list of activities of the slaves, as discussed during the focus groups, can be quite long, including generally agricultural activities (such as cattle rearing, gardening, or the processing of milk products), trading activities (selling village production), or domestic work (such as gathering water, finding firewood, milling the grain, cooking, preparing the master's bed, washing his clothes, bathing his children, massaging his feet, playing music to distract him, and—for women—satisfying his sexual appetite). Slaves estimate that, on average, they work about 16 hours per day. They wake up before the master and are the last to go to sleep. According to one testimony, "there is always something to do until we go to bed." By contrast, the masters—who may own an average of 10 slaves in Tchintabaraden—generally do not work at all.

Masters do not pay slaves any monetary wages or remuneration. In fact, slaves provide free work and services to their masters in exchange only for food and housing (they generally sleep on the floor in or around the masters' houses). Slaves are typically sanctioned if their masters are unsatisfied with the quality of their work. Some victims have reported food privation for one day. The NGO Timidria has also reported the case of a slave who allegedly ran away because his master threatened to castrate him. At the same time, slaves also face a number of additional social and customary barriers. In particular, they are not allowed to marry nonslaves, ensuring that their children will remain of "pure" slave descent, and they are rarely allowed to own land.

## Findings (2): Sedentary Niger

In the sedentary regions of Niger, the legacy of slavery is more complex and ambiguous. The strong resilience of "traditional values" in sedentary Niger (see Fuglestad 1983) may explain why even in these regions, traditional slavery has not disappeared but rather has mutated into a system of discrimination against people of slave descent. This system is not without reminders of the caste system in India or of the discrimination against indigenous peoples in some countries of Latin America. It can involve a whole spectrum of situations: from ordinary racism, ostracism, and social exclusion to the most exploitative forced labor.

Key informants consider that discrimination against people of slave descent is strongest with respect to marriage and access to landownership. So, for example, people of slave descent often find it impossible, for customary reasons, to marry a person with a higher social status. This came out clearly in our interviews. Among the 396 people interviewed who were not of slave descent, more than 90 percent said they would refuse to let their daughter marry a man of slave descent. When asked why, the respondents said they wanted to "conform to the tradition" and "preserve the family's honor and dignity." In matters of landownership, people of slave descent also feel discriminated against. In Niger, it is often considered that land—as well as the cattle and houses that are attached to the land—simply "cannot" belong to people of slave descent. Hence, they often belong de facto to their "masters."

What about employment relations between people of slave descent and their former "masters"? Here we must point out that in the sedentary regions of Niger, the employment relationship between former "masters" and former "slaves" has evolved into many different and complex situations. It is possible that a minority of people of slave descent continue to work, as unpaid domestic helpers or as agricultural workers, for their former masters in situations analogous to that of master and slave, with people being unable to control their own lives. In most cases, however, the relationship between masters and slaves has become more complex. When former masters continue to own the land of the people of slave descent, past slavery has often transformed into a system of sharecropping, in which the latter provide the former with a share of the harvest. This share of the harvest, which can sometimes be as high as 75 percent, is usually called the "tithe" (*la dime*), reminding us of the institution of serfdom. These practices are perpetuated by the customary system of land tenure, which prevents people of slave descent from ever owning their own land to gain independence. As a result, people of slave descent are locked into situations that resemble bonded labor in other parts of the world (see Chapter 3).

To put things into perspective, it must be emphasized that most people of slave descent have no employment or work relationship with any master whatsoever. But even then, the legacy of slavery can remain visible. So, for example, we came across people of slave descent who, although working and living independently of their masters, spontaneously harvest the land of the latter as a tribute to their past slavery. This occurs without any visible or direct form of coercion, outside of the invisible hand of tradition. In other cases, even when no master seems to influence the lives of former slaves, society seems to have confined people of slave descent to certain types of specific low-skilled occupations, in a form of occupational discrimination.

There are some important exceptions, of course. It is a well-known fact that some ethnic Songhaï-Djerma or Tuareg people of slave descent have made impressive careers in Niger's public administration. In those cases, it is "only" the stigma associated with their slave origin that remains—which explains why many of them do not like to return from the capital city, Niamey, to their places of origin, where they run the risk of being reminded of their social origin. In the majority of cases, however, people of slave descent remain at the bottom of the social pyramid, subjected to cruel forms of discrimination. Indeed, in most cases, these traditional practices prevent any kind of significant upward social mobility, locking people of slave descent in poverty and disadvantage.

To illustrate the lives of people of slave descent—and the variety of situations discussed in the above sections—we next present summaries of our case studies in the three villages of Gabou, Boukou, and Azarori. These summaries provide an overview of situations on a spectrum ordered from the least to the most exploitative. All these villages are located in the sedentary parts of Niger.

### The Village of Gabou

Gabou is a small village of 1,305 inhabitants located along the road from Til-labéri to Ayérou, in the region of Tillabéri. The village, created by a Tuareg community from Mali, is divided into six neighborhoods that look like little hamlets,[3] some of which are at a distance of about 5 kilometers from the center of the village. In Gabou, as in other Tuareg communities, the social organization is very hierarchical. The village has two distinct categories of people: those who belong to the nobility and those who are nonnobles, which also includes people of slave descent.

During our study, we interviewed a total of 36 households, of which there were 20 that we classified as "poor" and 16 that we classified as "nonpoor" (according to the definition discussed earlier). We found that about 40 percent of the households in our sample were households of slave descent. We also noted that all nine households of the nearby hamlet of Moulkouche were people of slave descent who, according to their oral history, had migrated from Mali in the 1970s together with their masters.

Despite their social origin, none of the people of slave descent whom we interviewed reported being forced to work. Interviews and focus group discussions revealed, however, that nearly all people of slave descent feel discriminated against owing to their social origin. Men of slave descent are not allowed to marry women from the nobility. Also, during wedding ceremonies or baptisms, some practices are exclusively reserved to the nobility. Discrimination is also clear at the level of landownership, and the children of people of slave descent cannot inherit any land after the death of their parents.

These structural rigidities, unsurprisingly, translate into high levels of poverty. The villagers are agropastoralists, but the village has faced chronic food shortages for many years.[4] During 2005, a year of generous rains, only 17 percent of households could produce enough food to satisfy their needs, whereas 60 percent of households produced less than half of their needs. The focus group discussions also revealed the extreme poverty and difficult living conditions of women of slave descent, who have to walk long distances to fetch water and to access the closest grain mills. In light of this situation, villagers have implemented coping strategies that include seeking help from richer parents, the exodus of young people, the sale of animals, and the gathering of wild plants. It seems unlikely that the situation will improve in the near future. As elsewhere, extensive farming has led to declining land productivity.

It is interesting that their social status was not identified by the villagers as a main challenge. Instead, the villagers mentioned lack of equipment and lack of capital to buy inputs, such as fertilizers. When asked about discrimination, people of slave descent remain admirably optimistic. They consider that such practices will disappear one day, but they have no idea of the time it will take. They agree that education could help, but unfortunately the enrollment rate in Gabou's primary school remains very low. The reasons, according to villagers, are the weak achievements in school and the difficulty of obtaining the school books and other materials.

## The Village of Boukou

Boukou is another small village of 813 inhabitants situated 7 kilometers from the urban community of Tillabéri, along the river Niger. All the inhabitants of Boukou are people of slave descent known as Horso people. According to the oral history of the village, as it was told to us by the chief, the first ancestor of the villagers was a slave who was living in one of the chiefdoms in the distant region of Zamaraganda. A few centuries ago, after a war, he was liberated and migrated south to create this village. Now, the people of Boukou live together in a relatively equitable social organization. There is no strong social stratification in the village.[5] As in Gabou, the villagers of Boukou are agropastoralists. Agriculture is the main economic activity, and animal husbandry is the second activity.[6]

In our study, we interviewed 20 randomly chosen heads of household, representing together about one-fourth of the total population. Our sample can therefore be considered as largely representative of the village. This sample includes 12 "poor" households and 8 "nonpoor" households. When asked about slavery, the villagers rejected slavery as an institution of the past. They considered that nowadays no one in the village is forced to work under coercion for any identifiable master.

At the same time, many of the villagers consider themselves victims of a whole series of discriminations and humiliations. Not only is their village known as Bagney Koiara, or "the village of the slaves," but in addition they are not allowed to marry a person from a higher social group. The Horso people can only marry people of the same social status, that is, people of slave descent. The main problem, however, is that the villagers from Boukou cannot own the land on which they work, nor the houses that they have built on it and in which they live. One villager whom we interviewed complained that "before, we were happy slaves; now we are chained."

To understand why the Horso people do not own their land, one needs to go back to the oral history of the village. According to the chief, when the Horsos arrived from Zarmaganga, they first settled on the island of Mara. In 1949 they then moved on to Boukou, which traditionally was part of the territory of the Diada populations. According to the verbal agreement of the time, the Diada agreed to let the Horso people settle on their territory on the understanding that they could never own any piece of Diada land. Ever since then, and although according to the law every citizen is entitled to buy land, the villagers of Boukou have to pay an annual "tithe" to the Diada people.

Following the local custom, this historical agreement also implies that the villagers of Boukou do not actually own the houses that they have built on the land and in which they live. Children of Boukou cannot inherit any land or any houses. During an alleged incident in 2006, a house was destroyed because it did not comply with the norms agreed upon by the Diada people. This dependency is also cultural. Indeed, there is no school in the village of Boukou. The children of the village have to attend school in the village of the Diada, but in practice the enrollment rate is very low, and many parents refuse to send their children to this school. All the household heads whom we interviewed were illiterate and, in light of this poor enrollment rate, this illiteracy is likely to continue in the future. The main source of worry, however, remains the land issue. The villagers complain that development projects are reluctant to work in Boukou because of the landownership problem. Villagers live under the constant threat of being expelled from the land on which they work, in which they invest, and on which they have built their houses—sometimes more than half a century ago.

In order to improve their economic welfare, here again households implement a variety of strategies that include obtaining support from richer parents established in the cities and sending their children to work in the cities or abroad. After the harvest, many young people migrate to nearby Nigeria, Togo, or Ghana.

### The Village of Azarori

Discrimination against people of slave descent is probably most striking in the Tuareg village of Azarori in the region of Tahoua, which has 3,000 inhabitants. In this village the land is dry and most villagers are poor. We interviewed 26 household heads, of which 23 were "poor" and 3 households were "nonpoor." Most of the heads of household were 40 years old or more, and as many as 38 percent of our sample were widows. Among the married households, 14 percent included more than one wife.

The Tuareg societies in general—and this community (called Kel Gress) in particular—are very hierarchical. The chief is very influential and is surrounded by an aristocracy that acts as a "council of wise people." Thus, social inequality is a strong characteristic. The village is divided into two main groups: on the one hand, the aristocracy, that is, the descendants of the masters who ruled with absolute power before colonialism and, on the other hand, the nonnobles, who constitute the people of slave descent and the members of so-called castes (professions of low social status). In our sample, 22 out of 26 households we interviewed admitted being of slave descent.

As in other villages, most people of slave descent complained that they cannot inherit land and that men of slave descent can never marry women from a higher social group. The existence of discrimination and a form of segregation also appeared clearly during our research. During a meeting with the women of the village, we noted how the dozen women of slave descent all sat together on one side of the room. Although the moderator gave them the opportunity to speak, they never dared to take the floor. Inequality is also clear in the area of education. The village has a school that was created in 1945 and that has contributed to the relatively high level of education of the children from the aristocracy, most of whom speak French. This contrasts with the children from our sample, where only 7 percent of households interviewed actually send their children to school.

The distinctive feature of Azarori, however, is the fact that some people of slave descent continue to work for their masters. A fraction of the people of slave descent seem to have been integrated into the households of the masters, who—in exchange for domestic work and services—provide food, clothes, and all expenses related to their marriages or other ceremonies. Others have converted to agriculture and do not actually live in the households of the masters. These farmers still consider that the people of slave descent always owe the master a share of the harvest, however—a situation that in effect transforms their relationship into something between a sharecropper and a serf.

Do these people want to break free from this apparently unfree relationship? This is a complicated issue. If we believe the "slaves," it would seem that working for a master is not perceived as a constraint or a form of coercion but rather as a way to honor the tradition and the customary norms. People of slave descent seem proud to serve their masters. The lack of alternatives is also mentioned: "We have no land and no animals; if we leave our masters we risk getting into situations that are even worse. And anyways, we don't know where to go." It is worth pointing out here that in a context of increasing poverty, masters sometimes face considerable difficulty in providing for the subsistence of all the "slaves" and may also have to undergo some financial sacrifice in order to uphold the tradition and their dominant social status.

## Conclusion

Our research has documented how people of slave descent in Niger continue to suffer from discrimination and forced labor practices. We have shown that in the nomadic parts of the countries, some people of slave descent continue to be attached to some aristocratic households. They work as household servants, tend livestock, or undertake agricultural tasks. Women also collect water, prepare food, and provide a range of other services to the masters. These people do not receive any wage payments and seem to fall under the category of forced laborers, defined by the ILO as "persons in a relationship resembling a slave-master relationship, lacking freedom to control their own lives" and "carrying out work for which they have not offered themselves voluntarily" (International Labour Organization 2003).

In other parts of the country, the problem is more complex and seems to have degenerated into a form of discrimination and exploitation sometimes called "passive slavery" in Niger. In these parts of the country, the reality seems to involve a spectrum of situations documented in our three case studies in the villages of Gabou, Boukou, and Azarori, going from ordinary racism to discrimination, segregation, and in some cases perhaps serfdomlike situations.

What is clear in any case is the need for both further research and strong policy measures to end these practices. Further research is necessary to produce a more complete understanding and geographical mapping of these practices in Niger, together with a better understanding of their magnitude in the different parts of the country. This would also settle the sometimes polemical debate about the numbers produced by NGOs. In this context, it would be desirable that these estimates and mappings be produced by the national statistical institute or some similar organization with a high level of credibility and technical expertise. More academic research is also needed on the qualitative aspects of forced labor and discrimination against people of slave descent in Niger and in other countries of West Africa.

The development of specific policy measures should be based on a recognition by government and development agencies that people of slave descent require special attention if they are to benefit from overall development and poverty reduction strategies. Without such recognition, the structural legacy of slavery will continue to weigh heavily on the shoulders of the poorest people in Niger.

# Notes

1. Letter no. 0303/DIRCAB/PM/CC/RP.
2. This part of the study was carried out by Saidou Abdoulkarimou.
3. These six hamlets are Gabou 1, Gabou 2, Tahagana, Bossa, Chantier, and Taloumbous.
4. The main activity is agriculture. Mil, niébé, and sorgho (millet, black-eyed peas, and sorghum) are the main crops, and marrows, onions, and sweet potatoes are the principal truck products. Rice is also produced on a small stretch of land, along the river. Animal husbandry is the secondary activity, practiced by about half the households, mostly with the use of one or two bovines or small ruminants.
5. The village is governed by a chief, assisted by the chiefs of the four neighborhoods (which are called Malloumbon Haoussa, Boukou Tchadoga, Koiratégui, and Mara Tchadoga).
6. Here again the main crops are mil, sorgho, and niébé. Both the soil and the vegetation show the marks of constant erosion and degradation. Along the river Niger and on the island of Malloumbon, the villagers cultivate floating rice and sorgho. Despite their proximity to the river, villagers do not grow vegetables; they say this is because of the lack of land surface and because they do not know the techniques. The recurrent droughts and the pauperization of the village explain why husbandry has lost some ground. Large herds have disappeared, and husbandry is now limited to a small number of two to four cattle. Many others have sold their animals or lost them owing to illnesses or lack of food. A study in 2005 showed that 45 percent of households are self-sufficient, which means that they covered or exceeded the production necessary for their own consumption.

# 5

## Trafficking for Forced Labor in Europe

### *Beate Andrees*

Forced labor in Europe today is largely a result of human trafficking and irregular migration. The ILO estimates that in 2005, out of 360,000 forced labor victims in industrialized countries (including Western Europe), 270,000 were trafficked (International Labour Organization 2005a). Media images of irregular migrants trying to enter the "fortress Europe"—from Albania to Italy or from Morocco to Spain—have spurred debate and concern over the protection of state borders. Although the protection of state borders against irregular migration has dominated European policy agendas in the past, the actual employment situation of irregular migrants, and in particular trafficked persons, is now moving gradually into the center of the debate. The European Union (EU) plan on best practice to combat trafficking in human beings, adopted in 2005, calls for a "reduction of demand" and an analysis of employment regulations and their impact on trafficking in human beings.

This chapter argues that deceptive recruitment mechanisms and exploitative systems of subcontracting are key factors in understanding the vulnerability of migrant workers to forced labor exploitation. Weak labor market regulations or enforcement and the lack of protection afforded to irregular migrant workers provide incentives to employers and intermediaries to use abusive practices. Easy profits can be made through deceptive job offers, illegal wage deductions, or nonpayment of wages. Some of the exploitation is organized by sophisticated criminal networks, but in the majority of cases, the exploitation of trafficked migrants takes place in the context of small-scale scam operations. Through complex subcontracting systems, trafficking penetrates mainstream economic sectors, such as agriculture, construction, or the service industry where there is a high demand for cheap and exploitable labor. Most migrant workers who work under hazardous conditions for low pay and without protection from labor law are not forced to work at gunpoint. There is a large enough pool of migrants who are willing to take high risks to enter Europe and who are determined to make their journey a success. But not all of them succeed, and some fall victim to various forms of coercion. Those who demand a better bargain for their labor are quickly replaced by more docile workers. The supply is huge and shifting gradually farther east and south.

This chapter is based on ILO research carried out between 2003 and 2007. It summarizes largely qualitative research from ten European source, transit, and destination countries.[1] It is therefore the result of a collective effort of researchers from many countries, and their studies will be quoted throughout this chapter. The purpose of this project was to close a gap in current research. Up to now most trafficking-related research has focused on trafficking of women for the purpose of sexual exploitation. Other forms of trafficking, such as those linked to forced labor in labor-intensive economic sectors, are still underresearched and undertheorized.[2]

The chapter is structured as follows: first, the methodology and limitations of trafficking research are explained; second, a typology of recruitment mechanisms is presented and described using case study examples; the remaining sections discuss forms of coercion and factors underlying the demand for exploitable migrant workers, followed by a brief summary of the chapter.

## Methodology

The research design varied between destination and source countries of trafficking and to a lesser extent between different destination countries. The main purpose of data collection was not to obtain representative results or reliable national estimates of trafficked persons. It was mainly designed to develop case studies. Researchers in both source and destination countries were asked to base their case studies on multiple data sources (triangulation), such as field observation, focus group interviews, questionnaires, or media research. Given the limitations to carry out such research in destination countries, owing to the sensitive nature of the subject, case studies collected in source or transit countries are often more reliable. As will be explained in more detail below, however, generalizations from these case studies should be made with care.

In principle, survey methods can be applied in source countries targeting households of (returned) migrants. Other possibilities are to interview returned migrants randomly, for example, at border crossing points or in migration information centers. Since this research was understood as a first assessment, aimed at understanding actual cases rather than obtaining representative data on trafficking, a different design was developed. It consisted of four components: (1) desk review of secondary sources reporting on trafficking in the country, (2) a standardized questionnaire with 160 returned migrants in each source country, (3) semistructured interviews with key informants, and (4) group discussions with select victims of trafficking identified in the second phase of the investigation (International Labour Organization 2002a). The countries covered by this research design were Albania, Moldova, Romania, and Ukraine.[3]

The main sampling method used was the so-called snowballing method, though returned migrants were also selected more randomly, for example, by directly approaching returned migrants in public spaces. Snowballing is generally described as a sampling method leading to nonprobability samples and is typically used when there is no preexisting sample frame. A researcher will start by contacting key informants who will then refer the researcher to other potential respondents and so on. The snowballing method was designed in such a way that it would include—to the extent possible—an equal number of returned migrant women and men (Andrees and van der Linden 2005).

In addition, an important distinction was made between "victims of trafficking" and "successful migrants." This distinction was introduced to understand specific factors that would explain why some are more vulnerable to exploitation and abuse than others. The key question used to differentiate between the two groups was: Were you free to leave your employment at any given point in time? Though "successful migrants" may have experienced some form of deception and abuse during their journey or final employment stage, they were free to leave without being faced by threats or the loss of any rights or privileges (e.g., nonpayment of wages or threat of violence against them or family members).

The questionnaire investigated the following main topics: demographic characteristics, the premigration situation of the respondent, recruitment, organization of the journey to the destination country, conditions of employment abroad, forms of coercion/exploitation encountered, awareness of assistance, and possibilities of exiting a situation of forced labor. With the exception of Albania, interviews with migrants were carried out by the NGO La Strada, which was thought to have access to respondents as well as knowledge about a victim-centered approach of interviewing. In Albania, the research, including interviews with victims, was undertaken by the International Catholic Migration Commission (ICMC). Researchers were asked to test the questionnaire in the field and to adjust it as necessary. The fourth pillar of the research design in source countries was the use of focus group interviews that helped to develop case studies as well as to corroborate results from the structured questionnaires.

The research design in transit and destination countries (France, Germany, Hungary, Portugal,[4] and Turkey) aimed primarily at the documentation of case studies. It was based on the following components: (1) literature review to collect available information on illegal employment of migrant workers, trafficking reports and statements of public authorities or civil society organizations (including the police, labor inspectors, NGOs, and trade unions), and academic research; (2) media review; (3) interviews of experts to obtain more data and to collect information on cases of forced labor and exploitation if the experts had encountered it in the context of their work (during the entry phase of the interview, forced labor was explained though it turned out to be more helpful to ask about the most blatant cases of exploitation among migrant workers); (4) study of court cases and case files managed by NGOs assisting victims (usually accessible when judicial proceedings had ended already); and (5) interviews with witnesses and victims of forced labor.

The report on Turkey also included semistructured interviews with employers of migrant workers. The research design for France and Hungary, similar to that for Turkey, was largely inspired by anthropological research methods such as participant and field observation. It involved several steps in developing a special interview technique, testing the semistructured interview guidelines, and field observations (Juhasz 2005). The research carried out in France focused on Chinese migrant workers.

The research design for the study on Russia was the most developed as far as methodological triangulation was concerned. The case studies compiled in the study on Russia were complemented by a random sample of interviews with 442 migrant workers carried out in three different regions of the country (158 in the Moscow region, 144 in the Stavropol region, and 140 in the Krasnodar region). The sample covered economic sectors with a high presence of migrant workers and known for exploitative labor practices as well as respondents with different nationalities and demographic characteristics (Tyuryukanova 2006).

Despite some attempts to collect information from random sampling, the results of the research studies are not representative. All samples have shortcomings. Those covering the four countries of southeastern Europe imply a certain bias in that snowballing was used to include an equal number of trafficking victims and successful migrants. The sample covering the Russian Federation, despite its merits, is still too small to lead to representative conclusions of the type that could be derived from a national survey. Case studies that were used in the remaining studies are generally not representative. Research results do, however, give important indications of the existence of forced labor as a result of human trafficking in all countries. They also provide detailed information about the process, circumstances, and consequences of trafficking, which could help direct further research on this subject and could lead to formulation of policy responses.[5]

The results of the primary research have been entered into two separate databases. A database on returned migrants includes 644 respondents, of whom 300 have been classified as forced labor victims on the basis of results of standardized questionnaires used in Albania, Moldova, Romania, and Ukraine. The second database includes 82 cases of forced labor victims collected in destination countries.[6] In addition, survey results covering 442 migrants in the Russian Federation are used in the analysis. The results from this primary research were complemented by secondary data sources.

## Recruitment Mechanisms

In industries that are characterized by low-skilled and often seasonal labor (e.g., agriculture and construction), employers are constantly faced with the need to recruit workers—often at short notice. On the one hand, they have a problem with retaining workers, as mobility in these sectors is significantly higher than in others; on the other hand, demand for workers varies owing to changing demands from customers, hence employers seek the flexibility to quickly lay off workers. Employers have three main options to recruit workers: through public employment services, through private employment agencies or other intermediaries, or on their own account—using either formal or more informal means.

In Western Europe, public employment service centers have gradually lost their monopoly over recruitment since the 1980s. Germany and Italy were among the last countries to change their legislation in order to allow private employment agencies to operate legally in the labor market. Although major private employment firms such as Adecco or Manpower act as brokers at both ends of the labor market—low and highly skilled—they have largely abstained from recruiting migrant workers. This has created a niche for small firms that were often set up by immigrants themselves and who quickly turned into important suppliers of migrant labor in many industries, in particular agriculture, construction, cleaning, mining, and transportation. The competitive advantage of these new "merchants of labour" (Kuptsch 2006) is twofold: knowledge of both demand and supply across countries, as well as flexibility due to their small size.

According to recent estimates, the number of private employment agencies recruiting for both the domestic and foreign market is increasing in all countries across Europe. In the "old" countries of the European Union (EU 15 plus Norway), temporary agency work accounts for 1.5 percent of total employment, involving between 2.5 and 3 million agency workers, employed by approximately 22,000 firms (Arrowsmith 2006). The emergence of private recruiters is closely linked to market opportunities and state regulations. Countries that had liberalized the market for private recruiters (or that had always had a liberal approach, such as the United Kingdom) witnessed a stark increase in particularly small recruitment firms in the 1990s. Many of them were involved in the recruitment of migrant workers, supplying them to local employers in a highly flexible manner. At the same time, irregular migration from the new transition countries of Eastern Europe to countries of Western Europe increased (Council of Europe 2006).

In source countries of migrant workers, a recruitment industry similarly emerged that became increasingly diversified and sophisticated. Although the industry is well developed in many Asian labor-sending countries, it is a completely new phenomenon in transition countries or other countries that have only recently opened up to global markets. As a consequence, most of these countries lack adequate regulations and the capacity to monitor the activities of these private recruiters. Although the recruitment industry also covers the domestic market, many have oriented their business toward countries with a demand for workers, in particular Western Europe and the Middle East.[7] Job matching across borders requires particular skills, which many of these newly emerging recruitment firms do not have. Even though entry costs into the market are low, competition for both job candidates and clients (employers) is harsh. In the absence of clear regulations and in light of the limited legal possibilities of recruiting across borders, many recruiters operate in a gray zone. Some are outright criminal (Andrees 2006).

Table 5.1 is an attempt to create a typology of these different types of recruiters (public and private) and their services and modus operandi in the labor market. Based on case studies and the limited surveys, it can be concluded that types 3, 4, and 5 are the most important ways of recruiting migrant workers in Europe. Given the small number of publicly organized recruitment programs between Eastern and Western Europe, it is perhaps not surprising that most of the information flows through informal channels.

The lines between legitimate, bona fide recruitment business and smuggling or trafficking networks can sometimes be blurred. Qualitative research has shown that recruiters—whether they are legal or illegal—use a wide range of channels to approach migrants. The Internet plays an increasing role in this. A male migrant worker in Russia, who was the victim of forced labor, explained how informal recruitment mechanisms work in practice: "I learnt from newspapers about work in Russia. An acquaintance recommended an intermediary to me, who demanded US$200 for his services and persuaded me that I would earn enough in Russia. Six more people came with me. In Russia, a person responsible for placing us in job was waiting for us. They sent us to work at different places" (Tyuryukanova 2006, p. 42).

Empirical findings support two major hypotheses: first, those migrants relying on an unspecified intermediary rather than their own family networks or formal recruitment structures are more likely to be abused during the recruitment process as well as in employment; second, the higher the constraints of migrants seeking employment abroad, the higher the probability that they are trafficked or otherwise abused. These constraints are typically of two sorts: lack of either money or social capital. Financial constraints arise out of the need to cover costs linked to finding employment abroad. Social capital constraints refer to the lack of access to information, knowledge, contacts, and reliable networks.

Figure 5.1 provides evidence for the first hypothesis—that it is risky to rely on an unspecified intermediary. We see that more than one-third of the victims of forced labor and successful migrants obtained job offers abroad via their social connections (respectively 37.6 percent and 41.8 percent). Victims of forced

**Table 5.1  Recruitment Mechanisms in Cross-border Labor Exchanges**

| Type of Intermediary | Means of Recruitment/Services | Type of Payment | Status: Legal or Illegal |
|---|---|---|---|
| 1. Public authorities (e.g., state migration bureau or public employment service) | Advertisement in local media or through public employment service but often limited outreach to local level; recruitment in the context of bilateral migration agreements; often lengthy and bureaucratic procedure and limited quotas that do not reflect full extent of demand. | Free of charge except for administrative fees, but problems of corruption have been reported. | Legal, but illegal practices linked to corruption have been reported. |
| 2. Private employment agencies (PEAs) | Recruitment for the domestic and international market; flexible recruitment as PEAs are in direct contact with employers; some PEAs also recruit to fill official labor migration quotas. Services can cover premigration training, handling of documents, transportation, placement, and return. | In principle, employers should pay the recruitment fee. In practice, fees are often charged to the job seekers. Fees can be inflated, and job offers can be false. | Legal. In countries with no legislation, they often operate in a legal vacuum. Certain practices may be illegal. |
| 3. Travel and other agencies (e.g., model, mail-order-bride, entertainment agencies) | Recruitment is a disguised activity, under the cover of travel services (e.g., transportation and handling of documents). Agencies may be a cover for trafficking activities. | Fees are collected and job offers may be sold as a "package deal" and are not bona fide. | Semilegal, often operating in a legal vacuum. Practices may degenerate into smuggling and trafficking. |

*(continues)*

**Table 5.1 Cont.**

| Type of Intermediary | Means of Recruitment/Services | Type of Payment | Status: Legal or Illegal |
|---|---|---|---|
| 4. Small opportunity networks and individual recruiters | Recruitment is often organized in the form of "gang labor," e.g., a returned migrant organizes a group of workers for a specific employer. Smugglers are often used to organize illegal transportation across the border. | Fees are charged, and the "gang leader" often keeps control over the group at the place of employment. | Informal and often illegal, especially if services of smugglers and illegal practices such as extortion are being used. |
| 5. Acquaintances (e.g., friends, neighbors, family) | Bona fide acquaintances that have been abroad before or have other contacts to employers abroad. This may also degenerate into trafficking, e.g., recruitment of relatives for forced labor exploitation. | Fees are usually not charged, but other forms of favors may be exchanged. | Informal and sometimes illegal, depending on the arrangement with employer and intention of the acquaintance. |
| 6. Organized smuggling and trafficking networks | Organized criminal networks are often involved in other criminal activities such as racketeering or drug trafficking. They establish contact with migrants via Internet, media, "friends," or directly. They organize travel/placement. Trafficking networks keep control over the migrant after the border crossing/job placement and use methods of deception as well as coercion. | High fees are charged and sometimes manipulated after arrival, which can lead to debt bondage in extreme cases. | Illegal. |

**Figure 5.1 Way of Obtaining a Job Offer Abroad**

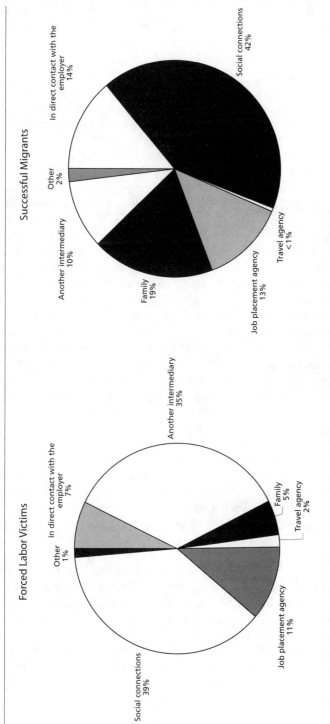

Forced Labor Victims

Successful Migrants

*Source:* Database prepared from study results with 644 returned migrants in Albania, Moldova, Romania, and Ukraine.

labor also obtained job offers via intermediaries (35.1 percent), however, which more successful migrants did to a much lesser extent (10.3 percent). Instead, successful migrants, after social connections, obtained job offers via family members (18.8 percent), which only a few forced labor victims did (5.4 percent). This suggests that successful migrants have more social resources than forced labor victims and therefore do not have to appeal to unreliable intermediaries.

The newer a particular migration route and the longer the distance, the more informational and financial constraints come into play. Over time, as migration networks become established, costs can decrease and access to information can be easier owing to the increasing number of actors competing in the emerging migration industry. Chinese migrants, for example, present a group of migrants that are, more than others, faced by informational and financial constraints. Gao and Poisson (2005) have identified three main modalities through which Chinese migrants organize their journeys and are inserted into the labor market of a particular destination country. First, the intermediary is a service provider who demands a high fee (about 20,000 euros for the trip to Europe), but this is considered as a fair market price. The dangers of the trip and even the violence of the smugglers are seen as inevitable. Second, the trip is organized by an agency. Migrants often leave by plane with a valid visa (tourist or business visa). This particular service is perceived as less dangerous, but abuses occur in relation to the exorbitant fees that have to be paid and services that may not materialize. Third, migrants are smuggled through a network where the intermediary in China is only loosely connected to intermediaries in transit or destination countries. In this case, migrants have reported frequent tragedies, such as rape, death, or other forms of violence.

Informational and financial constraints can also affect migrant workers who move across EU member states. For example, serious violations of labor rights of Portuguese migrant workers abroad are largely linked to temporary employment agencies that are not legally registered. Portuguese construction firms act as subcontractors and supply labor to their counterparts in the Spanish construction industry. These subcontractors are very small, often managed by former migrant workers, and they close down frequently. The most commonly mentioned abuses are deception in terms of wages and of working and living conditions. Recruiters approach potential migrants in their village or hometown and make unrealistic promises. Contracts are often not signed or only upon arrival in the destination country, where the promises are easily broken. Other abuses include illegal wage deductions by charging migrants exorbitant fees for transportation, housing, and sometimes even working tools. Cases of trafficked migrants from Portugal show that agencies can often maintain a high degree of control over workers once they are placed in the job (Pereira and Vasconcelos 2008).

To conclude, the more potential migrants are faced by informational and financial constraints, the more likely it is that they will become victims of trafficking and forced labor. Socioeconomic exclusion and discrimination affecting particularly women and ethnic minorities are key factors in creating vulnerability. Intermediaries exploit these constraints and often reap large profits on the expense of migrants. The more informal their operations—which are influenced by the existing regulatory framework in both source and destination countries— the more likely it is that abuses will occur. The exception is family connections that can play both in favor of and against the migrant. Research indicates that intermediaries are also able to exploit migrants who can theoretically move freely between two particular countries and seek employment legally (e.g., within the EU). The lack of awareness, loopholes in employment regulations, or weak enforcement plays into the hands of these intermediaries.

## Forms of Coercion: Wage Manipulations, Debts, and Threats

The results of the survey with returned migrants have shown that employers use a wide range of coercive measures against trafficked migrants. The ultimate aim is to avoid paying wages at market price or paying any wages at all.

The main forms of wage manipulation are the following: payment below minimum wage (or what is sometimes called "starvation wages"), late and irregular payment of wages, illegal wage deductions, withholding of wages, and no payment at all.

Migrants with debts are particularly vulnerable to wage manipulations. Debts typically arise out of the arrangement with an intermediary or family member who advances money for the trip. Since these arrangements are often informal, debts can easily be manipulated. In a situation similar to that of their often nonexisting employment contract, migrants know that they cannot enforce the "contract" made with their creditor. It is based on trust, and the creditor can exploit this trust because he does not depend on it in order to carry out his "business." Although debts were frequently reported by returned migrants, the existence of debts was best documented in reports from destination countries, as illustrated by the following case studies from Russia, Portugal, and France.

### Case 1: Russia

Research results from Russia indicate that debt bondage is closely linked to the nonpayment of wages, illegal wage deductions, and corruption as well as criminal networks. Tyuryukanova (2006) presented examples of how irregular migrant workers said they ended up in debt bondage: "Two years ago, they arrested me and I spent a night at Leninsky police station. The boss came and bailed me out, then I had to work off the debt" (p. 63). "I cannot change work, I cannot leave, I receive very little, have no money, my debt is increasing—I do not know why" (p. 125).

In some cases, migrants were informed about an accumulated "debt" they owed to their traffickers after arrival in the destination country. An analysis of the case studies indicates, however, that most of the debts were incurred during the employment stage. Owing to relatively easy travel within Commonwealth of Independent States (CIS) countries, real or manipulated transportation fees seem to play a less prominent role. In our sample, 12 percent of all interviewed migrants replied that they could not leave their employment as they had to work off a debt, 39 percent experienced a delay in the payment of wages, and 24 percent were not paid at all. Half of the 14 qualitative case studies that were analyzed in the report can be related to debt bondage. Ten of the 34 interviewed experts said they had encountered situations of debt bondage in their work (Tyuryukanova 2006, p. 71).

A breakdown of sectors showed that debt bondage is most pervasive in entertainment, domestic work, and construction. In Russia, migrants have to survive in an environment where labor law infringements are frequent, in particular, nonpayment of wages or illegal wage deductions, and the enforcement of labor law is hampered by a lack of resources. Corruption among law enforcement officials and a generally dismissive attitude toward complaints of irregular migrant workers play into the hand of employers.

### Case 2: Portugal

Research results from Portugal provide an example of migrant workers who were subjected to double exploitation imposed by their employers as well as criminal networks of their own national group. Though not debt bondage in the strict legal sense of the term, this created de facto situations of bondage where migrants were afraid to resist or to leave employment. The cases refer largely to irregular migrants from Eastern Europe (e.g., Ukrainians, Russians, Moldavians, and Romanians), but similar reports were also received from Brazilian migrants.

Most of the Eastern European migrants were men between 20 and 50 years of age with various professional backgrounds. They paid between US$450 and $1,500 for a "package deal" to a travel agent in their home country that would cover transportation, documents (usually tourist visa), and the promise of a job in Portugal. Upon arrival, most of them were quickly inserted into the labor market, sometimes for an additional fee. They then experienced reduced wage payments or wage deductions combined with blackmailing and extortion by criminal migration networks that aimed at making quick profits. Migrants also found that they had to pay additional fees for invented services, such as obtaining a tax identification number or changing the employer. Portuguese law enforcement authorities were able to dismantle most of these networks once they were alerted by an increase in the number of homicides and other violent incidences affecting migrant workers. Subsequently, the research brought to light only two cases of debt bondage (out of a total of 25 cases of coercive employment). The most common form of coercion was nonpayment or late payment of wages.

### Case 3: Chinese Migrants in France

Debt bondage among Chinese migrants has been widely discussed in the migration literature, and there are diverging opinions about its true nature. The debate was stimulated by reports about high smuggling fees that Chinese migrants have to pay in order to enter Western Europe or North America.[8] Some authors claim that these informal arrangements between smuggler and migrant are transparent and similar to other informal business transactions (Pieke et al. 2004). Others refer to the existence of violence, manipulation, and risks that are completely borne by the migrants and that make this a very unequal business relationship. They also emphasize the distorted balance between debts and potential earnings that makes it very difficult for the worker to escape the burden of debts within a reasonable amount of time (Kwong 1997).

ILO research carried out among migrant workers in France presented debt as a key factor that renders Chinese migrants servile and exploitable (Yun and Poisson 2005). Eleven out of 13 forced labor cases documented in the report can be linked to debt bondage (among other forms of coercion). According to another survey, based on 1,000 respondents of Chinese origin in France, 81 percent had to repay debts (Pina-Guerassimoff et al. 2002). The fact that most Chinese migrants borrow money from family members makes it difficult to establish a clear-cut situation of debt bondage, as the migrant is bonded not to the employer or smuggler but to family members. These moral obligations towards the family can be as effective as legal or illegal obligations vis-à-vis a creditor/usurer.

The average time to work off the debt is three to ten years. During this period of time, Chinese migrants work extremely long hours, are at the mercy of their employers, and live in fear of being detected by the police. Evidence suggests that some of them remain dependent on their employer even after they have repaid their debts, as they require support for obtaining residence and work permits. Like Eastern European migrants in Portugal, Chinese migrants in France are subject to blackmailing, extortion, racketeering, and violence carried out by criminal gangs that take advantage of these workers' irregular status.

### Exploiting Workers Through Threats and Debt

These three case studies illustrate the difficulty of establishing evidence of debt bondage that is systematically imposed by the employer/trafficker in order to retain and exploit workers. The evidence suggests a rather confusing relationship among smugglers/traffickers, criminal extortion networks, and corrupt law enforcement officials that forces migrants to stay with an employer to pay off debts or illegal fees. Although a spiraling debt with little opportunities to earn a decent wage does not constitute debt bondage in the strict legal sense of the term, it renders migrants vulnerable and docile, always hoping that one day they would return home as rich people.

Employers who pay extremely low wages or no wages at all often use threats against irregular migrant workers. These threats can be very subtle and indirect, but they are very effective. For example, women trafficked to the former Yugoslavia for the purpose of commercial sexual exploitation were threatened with resale to the military zone—where conditions were known to be much harder—if they did not obey (Kiryan and van der Linden 2005).

Threats can take on many different forms: threats of violence against oneself or others, threats of denunciation to the police or immigration authorities and subsequent deportation, or threats against family members. These threats can be used directly by the employer to exact labor or services from a worker or by criminal extortion networks.

Threats can also be effective by using a person's sense of shame—such as in the case of a woman forced into prostitution or a man humiliated in front of others. In fact, threats can only be understood by taking the perspective of those who are subjected to them and by analyzing the cultural background of the threatened person. This has been discussed in the context of prostitution and the varying attitudes attached to this activity in different societies (Anderson and O'Connell Davidson 2003). Others have analyzed the role of religious beliefs in keeping a person in bondage. Women from Nigeria, for example, are sometimes threatened with supernatural retaliation if they do not comply with the demands of their traffickers (Carling 2006).

Threats are so effective because migrants, and in particular irregular migrants, are faced with informational and financial constraints, as discussed previously. The threat of denunciation and deportation can lead to a situation where the migrant is not physically constrained to leave the work site but subjectively perceives a lack of freedom of movement. In our research, the respondents cited lack of freedom of movement as the most frequent coercive factor. Focus group interviews and case studies from destination countries, however, revealed that most trafficked persons are not physically confined to their workplaces, though in some cases employers monitor their movement. Limited freedom of movement is related to retention of identity documents and the absence of a legal work permit as well as a corruption. Tyuryukanova (2006) again illustrated this with a quote from a worker in Russia: "I partially work without payment . . . as I work for persons who legalize my status and the status of other migrants. Usually registration is arranged for 3–6 months. My boss has a man who is doing it. Without it, in effect, I cannot go to the city" (p. 67).

## Factors Underlying the Demand for Exploitable Migrant Workers

In the Introduction, three factors were identified that explain crime: a suitable target, a motivated offender, and a weak guardian. This section looks at the demand side of trafficking, and in particular the motivation of potential offenders. It is based on the premise that there would be no forced labor without the demand for goods and services that are either illicit or sold so cheaply that their price does not reflect production costs at decent wages and working conditions. There is an increasing body of research on the demand for sexual services and how suppliers, for example, pimps, have responded to changing patterns of demand. But patterns of demand—which are influenced by social, economic, and cultural factors—have also changed in other economic sectors. For example, a rising middle class and the insertion of women into the labor force have increased the demand for domestic workers. Discount supermarkets have stimulated the demand for cheap food products.

It would go beyond the purpose of this chapter to analyze the correlation of these factors with the supply of migrant workers. Our research mainly focuses on migrant workers and not on employers or consumers. Nonetheless, we discuss some factors that may underlie the demand for exploitable migrant workers as well as incentives of employers to use migrant labor at the lowest costs possible. This discussion largely draws on qualitative data from ILO research in European destination countries as well as other reports.[9]

According to the ILO research, the following sectors other than the sex industry are particularly vulnerable to forced labor and other exploitative practices: construction, agriculture, textiles and garments, restaurants and catering services, and domestic and care work. Many of these sectors now employ irregular migrant workers. In the following paragraphs, two examples are provided to illustrate this trend.

The first example refers to the garment industry in France. The number of large firms with 500 employees or more has shrunk by almost a third since 1990, and the proportion of subcontractors grew from a fifth to a third of all firms in the 1990s (Iskander 2000). Retailers have tightened the turnaround time they allow for orders to respond to changes in the fashion industry. The competition among supply firms has consequently intensified. Although large orders are imported (in particular from China), products at the high end of the fashion market are still produced in France. This niche is filled by small garment workshops that are largely run by Chinese immigrants (Gao and Poisson 2005).

The second example is also illustrative of the trend described above.[10] In 2003, there were an estimated 5,100 horticulture producers in the UK as compared to 6,200 in 1996. The sector generates about £2 billion per year, which accounts for 39 percent of all fruits and vegetables produced for UK households.

There are an estimated 20,000 workers in the sector, many of whom work on a temporary basis and are employed by labor providers ("gangmasters"). Retailers, including major supermarkets, were accused of squeezing prices and increasing orders of large stocks on short notice. Gangmasters responded to the pressure by reducing labor costs and by largely hiring irregular migrant workers. This was facilitated by the absence of effective legal regulations and a large supply of migrants from Eastern Europe.

In 2004, after a tragic incident involving the death of 23 Chinese cockle pickers and other cases of serious exploitation that came to public attention through a countrywide media campaign, public opinion changed. As a consequence, the Gangmasters (Licensing) Act was adopted in 2005 as well as a voluntary code of conduct. The impact assessment study carried out by the Ethical Trading Initiative (ETI) in 2006 revealed that suppliers were pleased with the new registration schemes and thought that good performance helped retain (if not increase) business. Some informants of the assessment study pointed out, however, that the conflict between retailer requirements and labor codes still persisted and that margins of suppliers were under pressure, which restricted their ability to improve labor standards (Ethical Trading Initiative 2006).

In the ILO study on Turkey, 15 employers were interviewed. They employed between 1 and 10 foreign workers in the following sectors: domestic service, entertainment/sex industry, textiles, construction, restaurant, and related services. They recruited these foreign workers through agencies but more often through informal methods, such as friends or the "foreign workers' bazaar" in Istanbul. Migrant workers, in particular those who are irregular, are easily inserted into the flourishing informal economy. Unregistered employment is also common among Turkish nationals. During the 1990s employers of small and medium-sized enterprises, in particular, responded to increases in taxes and insurance premiums by replacing regular with irregular workers. At the same time, sectors such as tourism, entertainment, and domestic service boomed during the 1990s, whereas the textile industry had to struggle with fierce international competition (İçduygu and Köser Akçapar 2004).

Among the main motivations for hiring foreign workers, employers cited the following: migrant workers are more disciplined and hardworking than Turkish workers; they are cheaper; speak many languages, and are generally better educated; they provide better services and do not complain; and Turkish customers request services of migrant workers, in particular of women in the entertainment industry. Employers also mentioned negative aspects of employing irregular migrant workers: their stay is only temporary; police checks lead to deportation of workers and high fines; problems can arise with insurance in the case of illness or death; there are communication problems and distrust.

There seem to be two opposing positions among employers when asked whether they were willing to employ migrant workers if they had to pay more taxes. Nearly all employers in the domestic service sector and textile industry answered positively along the following lines: "I believe that they are not any different than we are so why should they be treated like that? Even if it means paying more, I would employ foreigners as it has many advantages" (İçduygu and Köser Akçapar 2004, p. 62). Employers from other industries, such as entertainment, construction, and restaurants, answered negatively: "Even the Turkish nationals working for me, they don't have insurance or any social security. So why should I give it to foreigners?" (İçduygu and Köser Akçapar 2004, p. 62).

It is possible that due to the seasonal nature of the work in the construction and catering industries, employers have less interest in retaining workers beyond the season. They are therefore less willing to regularize their status and to pay taxes and social contributions. In entertainment and domestic service, social protection linked to work permits did not exist when this research was conducted.[11] Hence the demand for irregular and thus easily exploitable workers varies across economic sectors.

In Russia,[12] the sample included 72 interviews with employers in the construction industry from four different regions (Moscow, St. Petersburg, Rostov, and Perm). The majority of respondents (89 percent) were convinced that there is a shortage of labor in the industry; of this majority, 34 percent believed that it was an acute shortage. A majority (74 percent) responded that migrant workers were largely employed seasonally and in low-skilled jobs. Two-thirds of all employers interviewed believed that migrants were treated differently than native workers, and some thought that differences were substantial. When asked about incentives to violate current immigration and labor law regulations, employers cited the following: easy availability of cheap migrant labor, high taxes, loopholes in legislation, and a cumbersome registration system for foreign workers. Among their motives to respect legislation, employers cited fear of sanctions, respect for the law, and social accountability as the most pertinent.

Employers in certain economic sectors operate within or at the margins of a large informal economy where labor rights, tax provisions, immigration, and social security regulations are hardly enforced. At the time when this research was conducted, the risk of detection was low, and sanctions did not act as an effective deterrent, owing to corruption or other enforcement problems.[13] In countries with well-developed labor inspection systems, such as Germany or Portugal, employers tend to transfer risks to subcontractors. These subcontractors can be bogus or "letterbox" companies that claim to be based abroad. Some of them vanish as soon as they are targeted by law enforcement. Others are officially registered, but they operate with very narrow margins of profits that force them to resort to illegal practices. Setting up a subcontracting firm in one of the economic sectors cited above requires very little entry capital or knowledge. Very often, subcontractors recruit workers and take care of all labor-related issues.[14] Workers and employers are not in direct contact anymore. As a consequence, although forced labor may occur within mainstream businesses, it is more common within the subcontracting chain.

Of course, irregular employment as such does not necessarily imply the use of force and coercion in an employment relationship. On the contrary, this research found many cases where such a relationship was based on a mutual agreement between employers and migrant workers. Both were complicit because migrants often seek short-term gains and care less for long-term social security protection. Moreover, tax evasion damages the state and not the worker. There are two main factors that explain why and when forced labor occurred largely within irregular employment: first, irregular migrant workers have very little bargaining power and do not know how to enforce their informal/illegal contracts; second, irregular employment is often related to informal recruitment.

The availability of vulnerable workers, and business strategies that make it relatively easy to conceal illegal practices, such as subcontracting, are two important factors determining transaction costs for employers. According to theories on the economics of crime (Fiorentini and Peltzman 1995), employers resort to illegal business practices if the expected profits are high and transaction costs low. Belser (2005) has estimated that trafficking in human beings generates $US32 billion in profits annually, which includes illegal migration fees as well as profits made through labor law violations (such as nonpayment or withholding of wages). A breakdown showed that margins of profit per capita are twice as high in the sex industry as in other economic sectors. Nonetheless, employers in other industries can make significant profits based on the large number of illegally employed workers for whom they do not pay any taxes and social contributions and to whom they pay very low or no wages. Given these numbers, it is clear that there is much to gain for employers, pimps, traffickers, subcontractors, and others involved in the exploitation of migrant workers.

## Conclusion

Forced labor in Europe is by and large an outcome of irregular migration processes. Smugglers and traffickers respond to a bottleneck in the supply of cheap and disposable labor in most EU member states, Russia, Turkey, and other countries that gradually become destination countries of migrant workers. Given that there are only limited legal channels of migration and that some employers remain competitive only by putting pressure on wages, migrants are highly vulnerable to exploitation. They are faced with financial and informational constraints and thus often rely on dubious recruitment practices.

This chapter has proposed a typology of recruitment mechanisms that captures the diversity of legal and illegal ways to enter European labor markets. Empirical findings from largely qualitative case studies suggest that recruitment is a key factor influencing the success or failure of a migration project. Migrants who had to rely on informal or outright illegal intermediaries were more likely to end up in forced labor than those who did not have to. Furthermore, the chapter explored practices of coercion related to threats and debt bondage that enable abusive employers to cut down on wages or pay no wages at all. Given that irregular migrant workers have no regular employment contract, they have little leverage to negotiate fair wages or at least obtain wages that were promised to them.

Early policy interventions against human trafficking were based on the understanding that trafficking was an organized crime hardly affecting mainstream industries, thereby neglecting important labor market aspects. Over recent years, however, a paradigm shift took place, which many international organizations, NGOs, and human rights groups, including the ILO, demanded. This chapter has shed light on some of the underlying labor market mechanisms that expose migrant workers to highly exploitative practices. The challenge is now to translate these findings into effective laws and policies.

## Notes

This chapter is based on Andrees (2008).

1. The following countries were part of this research program: Albania, France, Germany, Hungary, Moldova, Portugal, Romania, Russian Federation, Turkey, and Ukraine.

2. In 2005, the International Organization for Migration (IOM) published a global survey on the "state of the art" in trafficking research. The bibliography on Europe includes mainly publications referring to sex trafficking (International Organization for Migration 2005). There are notable exceptions, though. In 2006, Anti-Slavery International published a series of research papers on trafficking for forced labor. The Victimology Society in Serbia, with support from the Organization for Security and Cooperation in Europe (OSCE), also addressed trafficking of men in a 2004 study (Nikolic-Ristanoviç et al. 2004).

3. A meeting was held in Geneva in 2002 to discuss the research design with research teams from each country and to make sure that it could be applied in a similar fashion (see also International Labour Organization 2002a).

4. Initially, the research was designed to study forced labor exploitation of migrant workers in Portugal. Information from key informants and other sources suggested, however, that Portuguese migrant workers were also subjected to severe forms of exploitation and that Portugal was both a source and a destination country.

5. For more information on the research design and methodology, see Andrees (2008).

6. The only cases entered in this database were those in which data on the forms of coercion were complete, in order to make a judgment about forced labor.

7. In the transition economies of Eastern Europe, reliable data are hard to find as private recruiters often act in a legal vacuum. In Ukraine, for example, there are about 400 licensed recruitment agencies recruiting for employment abroad. The number of agencies operating in the domestic market is unknown as no licensing scheme exists. In Albania, the number of licensed agencies grew from 2 to 20 over recent years (information from ILO country offices).

8. The price ranges between 3,000 and 20,000 euros per person, depending on the place of origin in China and country of destination.

9. The main focus here is on sectors other than the sex industry. IOM has sponsored pioneering research into demand patterns in the sex industry and in domestic work. All studies are based on small, nonrepresentative samples (Anderson and O'Connell Davidson 2003; Bianchi, Popper, and Luksik 2007).

10. The following is based on the Ethical Trading Initiative's impact assessment (Ethical Trading Initiative 2006), a Temporary Labour Working Group publication (Temporary Labour Working Group 2004), and information provided to the ILO in the context of an EU/AGIS-funded project, "Capacity Building to Combat the Forced Labour Outcomes of Human Trafficking in Europe," cofunded by the UK Department for Work and Pensions.

11. As for domestic services, the situation changed with the introduction of a new regulation on work permits in 2003.

12. The following data are from a draft report that the ILO commissioned in cooperation with the European Bank for Reconstruction and Development (EBRD) in 2006.

13. A new law adopted in Russia in November 2006 significantly increased sanctions for employers using irregular migrant workers, but protection mechanisms for migrants who have been exploited are not yet in place.

14. This is the case in "triangular" employment relationships where a labor contract exists between the worker and agency/subcontractor and a civil contract between the employer and the agency/subcontractor.

# 6

# Strengthening Labor Market Governance Against Forced Labor

*Beate Andrees and Patrick Belser*

The case studies in this book provide insights into the overall political context in which forced labor continues to strive. Forced labor exists owing to a mix of root causes, with weak enforcement of laws being one main cause. This chapter focuses on national policies and law enforcement responses that are aimed at ending the impunity of those benefiting from exploitation. Evidence from the case studies has shown that unscrupulous employers using forced labor seek to minimize the risk of detection, and indeed they often get away with it. Impunity means few prosecutions, but also few victims who are identified and assisted.

It is often argued that forced labor is a crime and that swift criminal law enforcement is the right answer against forced labor. Indeed, this approach was also adopted by the ILO Forced Labour Convention, 1930 (No. 29). Although criminal prosecutions are important, they are by definition reactive. Criminal law enforcement has limited preventive power and operates on the basis of a binary logic: victims and offenders. The reality of forced labor today, however, is more complex and rather colored in gray. As the case studies of this book demonstrate, there is a continuum of exploitation with clearly criminal practices at one end and more subtle forms of exploitation and discrimination at the other. The purpose of this chapter is therefore not to discuss how deviant behavior or greed can be best punished but rather to look at the institutions that underpin such abusive practices.

We argue that forced labor is first and foremost a failure of labor market governance. We further argue that strategies against forced labor and human trafficking will not succeed as long as they are narrowly focusing on criminal law enforcement without addressing the structural deficiencies in current labor market governance. Countries have adopted various modes of labor market governance. In essence, modes of labor market governance reflect the balance of power between market, state, and civil society actors. Hence, a set of labor institutions results in a specific system of labor market governance. According to Berg and Kucera (2008, p. 11), "labour institutions comprise rules, practices and policies—whether formal or informal, written or unwritten—all of which affect how the labour market works."

Institutions are embedded in historical, social, and cultural settings, and they are present in all countries, independent of their development. The *peshgi* system in Pakistan and the *engache* system in Peru are examples of informal labor institutions that impose certain rules on workers and employers. Although these systems of wage advances are not necessarily leading into bonded labor, they are nonetheless characterized by an unequal relationship of power. Workers are easily deceived about the nature of their debts and then forced to work them off on conditions they cannot choose freely. In response to these exploitative practices, labor market institutions have emerged that aim at mitigating the unequal bargaining power between workers and employers. This subset of labor institutions comprises, for example, labor law to protect workers, labor administration to formulate labor market policies, labor inspection systems to enforce the law, and trade unions and employers' organizations as well as employment tribunals.

Throughout this book, we have put emphasis on two labor institutions: wage and recruitment systems. In this chapter, we will look at formal labor market institutions that have been set up to protect workers from wage manipulations and deceptive recruitment practices. We analyze regulations and their enforcement through labor inspectors or other actors. We also discuss shortcomings of these institutions. Of course, many other institutions would be relevant for this discussion, for example, regulations on working time, subcontracting in global supply chains, or gender issues. We decided to add only one additional dimension to this discussion, however, since it is an important part of the policy response against forced labor: the role of trade unions and employment tribunals. They empower workers to stand up for their inalienable right: the right to freely choose employment.

The chapter is divided into two parts. The first part discusses national policies against forced labor, their overall strategy, and the role that has been assigned to labor market institutions. The second part analyzes strengths and weaknesses of relevant labor market institutions, namely labor inspection, recruitment systems, and institutions that protect the interests of victims. The chapter concludes with directions for further research and action.

## Regional and National Policies
## Against Forced Labor and Trafficking

In recent years, there has been increasing awareness about forced labor and the forced labor outcomes of human trafficking. International pressure has augmented and often resulted in the adoption of new laws and national action plans. Little research has been carried out so far to understand the impact of these national policies as well as to analyze factors that determine their successful implementation. Experts and policymakers often stress the need for a holistic approach against forced labor that requires cooperation with different stakeholders. In practice, however, implementation of complex policies is often hampered by a lack of political will, resources, and coordination.

Despite growing international commitment to fight forced labor and trafficking, only a few countries have developed a clear national policy, though many are in the process of doing so. For the purpose of this chapter, we have analyzed 28 national action plans (NAPs) against forced labor or trafficking.[1] Most of the existing NAPs to date focus on human trafficking, which reflects international attention to this subject and the fact that trafficking affects almost every country in the world today. The NAPs have been analyzed at two levels: the strategic level (vision, approach, definition of the problem, data, coordination structure, government ownership, legal framework, civil society participation, and budget allocations) as well as the operational level (prevention, protection, and prosecution).[2]

The results of this very limited assessment show that many NAPs lack a strategy that includes labor market governance and engages labor market institutions. There are, however, exceptions to this. The 2007 Action Plan on Tackling Human Trafficking of the United Kingdom, for example, recognizes that

> up to now, our effort has focused mainly on trafficking for sexual exploitation. We now need to move beyond this and also spotlight other forms of trafficking for increased attention, such as child trafficking and trafficking for forced labour. . . .
> We need to understand better how to recognise this form of trafficking and we need to raise awareness, through training and the provision of guidance to workplace enforcement agencies, law enforcement, immigration and other front line organisations so that potential victims of trafficking can be identified. (United Kingdom 2007, pp. 5–6)

The Human Trafficking Centre in the UK made trafficking for labor exploitation one of its core areas for training and action in 2008.

In some countries, separate discourses on forced/bonded labor and trafficking have led to the creation of two action plans. Pakistan, for example, first adopted a National Policy and Plan of Action (NPPA) for the Abolition of Bonded Labour and the Rehabilitation of Freed Bonded Labourers in 2001. The NPPA systematically involves labor market actors, such as social partners, labor inspectors in cooperation with vigilance committees, and other players. This is not surprising, since the lead ministry is the Ministry of Labour. Following the adoption of a new law against human trafficking, the Ministry of Interior drafted an NAP titled "Combating Human Trafficking." Even though the plan focuses on prevention and reintegration alongside law enforcement and prosecution issues, the Ministry of Labour has limited responsibility, not to mention more specialized labor agencies and social partners. This divide is often instigated or perpetuated by international organizations and donor agencies that tend to rely on their particular framing of the problem.

The lack of sound statistical data is a common problem to all action plans. Only 2 out of 28 NAPs are based on statistical data, and most deplore the absence of data that makes policy planning very difficult (see Chapter 9). Most of the reviewed NAPs have a clear government ownership (at least on paper), and the lead is assigned to a specific ministry, usually a ministry of interior as far as trafficking is concerned and a ministry of labor for other forms of forced labor. Some countries have appointed a coordinator or rapporteur. The majority of NAPs acknowledge the important role of civil society organizations in the fight against forced labor and trafficking, especially with regard to victim identification and protection. Many of them are silent about trade unions and employers' organizations, however.

For national policies to be effective, they have to be supported by an adequate legal and institutional framework as well as financial resources. Many NAPs fall short of this requirement. Only seven NAPs state a clear source and quota of budgetary allocations. The others are rather vague about it or do not mention it at all. Likewise, many policies are not linked to necessary legal reform processes. There is often a gap between action initiated by the government administration and action of the legislature. One is often lagging behind the other. Even more striking is the absence of clear indicators to measure progress over time. Many NAPs state highly ambitious objectives but remain silent about their implementation.

Countries that have gone through a series of policy revisions, however, show more mature instruments. Ukraine, for example, was one of the first countries to adopt an NAP against human trafficking. Although earlier plans were imbalanced in terms of policy priorities and not attached with indicators and budget allocations, the current NAP is very comprehensive and linked to a budget for the first time. The central government has also initiated roundtables at the district (*oblast*) level to ensure implementation across the country. It currently aims to develop a monitoring mechanism in order to measure progress over time.[3] The example of Ukraine also shows progressive change in policies. The first NAP adopted in 1999 was dominated by a strict criminal law enforcement approach (and resources primarily channeled to the training of police, border guards, and prosecutors), whereas the third NAP, adopted in 2007, involves labor market institutions for at least half of all planned activities.

With NAPs often lacking a clear strategy, it is not surprising that even law enforcement responses are insufficient. This is mainly owing to the fact that policy development has often been dissociated from legislative reforms. Some countries were under pressure to change laws rather quickly because of the ratification of the Palermo Protocol, EU directives, or pressure through the annual US *Trafficking in Persons Report* that classifies countries in a three-tier system. But enforcement of these new laws remained weak because law enforcement authorities did not receive clear guidelines and training. Moreover, law enforcement measures often failed in the long term because they were not accompanied by strong victim protection measures, prevention, and alternative income-generating measures. Experience from countries in southeastern Europe has shown that swift law enforcement action was crucial in sending a clear message to criminal groups involved in trafficking in human beings. It did not succeed, however, in suppressing trafficking as such, as criminals have adapted their strategies and victims were often left without sufficient protection (Limanowska 2005; ICMPD 2007).

Ideally, national policies should be embedded in a regional approach to ensure policy coherence. Unfortunately, regional cooperation is hampered by many obstacles, as national policies vary greatly and transaction costs to share information are high. The following examples represent attempts to coordinate action at a regional level. Implementation of these regional action plans is still in the beginning stage, and they have not yet yielded effective results. As can be seen from the examples, with the exception of Latin America, the emphasis is on trafficking in human beings.

In 2001, the Economic Community of West African States (ECOWAS) adopted the ECOWAS Initial Plan of Action Against Trafficking in Persons, with a focus on criminal justice responses. The ECOWAS plan of action directs the executive secretariat to prepare proposals to progressively eliminate trafficking in persons in the subregion, with special consideration of the situation of trafficked children.

In 2004, member countries of the Association of Southeast Asian Nations (ASEAN) adopted a Declaration Against Trafficking in Persons, Particularly Women and Children. They expressed the urgent need for a comprehensive regional approach to prevent and to combat trafficking in persons as well as to undertake action to safeguard the human rights of victims.

In 2005, the fourth Summit of the Americas led to the adoption of an action plan, which aims, inter alia, "to eliminate forced labour before 2010" by strengthening measures and policies and to enable those countries that have not already done so to achieve this goal. It also encouraged the drafting of national action plans.

In Europe, regional coordination of action against human trafficking is led by the European Union, the Council of Europe, and the OSCE. The permanent council of the OSCE was the first to adopt a regional action plan in 2003. In 2005, the Council of the EU adopted the Plan on Best Practices, Standards, and Procedures for Combating and Preventing Trafficking in Human Beings (EU Action Plan, 20005/C311/01). In February 2008, the Council of Europe Convention on Action Against Trafficking in Human Beings entered into force with the ratification of ten member states. In 2006, a first interregional Plan Against Trafficking in Human Beings, Especially Women and Children, was adopted by the European Union and African States in Tripoli by the Ministerial Conference on Migration and Development.

Despite the fact that these regional plans are not supported by direct budget allocations, they have been important in spearheading action at the national level and in raising global awareness about forced labor and trafficking. In addition, there are many bilateral and multilateral cooperation agreements. Though sometimes very specific and concrete, they often fail to be implemented owing to a lack of funding and of the political will to make cross-border cooperation effective—especially when it comes to trafficking for labor exploitation.

## The Role of Labor Market Institutions

### The Strengths and Weaknesses of Labor Inspection

It is often argued that forced labor takes place in the informal or illicit economy, which is out of reach for labor inspectors or other formal labor market institutions. Case studies in this book demonstrate, however, that forced labor can also penetrate mainstream economic sectors. Although it may be true that the majority of forced labor takes place outside formal workplace arrangements, it is argued here that forced labor also occurs in the formal sector due to weak labor market regulation and labor law enforcement. Instead of focusing narrowly on the worst cases of exploitation often linked to criminal activities, governments should strengthen the overall floor of labor protection and labor law enforcement. Many countries face serious difficulties in doing so, however, because they have dismantled labor inspection services or because inspection functions are highly fragmented.

The history of labor inspection is very closely related to concerns over core labor standards. In France, for example, a law in 1892 set up a special body of civil servants charged with the inspections of labor conditions and most of all with the implementation of the 1841 law on child labor. In Great Britain, voluntary labor commissions became part of the government's administration in 1844 in order to counter the worst excesses of the Industrial Revolution. In Latin America, the development of strong labor administration systems, including labor inspection, was linked to the insertion of social clauses into national constitutions at the beginning of the twentieth century.

In 1947, the ILO adopted the Labour Inspection Convention (No. 81). Convention No. 81 provides an overall guideline to labor inspection, taking into account divergence in labor law as well as different cultures with regard to workplace inspection. The most crucial element of Convention No. 81 is a provision that empowers labor inspectors to enter any workplace liable to inspection without prior notice. This makes labor inspectors especially valuable in efforts to enforce laws against forced labor. In addition, labor inspectors have a wide range of dissuasive measures at their disposal in order to bring employers into compliance. Some economists have argued that compliance of private firms is influenced by two important variables: the probability of inspection and the severity of sanctions (Squire and Suthiwart-Narueput 1997). Research based on interviews with employers that has been cited throughout the case studies of this book also indicates that low risks of detection and sanctions are the main factors influencing employers' behavior. Indeed, some of the qualitative case studies show how employers first test their victims and then force them into a spiral of dependency and exploitation over time.

Despite their important role, recognized in international and national law, labor inspectors face many obstacles. The most serious obstacle is the lack of political will to adequately staff and train labor inspection services, which is often linked to an overall weak labor administration system. In some developing countries, the whole labor administration system receives less than 1 percent of the national budget and sometimes a mere 0.1 percent; it does not take much effort to calculate how understaffed and underresourced labor inspections are in those countries (ILO 2002b).

One tentative study has recently estimated that there is a global shortfall of more than 45,000 labor inspectors (Belser et al. unpublished). This estimate is based on the gap between the estimated number of labor inspectors per region and ILO benchmarks for a minimum number of labor inspectors according to the number of workers and the development stage of the country. Industrial market economies, for example, should have one inspector for every 10,000 workers, transition countries one for every 20,000, and less developed countries one for every 40,000. The shortfall is calculated per country and multiplied by a population expansion factor. Table 6.1 shows that the gap is highest in industrialized countries (partly owing to their high benchmark) as well as in Asia (owing to its large populations).

Apart from this shortfall of labor inspectors, there are other limitations that are not strictly related to their numbers. Barriers to effective labor law enforcement are also related to cultural, economic, and political factors at different levels. Probably the most important issue is the lack of clear legislation and operational guidelines that would actually empower labor inspectors to focus on forced labor issues. Although most countries have ratified ILO forced labor conventions, provisions in national law are often too vague or entirely absent (see ILO 2007a). National antitrafficking laws, often enacted upon ratification of the Palermo Protocol, however, focus narrowly on criminal law enforcement without considering the important role of labor inspectors (see Chapter 7). It has also been noted in the preceding section that labor inspectors are largely absent in national action plans or policy consultations against forced labor/ trafficking. Again, there is a divide between action plans focusing on forced

**Table 6.1  Shortfall of Labor Inspectors**

|  | Total Number of Labor Inspectors in the World (estimated range) | Estimated Global Shortfall in the Number of Labor Inspectors |
|---|---|---|
| Industrialized economies | 18,393–20,306 | 20,703 |
| Transition economies | 10,805–12,495 | 4,623 |
| Middle East and North Africa | 3,686–4,423 | 500 |
| Asia and the Pacific | 47,711–78,344 | 14,127 |
| Latin America and the Caribbean | 5,433–6,332 | 1,334 |
| Sub-Saharan Africa | 1,550–2,114 | 3,939 |
| Total | 89,071–119,740 | 45,226 |

*Source:* Belser et al. (unpublished). Column 2 is estimated on the basis of a sample of the number of labor inspectors in 63 countries. Column 3 is obtained by using the difference in the 63 countries between the actual number of labor inspectors and the benchmarks discussed in the text.

labor and those focusing on trafficking. Action plans against forced labor tend to recognize the role of labor inspectors more often.

Without a clear mandate, labor inspectors cannot act. In addition to the need to recognize the role of labor inspectors in laws and policies, there have to be operational guidelines that would allow front-line inspectors to assess specific situations and to act upon them. Although these operational guidelines have been developed for specialized police units against trafficking in many countries, they hardly exist for labor inspectors. There are a few exceptions, such as Italy, where police and labor inspectors work in joint teams and have developed indicators to guide their operations.[4] Political support for labor inspectors also requires investment in training and ensuring the safety of inspectors. Situations of forced labor can be dangerous. In 2004, three labor inspectors and a driver were killed in Brazil. They were ambushed by armed men on their way to inspection sites. In the same year, two inspectors were killed in southern France when they visited a farm supposedly employing irregular migrant workers. These tragic incidents demonstrate that inspectors need the support of the police in such critical situations and that they need to be trained on safety issues.

In addition, labor inspection is often fragmented, even though the ILO has noticed a trend toward integrated inspection systems over recent years (International Labour Organization 2006a). In many countries, there is a divide between factory inspectors concerned with issues of occupational safety and health (often fragmented themselves) and inspectors responsible for illegal employment, employment contracts, and related issues. In general, however, labor inspection activities tend to focus on workers in the formal rather than informal economy despite the principle that labor law should have universal coverage. Likely victims of forced labor often work in informal and "invisible" places of employment, such as private premises of their employer or geographically isolated areas. This is particularly true for small illegal sweatshops, domestic work, prostitution, and agricultural farms. In order to reach out to those vulnerable workers, labor inspectors have to develop strategies to work jointly with community-based organizations, trade unions, and the police.

Cultural obstacles may also prevent a more active role of labor inspectors in the fight against forced labor. Forced labor may be perceived as a minor issue as compared to inspection tasks that are relevant to the majority of workers, such as occupational safety and health. Victims of forced labor often come from discriminated groups of society, such as bonded laborers in Southeast Asia, irregular migrant workers in Europe, indigenous people in Latin America, or descendants of slaves in Africa. They are not only invisible to inspectors in the world of work but in society at large. The exploitation they suffer is sometimes blamed on them; this is often manifested in the attitude toward irregular migrant workers who are supposed to know what they are getting into by entering a country illegally. Even though labor inspectors tend to have a work ethic that is focused on bringing employers into compliance and protecting workers, they may not be entirely free from these discriminatory attitudes. There are examples of inspectors in Bolivia who have helped employers to find indigenous workers who escaped debt bondage instead of protecting the rights of the workers (see Chapter 2).

In the following sections, we present two examples that highlight the importance of labor inspectors in the prevention as well as elimination of forced labor and trafficking.

*Mobile Inspection Units in Brazil.* The Mobile Inspection Group was created by the federal government in 1995, following an official recognition of the problem of what is called "slave labor" in Brazil.[5] The group receives complaints from workers or more frequently from an NGO called the Pastoral Land Commission (CPT), the federal police, trade unions, or work cooperatives. It can mobilize a Mobile Inspection Unit (MIU) to travel to suspected work sites. Control rests with the labor inspection section of the Ministry of Labour and Employment in order to guarantee that denunciations and preparations for inspections are kept completely secret. Between 1995 and 2007, the MIUs received 31,158 complaints, inspected 1,789 farms, and rescued 25,064 workers (see Chapter 1).

What make the MIUs unique are their interagency composition and their power to impose penalties on the spot. In 2007, there were seven inspection units covering the whole country. Each unit is usually composed of labor inspectors from the Ministry of Labour and Employment and police agents and district commissioners of the federal police as well as labor attorneys. MIUs can file notices of labor code violations and impose appropriate fines as well as obligations to pay workers the wage arrears and other benefits due to them. The federal police are responsible for the security of the team and for initiating criminal investigations, such as under the country's provisions against slave labor.

The collaboration among the labor inspectors, the attorneys, and the federal police has been institutionalized, and the cooperation among these different agencies and ministries has become routine. This has not always been the case. Although labor attorneys have participated in inspections since 1995, it is only since 2002 that the involvement of labor attorneys has become more systematic. In 2003, they participated in 80 percent of the operations; the following year, the figure was more than 90 percent. Apart from lending their support to the MIU, labor attorneys have also brought public and collective civil actions to court in order to force offenders to pay compensation for wage arrears and other violations of labor law. As judges are receiving more suits and are becoming more sensitive to the issue of slave labor, the number of condemnations and settlements has also increased.[6]

*Inspection of Qualified Industrial Zones in Jordan.*  Since 1997, following an agreement on the establishment of Qualified Industrial Zones (QIZ), Jordan has benefited from a significant inflow of foreign investments, especially into the garment sector. Since the late 1990s, the textiles and garment sector has become an engine of growth in Jordan. It accounts for 30 percent of all exports from Jordan and 90 percent of exports to the United States, thanks to a bilateral free trade agreement (FTA) concluded in 2000. The FTA is designed to ensure that both countries uphold ILO core labor standards, including the prohibition of forced labor.

In 2006, the US-based National Labor Committee (NLC) investigated labor practices in the QIZ and denounced abusive working conditions, including forced labor, in a highly publicized report (National Labor Committee 2006). The study looked at factories, which benefited from preferential access to the US market. According to the Jordanian Ministry of Labour, there are nine QIZ with 114 companies, of which 59 export to the United States and 55 are subcontracting companies. They employ a total of 54,077 workers, of which 36,149 are migrant workers coming largely from India, Bangladesh, China, and Sri Lanka.[7]

The NLC report caused great concern in Jordan, and the Ministry of Labour initiated an inspection campaign shortly after. Inspections covered companies reviewed in the NLC report as well as other establishments in the QIZ. Inspectors were accompanied by embassy staff to ensure translation and media coverage on some occasions. As a result of the campaign, a total of 114 penalties were issued and two establishments were closed. Apart from these immediate remedies, the inspection report of the Ministry of Labour highlighted some important conclusions.

Although some of the accusations of the NLC, especially those regarding physical violence and restriction of freedom of movement, could not be proven, it was noted that migrant workers may have been intimidated prior and during the interviews. Hence, there is a need to develop other measures, such as anonymous hotlines to receive complaints. It was further noted that enforcement tends to focus on violation of work permits of migrant workers instead of labor violations such as forced overtime or irregularities in wage payments. Furthermore, the insufficient number of labor inspectors and their weak capacity to regularly inspect QIZ were noted. Finally, the campaign also highlighted the need for policy coherence among the Jordan Investment Board (which issues licenses for companies in the QIZ), the Ministry of Labour, and the Ministry of Interior. Following the campaign, collaboration between the ILO and the Ministry of Labour was fostered through capacity-building measures on migration management, awareness-raising on forced labor and trafficking, and other ongoing measures.

* * *

These two examples demonstrate that labor inspectors play a key role in the prevention and identification of forced labor practices that can be extremely damaging not only to a specific industry but also to a country as a whole. Unfortunately, the weakness or complete absence of labor inspection in many countries is an obstacle to the enforcement of anti–forced labor legislation. In order to follow up on forced labor complaints, some governments have set up special inspection units or local vigilance committees. Even though this may be a useful strategy to use to respond to the specific challenges of identifying forced labor, it is important to fully integrate inspection services. Otherwise, responses will remain ad hoc, fragmented, and piecemeal.

In Pakistan, for example, the local government of Sindh province has stopped unannounced labor inspections in an attempt to attract foreign investments. Bonded labor is still common in the province. In India, labor inspection covers the whole country in principle, but its reach in rural areas where bonded labor continues to exist is limited. In both India and Pakistan, vigilance committees have been established at the community level to monitor the situation of bonded labor and to bring cases to court. Despite these efforts, vigilance committees are often ineffective in identifying the victims and rehabilitating them. Enforcement systems, such as labor inspection, should therefore be strengthened to work hand in hand with vigilance committees at the local level. For example, by active enforcement of the Minimum Wages Act in India, combined with regulation of production units (under the Factories Act), debt bondage can be prevented. Labor administration and the factory department should make periodic inspections of work sites and establishments and register complaints with senior officials regarding nonpayment of minimum wages and back wages.[8]

*Monitoring Abusive Recruitment Practices*

Case studies in this book highlight differences and commonalities in the recruitment of potential forced labor victims. There are four main ways into forced labor: (1) through traditional relations between tenants and landowners or between former slaves and masters that are passed on to the next generation, (2) through kidnapping and abduction (relevant mainly in the context of civil war), (3) through formal and informal recruiters operating in domestic labor markets, and (4) through formal and informal recruiters facilitating cross-border labor exchanges. There may be overlaps but by and large those categories are most relevant. In this section we discuss the importance of strong labor market institutions to monitor the recruitment process within a country and especially across borders.

Throughout history, labor recruitment agents have had to struggle against their negative image. Whether private or public, formal or informal, legal or illegal, recruiters are the link between labor supply and demand. They respond to a particular market failure, namely the fact that both employers and workers have imperfect information about vacancies and appropriate candidates. This imperfection is exacerbated in the international context where private agents are often needed to scout for foreign job opportunities and to place workers abroad (Martin 2006).

For a long time, ILO standards have promoted a state monopoly on recruitment in order to protect workers from abuse. Following decisions in an increasing number of member states to abolish this monopoly (or not to establish it in the first place) and to allow private recruiters to operate in the market, the ILO adopted a new convention in 1997 that acknowledges the legitimate role that private employment agencies can play in the labor market.[9] The new convention assigns the role of monitoring and inspecting private employment agencies to labor inspectors; however, a specialized authority could also be appropriate.

The logic of reinforcing regulations and monitoring private employment agencies as part of an anti–forced labor/trafficking strategy is twofold. First, it sends out a clear signal that not only those profiting from the employment of forced laborers but also those knowingly facilitating the recruitment into coercive employment will be held responsible. Second, it helps to prevent forced labor by clamping down on unfair competition in the recruitment industry and by progressively driving illegal recruiters out of the market. This should be seen as a long-term process that has to start with clear legislation, the establishment of a properly resourced monitoring institution, and the effective punishment of offenders. We give two examples to show the relevance of this approach to the prevention of human trafficking. So far, we have only limited experience of how this could be applied to situations of traditional forced labor.

*Regulating "gangmasters" in the United Kingdom.* The UK government has always allowed private recruiters to operate in the labor market under the 1973 Employment Act. In agriculture and food processing, private intermediaries are called "gangmasters," and they play an important role in job matching and outsourcing. In the 1990s, gangmasters became increasingly involved in the recruitment of foreign migrant labor, such as from Eastern Europe. Since it was fairly easy to register as a gangmaster, foreign workers themselves became involved in this business, operating in the UK and in their home countries. At the same time, trade unions and other actors called for better regulation of gangmasters following the detection of abuses of workers' rights.

In 2005, a tragic incident involving the death of 23 migrant cockle pickers recruited through gangmasters, followed by an intense media campaign, changed the UK approach. The government-sponsored Ethical Trading Initiative (ETI) had already initiated consultations with relevant stakeholders, which led to the establishment of the Temporary Labour Working Group (TLWG) in 2002. Its members include major retailers, trade unions, and government agencies, among others. The TLWG drafted a voluntary code of conduct that was used as a benchmark prior to the adoption of the Gangmasters (Licensing) Act in 2005, which made the licensing of gangmasters compulsory. According to the new act, the Gangmasters Licensing Authority (GLA) was established in May 2005. The GLA is responsible for licensing existing and prospective gangmasters. The act clearly sets out that gangmasters offering their services without having obtained a license before operating their business will be guilty of an offense. Additionally, those employers ("labor users") who use the services of nonlicensed gangmasters will be equally punished.

The GLA published a consultation document in October 2005 on the specific conditions for issuing a license.[10] In 2008, the GLA issued more than 1,000 licenses and revoked 55. The following is a recent example of how the GLA operates in practice. An unannounced raid targeted labor providers in the flower, plant, and bulb industry around Spalding and Boston in the run-up to Easter and Mother's Day. GLA officers entered the premises of a number of nurseries, inspected vehicles used to transport workers, and carried out worker interviews on several daffodil fields in the area. The gangmasters were supplying hundreds of mainly English, Polish, and Slovakian workers to pick daffodils and work in the nurseries. The GLA officers found gangmasters who retained passports of their workers and charged them high fees for accommodations and transportation that could lead into debt bondage, among other violations of the law.[11]

The GLA is seeking to follow a proportionate approach to scoring compliance, with categories such as critical (safety), critical (other), reportable, and correctable. Against these criteria, compliance and the possible risk factor will be scored on the basis of, for example, interviews with workers and labor providers, data collected from labor providers, or evidence collected by the GLA's officers. On the whole, the risk assessment process is aimed at lowering the cost of the overall licensing regime, as compliant labor providers will not be burdened with inspection and auditing costs. Additionally, only those labor providers are targeted who are believed to constitute a risk to workers.

This process has been accompanied by increased cooperation between various authorities, as well as between the private and public sector. It has also triggered the adoption of a National Action Plan Against Human Trafficking that highlights the need to address abusive recruitment and contract labor practices. Although the GLA has made progress in closing down illegal gangmasters and punishing offenders, there remain important gaps with regard to victim protection in UK law. As a rule, irregular migrant workers are denied any rights that could arise out of an irregular employment relationship. This creates obstacles to the enforcement of labor law. It should also be noted that the GLA has no mandate to cover industries other than agriculture and food processing.

*The Philippine Overseas Employment Administration.* This example offers the perspective of a source country of migration. The government of the Philippines has long since adopted an active labor export strategy; it deploys around one million workers per year abroad. NGOs have criticized the government for its labor export strategies and the many abuses that Philippine migrants suffer abroad. At the same time, the government has established one of the strongest institutions to protect migrant workers—the Philippine Overseas Employment Administration (POEA). The POEA monitors recruitment agencies, checks employment contracts, provides predeparture training, and follows up on complaints of migrant workers. It works together with a number of labor attachés deployed in Philippine embassies in major destination countries.

Between 1992 and 2002, the POEA filed 650 cases alleging illegal recruitment, but only 66 of the cases that were recommended for prosecution resulted in a criminal conviction, a result attributed to the inefficiency of the Philippine court system and the reluctance of many migrant victims to file formal charges and to testify in court. Some victims refuse to testify because the recruiter is a relative, friend, or resident of their town, and in other cases victims who initially allege that they had to wait too long to be deployed are in fact sent abroad, which stops the case.

Many violations of POEA regulations occur overseas, as when a migrant is required to sign a supplemental contract that requires the payment of additional fees. Migrants in such cases could complain to labor attachés at local consulates, but most do not, fearing that they could be dismissed by the employer and required to return the debts they incurred to go abroad. To protect migrants in such situations, Philippine law makes Filipino recruiters jointly liable with foreign employers to fulfill the provisions of the contracts that each migrant leaving legally must have. This helps to protect migrants but prompts some recruiters to complain that their revenues and profits depend on deploying migrants to employers abroad whom they may not know well.[12]

## Voice and Empowerment—The Role of
## Labor Market Institutions in Victim Protection

So far, we have discussed the role of labor market institutions in the identification of forced labor practices and the punishment of offending employers as well as recruiters. In the remaining sections, we emphasize a victim-centered approach and discuss the contributions of labor market institutions to victim protection and to the prevention of forced labor. Criminal justice approaches have to operate within the paradigm of victims versus offenders. From a labor law perspective, however, victims are first of all workers, and as such, they are active agents in the labor market and not passive victims. Strategies that include labor market institutions should therefore be based on an empowerment of workers who may be vulnerable to forced labor but who are still able to act. The key challenge is to widen workers' choices when accessing the labor market and to support institutions through which they can channel their complaints. The role of employment tribunals and trade unions is crucial.

*Employment tribunals.* Labor courts provide an important venue in which workers may file claims against employers engaging in abusive workplace practices.[13] Many abusive practices, including illegal working hours, withholding or underpayment of wages, and poor work conditions, are reflective of situations where workers have little or no bargaining power vis-à-vis their employer. Undocumented and irregular migrants who are smuggled into a destination country are particularly vulnerable to such practices. Thus, even if an employer does not use forced labor, many migrants are likely to endure poor working conditions and labor rights violations at the hands of their employer. This can be explained by the vulnerability of the worker, whether due to continued irregular status, poverty, or isolation. In any case, it is often difficult for victims of forced labor exploitation to seek redress through criminal prosecutions and civil compensation (see Chapter 7). Labor courts, however, provide workers who endure violations of their rights, and who may or may not also be victims of forced labor, with an opportunity to contest the working conditions imposed by their employers through administrative proceedings.

Unfortunately, in many destination countries of trafficked victims, immigration law has been seen as limiting the labor rights of undocumented migrants guaranteed under international human rights law. In 2002, the US Supreme Court ruled in *Hoffman Plastics v. National Labor Relations Board,* 535 U.S. 137, that although undocumented migrants may have a right to appear before the National Labor Relations Board (the US equivalent of an employment tribunal), immigration law prohibits an award of back pay as a remedy to an appellant who was undocumented because it would contravene federal immigration law. In the *Hoffman* case, an undocumented migrant was fired from his job for attempting to organize a union; in this case, the dismissal directly contravened the National Labor Relations Act, which prohibits retaliation against an employee for union-organizing activities. Nevertheless, the employer was exculpated because the defendant successfully argued that an undocumented migrant is forbidden from recovering compensation owing to his or her illegal status in the United States.

Other rulings have reviewed *Hoffman* and sought to limit its applicability. In 2003, in an advisory opinion filed by the Inter-American Court for Human Rights at the behest of Mexico, the court ruled that "if undocumented workers are contracted to work, they immediately are entitled to the same rights as all workers . . . this is of maximum importance, since one of the major problems that come from lack of immigration status is that workers without work permits are hired in unfavourable conditions, compared to other workers." Thus, the Inter-American Court held that a number of rights must be furnished to undocumented migrant workers, regardless of whether they are legally in the country or not. In the case of migrant workers, there are certain rights that assume a fundamental importance and that nevertheless are frequently violated, including the prohibition against forced labor, the prohibition and abolition of child labor, special attention for women who work, rights that correspond to association and union freedom, collective bargaining, a just salary for work performed, social security, administrative and judicial guarantees, a reasonable workday length, and adequate labor conditions (safety and hygiene), rest, and back pay.[14]

Other barriers prevent undocumented migrants from using tribunals. Even if employment tribunals are not compelled to report undocumented migrants, most undocumented workers are still reluctant to appear before labor tribunals because of the assumption that they will be deported. Many others fail to use labor tribunals because of a lack of knowledge and awareness about the tribunal's purpose or function. In other cases, employment tribunals refuse to hear cases, stating that it is more appropriate for the source country of the victim to file claims. Finally, many undocumented migrants have a difficult time filing cases because they do not have a legally binding contract to establish a formal working relationship between themselves and an employer; most courts view these contracts as unenforceable since they were entered into as a breach of national provisions permitting employment.

Spanish courts have recognized a similar right for undocumented workers to seek compensation from industrial tribunals. In a case before the Supreme Court of Catalonia in 2002, the courts found that workers, regardless of their immigration status, have certain inalienable labor rights and have the right to appear before a court to claim these rights. Since then, industrial tribunals have adjudicated cases on behalf of migrant workers without inquiring into their immigration status in Spain.

Does providing migrant workers with the right to appear before an industrial tribunal reduce forced labor practices? Although there is no systematic empirical evidence, we believe that holding employers responsible for labor violations improves the ability of all workers to work under fair conditions and discourages employers from violating the rights of undocumented workers. Although such rights violations may not constitute forced labor at the outset, it may become coercive over time if the employee eventually resigns himself or herself to continue working in that place of employment owing to some vulnerability (e.g., poverty, isolation) that makes the victim believe that he or she has no real and acceptable alternative. A second reason to encourage interaction between migrants and tribunals is that it may reduce the economic incentive for employers to hire undocumented migrants for the sole purpose of reducing wage costs. If employers are compelled to pay monetary penalties and face legal sanction, they will be deterred from engaging in exploitive and forced labor practices. Finally, improving interactions between migrants and the government is likely to increase the level of trust between law enforcement and migrants and may encourage more migrants to report forced labor practices that are otherwise impossible to detect.

*Trade unions.*   Many complaints that are brought to court are supported by trade unions. As this is not the place to discuss the strengths and weaknesses of trade unions as such, or their policies and campaigns, we will simply highlight some practical examples of trade union action to support forced labor and trafficking victims. Like any other labor market institution, trade unions face important challenges: limited resources, global competition, and weakening bargaining power. In addition, trade unions are membership-based organizations and therefore less inclined to serve vulnerable workers such as migrant or rural workers, who tend to be unorganized. Many trade union campaigns have targeted these challenging areas, such as domestic work and subcontracting, however. Like NGOs who are at the forefront of protecting victims of human trafficking or bonded labor, trade unions require capacity and funding to carry out activities that are not strictly related to their core mandate.

Nonetheless, as a strategy to reach out to unorganized workers and to prevent undercutting of labor standards, trade unions have detected forced labor cases in the past and initiated remedial action. They are also involved in the prevention of forced labor and trafficking through their work with undocumented migrants or their campaign to organize workers in vulnerable sectors. The Spanish Comisiones Obreras trade union, for example, has been able to obtain indemnities for family members of irregular migrant workers who have been killed while working in Spain. The union has also defended and won a number of cases in industrial tribunals involving irregular migrant workers who have filed complaints against their employers (Platform for International Co-operation on Undocumented Migrants 2005). The Nepalese Transport Workers Union Yatayat Mazadoor Sangh provides advice and support to people traveling to India across the open border in search of work. It has trained its members to look out for signs of trafficking, especially involving young women, who are trafficked for sex work. It has established kiosks at bus stations along the border with India where advice is given to travelers.

In the Russian Federation, trade unions have changed their strategy in order to provide support for irregular migrant workers from Central Asia and other countries. Despite widespread discrimination against workers from Central Asia, trade unions have adopted a policy in favor of regulated migration. A bilateral cooperation agreement was signed between construction industry unions in Tajikistan and Russia through which 2,872 migrants became members of the Russian trade union. In addition, after the intervention by unions, more than 5 million rubles of back wages have been recovered since 2005.[15]

## Conclusions

With growing global awareness that forced labor, slavery-like practices, and human trafficking continue to exist in the twenty-first century, alliances are forged that aim at addressing the crime from a holistic perspective. This chapter argues that labor market institutions should be an integral part of these global, regional, and national alliances. In order to take effective action, however, these institutions need a mandate based on national laws and policies as well as training and resources. In many countries, this is often lacking despite significant investments to combat forced labor and trafficking. Empirical research has shown that forced labor often occurs against the backdrop of weak labor market regulation and governance. Fragmented approaches that privilege the fight against forced labor and trafficking at the expense of labor market governance will not work in the long run.

This chapter also shows gaps that should be addressed by further research, such as analyzing the impact of anti–forced labor programs. In addition, a deeper understanding of labor market institutions and their potential as well as actual role in the prevention and prosecution of forced labor is necessary. This research should focus on civil society action, including NGOs and trade unions, and on the role of business, labor inspectors, and labor administration more generally. Finally, as forced labor is a truly global concern, we need a better understanding of how global advocacy networks work and their impact and potential for future action. It is only through coordinated action involving a broad range of players that a future without forced labor will be possible.

## Notes

We would like to thank Ana Andreati for her work in setting up the database as well as for her contributions in analyzing the data. We also thank Rohit Malpani and Leonardo Sakamoto for providing input to this chapter.

1. Action plans were selected according to regional distribution and focus (forced labor/trafficking). Six were from African countries (mainly western African countries), 6 from Asia (Mekong countries), 5 from Latin America (Andean countries and Brazil), and 11 from Europe (mainly Eastern Europe). The focus also varied: only 5 NAPs were on forced and bonded labor; the rest focused on trafficking for labor and sexual exploitation, and of these, 6 were explicitly on sex trafficking.

2. The analytical criteria are based on the guidelines in ICMPD (2006).

3. This information is based on a joint ILO–International Centre for Migrant Policy Development (ICMPD) project, "Elimination of Human Trafficking in Ukraine and Moldova Through Labour Market Based Measures," 2006-09, EU/AENEAS.

4. This information is based on an ILO labor inspection expert meeting, December 2007. For a detailed discussion of challenges and strategies of labor inspectors in combating forced labor and trafficking in Europe, see von Richthofen (2007).

5. This section is based on Sakamoto (2005).

6. In 2002, Judge Jorge Vieira, the judge of the Second Court of Maraba, passed the first sentence for slave labor in the history of the Labour Courts and was immediately threatened with death.

7. For more information, see "Ministry of Labour Report on Status of Migrant Workers in Qualified Industrial Zones," Amman, May 2006.

8. For a detailed discussion of this topic, see Sathya (2005).

9. For more information on the 1997 Private Employment Convention No. 181, see ILO (2007b).

10. The document is available at www.gla.gov.uk.

11. For more information, see www.gla.gov.uk.

12. For more information, see www.poea.org as well as Averia (2006).

13. This section on employment tribunals is taken from Malpani (2006). It is included in this chapter with permission of the author. The focus is on likely victims of human trafficking.

14. See Inter-American Court for Human Rights, Legal Condition and Rights of Undocumented Migrant Workers, Consultative Opinion OC-18/03 (September 17, 2003). Available at www.hrw.org.

15. This information comes from the ILO Moscow office.

# 7

## Criminalizing Human Trafficking and Protecting the Victims

### Rohit Malpani

Since 2000, there have been rapid changes across Europe in the legal approaches utilized to combat trafficking in persons. This was mostly spurred by enactment of a new United Nations convention in 2000 to combat organized crime, with an accompanying protocol to combat illicit trafficking, known as the Protocol to Prevent, Suppress, and Punish Trafficking in Persons, Especially Women and Children (hereafter known as the Palermo Protocol). The Palermo Protocol conveyed a growing consensus that trafficking in persons included trafficking for purposes other than sexual exploitation, such as forced labor, slavery, servitude, and organ removal.

The ILO 2005 global report, *A Global Alliance Against Forced Labour* (2005a), also drew specific attention to the concerns of trafficking for the purpose of forced labor in Europe and other countries. Moreover, it highlighted two major problems that impede more effective action against forced labor. First, with few exceptions, forced labor is not defined in any detail in national legislation, making it difficult for law enforcement agents to identify and prosecute the offense. Second, and in consequence of this, there have been very few prosecutions for forced labor offenses in the world.[1]

This chapter precisely addresses these issues. The chapter examines new developments in laws designed to combat trafficking for forced labor across Europe, including new policies and laws of the European Union and Council of Europe and, where appropriate, in the United States, which faces similar challenges. Thus, the chapter provides an in-depth analysis of penal code revisions and whether they have been effective tools to prosecute trafficking and forced labor exploitation. Second, the chapter explores whether countries have fulfilled human rights standards related to protection of trafficking victims, including a state's obligation to protect victims of trafficking and to provide victims with the right to seek redress.

## Legislation to Combat Trafficking for Forced Labor

One of the compelling reasons to examine how European countries have adopted the Palermo Protocol is the diversity of legislative approaches across Europe to combat trafficking in persons. The chief reasons for divergent approaches are (1) membership (or lack thereof) in the European Union; (2) a country's self-perception as either a source, transit, or destination country; and (3) whether the country relies upon common or civil law. The European Union's passage, on July 19, 2002, of Council Framework Decision 2002/629/ JHA obligated all member states to take necessary measures to punish all forms of trafficking in persons in line with the standards advocated by the Palermo Protocol.

One push factor encouraging a common approach to trafficking in persons across Europe, besides further enlargement of the European Union, has been the Council of Europe, whose membership includes nearly all countries in Europe. The Council of Europe recently drafted a regional convention entitled Convention on Action Against Trafficking in Human Beings, which entered into force in February 2008.[2] The definition of trafficking in human beings is identical to the protocol's definition of trafficking in persons,[3] and ratifying parties to the Council of Europe Convention, under Article 19, must accordingly criminalize trafficking in human beings. A second factor encouraging a common approach is the increasing realization among traditional source countries, which are mostly outside the EU, that they have become both source and destination countries and must adopt legislation to reflect this new reality.

Thus, many countries in Europe have made changes to their criminal codes to satisfy their obligations under the Palermo Protocol, but their approaches have varied. In some countries, different penal code provisions have been introduced or used to charge offenders with trafficking for forced labor offenses. In particular, some countries have identified seizure of identity documents as the preferred modus operandi of many traffickers and have criminalized seizure of identity documents (without reasonable excuse). On the contrary, a few countries have not criminalized all forms of trafficking for forced labor but are in the process of drafting laws that will enable prosecutions in the future; others do not consider themselves to be destination countries of trafficking for forced labor and their laws reflect this self-perception.

### *"Abuse of Vulnerability" as a Mode of Coercion*

"Abuse of vulnerability" was introduced as a means of coercion in the Palermo Protocol in recognition of the propensity of traffickers to coerce individuals into performing labor or services, including sexual services, without relying upon direct physical abuse, threats, or fraud. Instead, traffickers take advantage of a specific vulnerability or vulnerabilities that many victims, including those who voluntarily move from source to destination country, experience.

Although the Palermo Protocol includes "abuse of vulnerability" as a means of coercion, the protocol itself does not define or explain "abuse of vulnerability" adequately. The *Travaux Préparatoires* states: "Abuse of vulnerability is understood to refer to any situation in which the person involved has *no real and acceptable alternative* but to submit to the abuse involved."[4] This standard has been adopted by the European Union, which mandated in 2002 that all EU countries adopt legislation criminalizing trafficking in persons. In particular, the Council Framework Decision of July 19, 2002, states that abuse of vulnerability is a situation in which a "person has no real and acceptable alternative but to submit to the abuse involved."[5] Neither the protocol nor the EU Council Framework Decision provides any further guidance as to the meaning of abuse of vulnerability. This chapter considers various approaches countries have adopted to tackle this ambiguity in the protocol.

An abuse of vulnerability, like other methods of coercion mentioned in the protocol, involves a conscious act by a trafficker to coerce an individual to perform labor or services, which in this case are acts that are designed to exert psychological control over the individual. Yet unlike other modes of coercion, an abuse of vulnerability also relies upon whether the victim was vulnerable or susceptible to the trafficker's abuses. Thus, there are two interrelated elements: (1) the vulnerability of the victim, and (2) the act of the trafficker that successfully coerces an individual by abusing that vulnerability.

The vulnerability of a victim can result from some innate characteristic of the victim (physical or mental deficiency, ill health, or youth) or may develop owing to the situation the victim finds himself or herself in within a destination country (poverty, precarious administrative status). Also, the actions of a trafficker could either create or worsen a victim's vulnerability (extremely low wages causing poverty, restricted movement causing isolation, seizure of identity documents causing fear of deportation). None of these forms of vulnerability is specifically mentioned in the protocol's definition of trafficking in persons, however; therefore, one cannot assume that any vulnerability (if not mentioned in the penal code) will be recognized by criminal courts as a form of vulnerability.

This chapter argues that, as most penal codes in Europe are currently written today, applying abuse of vulnerability as a mode of coercion to punish traffickers is highly difficult because common forms of vulnerability, and common forms of abuse exerted by traffickers to abuse victims, are neither specified nor included in these penal codes. Instead, penal laws are as ambiguous as the Trafficking Protocol and do not provide any useful legislative guidance, which means that judges are forced to make these determinations "blindly." Generally, this chapter argues that there are two major shortcomings in how penal laws in Europe define abuse of vulnerability:

1. Penal codes do not provide specific examples of vulnerabilities that traffickers will take advantage of to compel a victim's involuntary consent, or

penal codes only provide a few specific examples of vulnerability that do not account for all forms of vulnerability that result in forced labor exploitation.

2. Most penal codes do not codify specific acts of traffickers—such as seizure of identity papers or forcing a victim into debt bondage—as prima facie criminal acts of trafficking for forced labor exploitation. A review of a few cases shows that judges are inclined to excuse criminal acts that should be punished if the offender also provided a few benefits or freedoms to the victim.

Instead of clarifying abuse of vulnerability through specific legislation, a number of countries have merely adopted the Trafficking Protocol's definition without providing additional guidance. Countries generally do not even acknowledge the protocol's explanatory notes, which define an abuse of vulnerability as having "no real and acceptable alternative," in their legislation. For example, the Netherlands defines abuse of vulnerability as abuse of a situation of dominance arising from given circumstances, or through abuse of a vulnerable situation. The Netherlands' legislation does not provide any additional guidance to police, prosecutors, or judges to recognize, prosecute, or convict traffickers who employ abuse of vulnerability as a mode of coercion.

The main difficulty with solely adopting the term *abuse of vulnerability* (without further clarification) is that it preserves the term's ambiguity, providing no guidance for judges to apply the two elements of the term as discussed above. Abuse of vulnerability is a concept that is difficult to apply in practice. In many cases the relationship of the employer and victim is not outwardly coercive, and the abuse is neither overwhelming nor constant. Often, the victim is granted certain "freedoms" or "benefits" that may color the judge's perception of the victim and the employer. Thus, the penal code should clearly and specifically define when an abuse of vulnerability constitutes a criminal act by defining the term's two elements: what the vulnerabilities are that cause an individual to be susceptible to coercion, and what types of acts of an offender are sufficiently abusive to cause that individual to thereby consent to the coercion. This is necessary because without guidance, some judges will not view a vulnerability of a victim and an act of a trafficker to abuse that vulnerability in a light that recognizes the victim's mental state and the effect of the act upon the victim's ability to make independent decisions.

In *Affaire Siliadin v. France,* a French court initially ruled that a victim of forced labor exploitation was not sufficiently vulnerable to involuntarily consent to coercion. In France, the law defines *abuse of vulnerability* in cases of forced labor exploitation as subjecting or obtaining the performance of services from a person "whose vulnerability or dependence is obvious or known to the offender" (Europol 2005, p. 45). As with legislation that only incorporates the term *abuse of vulnerability* into the penal code without further explanation, the French law neither defines nor specifies either vulnerability or dependence. The case was overturned by the European Court for Human Rights

(ECHR) for failing to recognize that the victim was entitled to protection and redress for forced labor abuses under Article 4 of the European Convention of Human Rights.[6] The court noted that the French law failed to recognize the victim's grievances because the law was too ambiguous to consistently address forced labor abuses. As the court stated, the law was "susceptible to widely varying interpretations from one tribunal to another, as was seen in this case," and the penal code provisions "would not assure a minor a concrete and effective protection against the acts (of exploitation) of which she was a victim."[7]

In the case, a 15-year-old Togolese girl had been invited to study and live with a French family. She was made to repay the family who sponsored her journey through domestic work. She was not properly credited for her work, however, and her passport was confiscated. Thereafter, she was sent to work for a second family, first during a period of time when her employer was pregnant, and then was made to stay thereafter against her will. She was made to work 12 hours every day of the week and was only allowed to leave on Sundays for a short period of time, increasing her sense of isolation. She was not paid at all for her work except that she received 500 French francs once or twice. Her immigration status was never regularized, and she continued not to have access to her travel documents, which according to her testimony left her constantly in fear of deportation. For a while she managed to escape these circumstances without her identity documents and worked for a friend for a fair salary. Pressure from her original hosts to return to the second family led her to return to work there, however, again without any change in her immigration status and without receiving any further salary. She finally managed to regain her passport and was able to seek the help of a nongovernmental organization.[8]

Here, there were several clear indicators of the victim's vulnerability that could all be considered prima facie evidence of her vulnerability, including her illegal status, isolation, dependence on money provided by the host families, fear of denunciation to the authorities, and fear of deportation. Despite clear evidence of her vulnerability, the French court found that she was in a state of neither vulnerability nor dependency. Instead, it declared that because she was able to leave her employment to work for a different family, was capable of calling her family in Togo from time to time, could speak French well, and had never complained about the terms of her employment, she was not sufficiently vulnerable to involuntary consent to forced labor exploitation.[9]

In overturning the decision, the ECHR noted that the victim was entirely at the mercy of her employer since she did not have possession of her identity papers, was mostly isolated, had been falsely promised resolution of her precarious administrative status, and did not move around freely because she feared detection and deportation.[10] The ECHR determined that criminal charges should have been upheld against the employers, that significantly more compensation should have been paid, and that the French penal law criminalizing forced labor was too ambiguous and was too open to multiple interpretations.[11]

In the case described above, there was no shortage of evidence establishing (1) the vulnerability of the victim and (2) actions taken by her employers to take advantage of that vulnerability.

The case also demonstrates that in nearly all employment relationships involving an abuse of vulnerability as the mode of coercion, there are instances where the employer will have provided some benefit to the victim, and instances where the victim had an opportunity to exercise at least some degree of freedom. By finding the offenders innocent, an important question is raised, namely: if these exceptional moments of freedom or goodwill on the part of the offender are usually sufficient to negate an abuse of vulnerability, when would a court actually find a trafficker or employer guilty of abusing the vulnerability of an individual? In all likelihood, the coercion and abuse would be so severe, and the vulnerability of the victim would be so obvious, that one of the other modes of coercion (threat, abuse, fraud, violence) provided in the definition of *trafficking in persons* under the Palermo Protocol would also be applicable. Thus, the term *abuse of vulnerability* would become meaningless.

Under this scenario, only by defining when an abuse of vulnerability constitutes a punishable act can a legislature ensure that judges will not strip the term of any real applicability as a mode of coercion. This would involve first, as mentioned above, providing specific examples of vulnerabilities that would leave an individual susceptible to coercion, and second, including examples of acts that are prima facie evidence of an abuse of vulnerability.

It is instructive to see how other countries have attempted to define *abuse of vulnerability* in lieu of only adopting the protocol definition verbatim and to see whether other countries have enacted laws that overcome any of the problems discussed above.

In Germany, *abuse of vulnerability,* under a new law enacted in 2005 that specifically criminalizes trafficking for forced labor exploitation, is defined as "taking advantage of a predicament or helplessness associated with the person's stay in a foreign country."[12] Thus, this law defines *vulnerability* as a *predicament* or *helplessness.* This law is just as ambiguous as the Palermo Protocol definition of trafficking in persons, however, since it neither specifies nor defines the forms of vulnerability that would constitute a predicament or helplessness. In addition, the law does not explain how to interpret "taking advantage" as a standard for measuring whether an employer's actions qualified as criminally abusive acts, although "taking advantage" indicates that a trafficker or employer could be criminally liable for actions that would not be viewed as coercion under a penal code that utilizes the term *abuse of vulnerability.* Finally, the law does not state whether personal freedoms granted to victims or "good intentions" of traffickers are to be weighed as mitigating considerations against guilt. In fact, some state criminal investigators and prosecutors in Germany have raised concern that they are uncertain how to utilize this new provision in forced labor cases.[13] Prosecutions are only carried out for clear-cut cases of forced labor exploitation or cases where traffickers employ physical force, heavily restrict the victim's movements, or threaten the victim with serious harm.[14]

In Italy, *abuse of vulnerability* is defined as "when anyone takes advantage of a situation of physical or mental inferiority or poverty."[15] This law defines vulnerability as physical or mental inferiority or poverty. Although this language provides specific examples of when a judge may find an abuse of vulnerability under the law, it limits the law's overall scope, since it only defines abuse of vulnerability in three respects. It might have been preferable for the legislation to state that the listed forms of vulnerability were nonexclusive and that other forms of vulnerability, although not enumerated in the law, could also be actionable in Italian courts. Furthermore, poverty is highly difficult to apply in practice. For example, how poor must an irregular migrant be to qualify as vulnerable? Does it make a difference if the irregular migrant has dependents, and must an employer know that an irregular migrant has dependents? In what ways may a trafficker take advantage of the poverty of a victim? If the trafficker recognizes that the migrant is poor and offers a substandard wage, without coercing the migrant to remain in the job (except that the migrant will lose his or her salary and will fall into even more dire poverty), is the employer abusing the vulnerability of the migrant?

A case from Belgium demonstrates the difficulty courts face in determining whether paying an impoverished individual a substandard wage constitutes an abuse of vulnerability. The former Belgian law punishing trafficking, or Article 77 of the Immigration Code, mentions that a precarious situation is a vulnerability. In the case, a family exploited for forced labor stated that they were in the country illegally, had absolutely no resources, and were constrained to accept awful working and living conditions imposed upon them. Victim testimony established that "the abuse consists of being paid a miserable remuneration, of about 1 euro per hour for 50 hours of work per week for numerous months, without benefits or social protection."[16]

The victims did not argue that the traffickers took advantage of their precarious administrative status; thus, their only vulnerability was their dire poverty, and the punishable abuse was the employer's unwillingness to pay them a fair wage for their labor. Does this constitute an abuse of vulnerability? Here, the employer clearly knew that the family was poor and needed a wage to survive as irregular migrants. And if the family did not accept the wages and working conditions imposed by the employer, they would not be able to survive. Thus, it can be argued that the family had no real or acceptable alternative to the terms of employment. This would be consistent with the intent of the protocol, which stated that abuse of vulnerability occurs when the victim has no real and acceptable alternative. On the other hand, the employer did not force the victims to continue working for him. In the case, the Belgian court ruled that no abuse was established and that the victims were not found to be in a particularly vulnerable situation.

The United States defines an *abuse of vulnerability* uniquely under the Victims of Trafficking and Violence Prevention Act (TVPA) of 2000 (amended). This was enacted prior to drafting of the Trafficking Protocol, which the United States ratified in December 2005. Under the act, a trafficker abuses the vulnerability of a victim "by means of any scheme, plan, or pattern intended to cause the person to believe that, if the person did not perform such labor or services, that person or another person would suffer serious harm or physical restraint" or "by means of the abuse or threatened abuse of law or the legal process."[17]

Here, the law differs from previously discussed examples by providing a measurable standard to determine whether psychological coercion results in a victim's involuntarily consenting to a trafficker's demands. Under the law, an individual is guilty of forced labor exploitation if he or she causes a victim to believe that his or her failure to comply with a trafficker's orders would result in serious harm to the victim or to other individuals. The law limits the scope of use of "abuse of vulnerability" as a mode of coercion, however, because the individual must believe that he or she would suffer serious harm or physical restraint. A further reason why the TVPA is a good law is that it acknowledges that abuse of vulnerability can occur by means of the abuse or threatened abuse of law, which presumably would include denunciation to immigration authorities. Finally, the act criminalizes unlawful possession of identity documents (of a victim) as prima facie evidence of trafficking for forced labor purposes, which is one type of abusive act consistently employed by traffickers.

As we have seen, countries have attempted to define abuse of vulnerability in greater detail than the drafters of the protocol. Specific definitions of abuse of vulnerability should not wholly exclude other forms of vulnerability that a legislature does not anticipate, however, and should only list specific types of vulnerability as examples of vulnerability. In addition, penal codes in Europe, for the most part, do not criminalize acts of traffickers that are prima facie evidence of an abuse of vulnerability, such as seizure of identity documents.

Hence, most countries do not criminalize any acts or abuses that employ psychological coercion to induce involuntary consent. The Palermo Protocol itself does not mention any acts as forms of psychological coercion that abuse the vulnerability of a victim, but it does provide under Article 5(1) that states should adopt legislative and other measures to establish criminal offenses for trafficking in persons. Thus, we need to ask what legislative measures—besides adoption of the definition of trafficking in persons into the penal code—could effectively establish criminal offenses for trafficking in persons. The ILO has provided guidance as to types of acts that cause a victim to involuntarily consent to forced labor exploitation. As previously mentioned, the ILO, under Convention No. 29, defines *coercion* as a situation where labor or services are "exacted from any person under the menace of any penalty."

Under Convention No. 29, work or services exacted from any person under the menace of any penalty means that, besides the threat or imposition of penal sanction, a penalty may "take the form of a loss of rights or privileges" (International Labour Organization 2005b, pp. 19–20). The following six acts, according to the ILO Committee of Experts, may indicate a forced labor situation: (1) physical or sexual violence, or threat of violence; (2) restriction of movement of the worker; (3) debt bondage or bonded labor; (4) withholding wages or refusing to pay the worker at all; (5) retention of passports and identity documents; and (6) threat of denunciation to the authorities. The latter four acts (namely, debt bondage, withholding of wages, retention of identity documents, and threat of denunciation to the authorities) are all acts that are designed to abuse the vulnerability of a victim. Each of these acts creates a fear or vulnerability or exacerbates a preexisting fear that can cause a victim to involuntarily consent to the demands of an offender.

## Criminalization of Wrongful Possession of Identity Documents

It is not uncommon for traffickers to seize the identity documents of migrant workers, particularly those who are irregular, to coerce the individual. This act leaves the victim fearful of detection, arrest, and deportation and powerless to leave an employer to either change jobs or to leave a country. A review of legislation shows that most countries have not enacted laws that penalize seizure of identity documents. One of the first countries to penalize this act was the United States under the Victims of Trafficking and Violence Protection Act of 2000, which penalizes seizure of identity documents with a five-year prison sentence. The provision states:

> Whoever knowingly destroys, conceals, removes, confiscates or possesses any actual or purported passport or other immigration document, or any other actual or purported government identification document, of another person, to prevent or restrict or to attempt to prevent or restrict, without lawful authority, the person's liberty to move or travel, in order to maintain the labor or services of that person, when the person is or has been a victim of a severe form of trafficking in persons, shall be fined under this title or imprisoned for not more than five years, or both.

Thus, the act of seizing, confiscating, concealing, or removing a victim's identity documents establishes the mode of coercion necessary to secure a conviction for trafficking in persons. In Europe, there has been little compunction to adopt this approach. Until recently, only a few countries had adopted or were considering laws that criminalize acts relating to travel or identity documents. In Macedonia, Article 418-a of the Criminal Code (Trafficking in Human Beings) states: "A person who withholds or destroys another person's identity card, passport or other identification document for the purpose of committing the crimes referred to in paragraph 1 and 2 (trafficking in persons), shall be punished with imprisonment of 6 months to five years."

The only shortcoming with the Macedonian provision, in comparison to the US provision, is that it does not include "purported" or false identity documents. Traffickers often provide fake documents to victims, who view these documents as their one form of security against deportation or arrest. This identity document is then seized and control of the document augments the trafficker's authority. By not including fake or manufactured documents, the legislation excludes a common ploy used by traffickers to exert control over victims.

Although national laws may not reflect the increasing use and abuse of identity documents to exploit migrant workers, the Council of Europe, in the recently created Council of Europe Convention on Action Against Trafficking in Human Beings, has stated in Article 20: "Each Party shall adopt such legislative and other measures as may be necessary to establish as criminal offences the following conducts, when committed intentionally and for the purpose of enabling the trafficking in human beings: forging a travel or identity document, procuring or providing such a document, or retaining, removing, concealing, damaging or destroying a travel or identity document of another person."[18] Thus, the new Council of Europe Convention, which entered into force February 1, 2008, compels all states to criminalize the use of identity documents as an end to further human trafficking.

### Withholding of Wages, Threat of Denunciation to the Authorities, and Debt Bondage

Other acts that the ILO has identified as strong indicators of a forced labor situation, such as withholding of wages, debt bondage, and threat of denunciation to the authorities, are not explicitly criminalized in penal codes across Europe. Although withholding of wages is probably implied as an abuse of vulnerability in the definition of trafficking of persons and has been recognized in courts as an abuse of vulnerability, it is not specifically criminalized (as is the seizure of identity documents). Threat of denunciation—which is used against irregular migrant workers—comes within the legal definition of blackmail in some jurisdictions. The standard definition of blackmail, as the ILO explains, occurs when "a person . . . with a view to gain for him or herself, or another or with the intent to cause loss to another . . . makes any unwarranted demand with menaces" (International Labour Organization 2005b, p. 21). For instance, Austria punishes abduction with use of blackmail under its penal code (Europol 2005, p. 3). Besides statutes punishing blackmail, other countries have included threat of denunciation to the authorities as a type of vulnerability under the definition of trafficking in persons. It is only recognized as an abuse of an individual's illegal administrative status (as in Luxembourg), however, or abuse of an individual's precarious situation.

## The Definition of Forced Labor

Another ambiguity with the definition of trafficking in persons in the Palermo Protocol is that the term *forced labor* is undefined. As previously mentioned, ILO Convention No. 29 defines *forced labor* as "all work or service, which is exacted under menace of any penalty and for which the said person has not offered himself voluntarily." Under Article 25 of the same convention, countries are obligated to criminalize forced labor exploitation through appropriate penal sanctions. This definition of forced labor is specifically limited to Convention No. 29, however, since Article 2(1) specifically states that the definition of forced labor is for the purposes of Convention No. 29. Nevertheless, parties to the convention are obligated to criminalize forced labor and to ensure that any criminal law penalizing forced labor is consistent with Article 2(1). At the time of writing, all countries in Europe had ratified Convention No. 29.

Although the ILO definition of trafficking for forced labor has been widely adopted, some countries have chosen to alter the definition of forced labor for the purposes of their penal code. In Germany, trafficking in persons for the purpose of forced labor is defined as "Whoever, by taking advantage of a predicament or helplessness associated with the person's stay in a foreign country, places another person in slavery or bondage, or brings him to take up or continue employment with him or a third person under working conditions that show a crass disparity to the working conditions of other employees performing the same or comparable tasks."[19]

Here, the German penal code provision changes the definition of forced labor by penalizing labor and services where the individual must work under conditions that show a crass disparity to the working conditions of others performing comparable tasks.

The trend of redefining forced labor is not limited to Germany. In France, there are three laws that criminalize forced labor exploitation, one specifically criminalizing the recruitment, trafficking, and lodging of the victim and two separate laws criminalizing the exploitation of the individual for forced labor in France. In all three laws, forced labor is defined differently than in ILO Convention No. 29. Under Article 225-4, which penalizes trafficking in persons, *forced labor* is defined as "conditions of work or living contrary to his or her dignity" (Europol 2005, p. 45). Under Article 225-13, *forced labor* is defined as "unpaid services or services against which a payment is made which clearly bears no relation to the importance of the work performed," and under Article 225-14, *forced labor* is "working or living conditions incompatible with human dignity" (p. 45).

Finally, the Belgian parliament passed a new trafficking-for-forced-labor law that defines *forced labor* as work "in conditions contrary to human dignity."[20] One difference between this and the other laws is that the Belgian parliament has defined "conditions contrary to human dignity" through the legislative record. During deliberations for the new law, the Minister of Justice provided testimony to specify those conditions the ministry considered contrary to human dignity, which included low wages or nonpayment of wages, long working hours, and unsafe working conditions.[21] Under this law, judges are compelled to include all forms of labor or services where prosecutors can demonstrate any or all of the working conditions listed above.

Although, as discussed above, Convention No. 29 defines *forced labor* as all labor and services that are provided involuntarily under menace of penalty, some countries have chosen to criminalize only those forms of labor or services that are contrary to human dignity. In a sense, this states an obvious relationship, or that most labor extracted through coercion is substandard or that it forces individuals to work under conditions contrary to human dignity. This standard could provide clearer guidance to law enforcement personnel to identify victims of forced labor, or it could provide greater guidance to judges within civil legal systems to issue consistent rulings as to whether forced labor exploitation has occurred.

### No Criminalization of Movement

As discussed, neither the French nor Belgian penal code punishes all forms of forced labor exploitation. Furthermore, both the French and Belgian laws exclude prosecution of traffickers who only engage in moving victims between intermediaries, where the receiving intermediary does not exploit a victim for labor or services. Thus, traffickers who only act as transfer agents appear to be excused from prosecution under both the French and Belgian penal codes (Comité Contre L'Esclavage Moderne 2005, p. 5). Article 225-4-1 of the French penal code states: "Trafficking in persons is the act . . . to recruit, transport, transfer, host or accommodate a person, to put him or her at the service of a third party, even unknown, in order either to facilitate against this person infractions of procurement, sexual aggression or harm, begging exploitation, working or living conditions contrary to human dignity" (Comité Contre L'Esclavage Moderne 2005).

Thus, unless the offender has directly transferred a victim to a trafficker who will exploit the victim for labor or services contrary to human dignity, the offender cannot be found guilty of trafficking in persons.

### Penal Laws in Countries Transitioning from Source to Destination Country

Until recently, countries on the eastern side of Europe were mostly characterized as source and transit countries. A 2005 US State Department classification of countries in Europe as a source, transit, or destination country (see Table 7.1) indicates that many recent entrants to the European Union, including Lithuania, Poland, Hungary, the Czech Republic, Bulgaria, and other countries in Eastern Europe (Bosnia-Herzegovina, Bulgaria, Kosovo, and Serbia), have also become destination countries (as well as continuing to be source countries).[22] Other countries, such as Estonia, Latvia, the Slovak Republic, and Slovenia, as new entrants to the European Union, and aspirants to the European Union (Ukraine and Turkey), although supplying cheap labor to other EU countries, will also attract numerous regular and irregular migrants from poorer countries.

Accordingly, all these countries will need laws that criminalize the recruitment of labor (for the purpose of forced labor exploitation in other countries) and penal laws that punish exploitation for forced labor purposes within their own territories. All countries that are members of the European Union must comply with the EU Council Framework Decision of July 19, 2002, and criminalize all forms of trafficking in persons.[23] Other countries in Eastern Europe have developed penal laws that punish forced labor exploitation in their own countries, and some countries have successfully prosecuted cases of forced labor exploitation. Moldova has enacted a new penal law that effectively criminalizes a set of illegal acts that result in compelling the involuntary consent of an individual for forced labor purposes. Nevertheless, considerable work must

**Table 7.1  Classification of Countries**

| Source Countries Group 1 | Source and Transit Countries Group 2 | Source, Transit, and Destination Countries Group 3 | Transit and Destination Countries Group 4 | Destination Countries Group 5 |
|---|---|---|---|---|
| Albania | Estonia | Bosnia-Herzegovina | Austria | Cyprus |
| Belarus | Georgia | Bulgaria | Belgium | France |
| | Latvia | Croatia | Denmark | Greece |
| | Moldova | Czech Republic | Finland | Israel |
| | Romania | Hungary | Germany | Luxembourg |
| | Slovak Republic | Lithuania | Italy | Norway |
| | Slovenia | Macedonia | The Netherlands | |
| | Ukraine | Poland | Portugal | |
| | | Russia | Spain | |
| | | Serbia and Montenegro | Sweden | |
| | | Kosovo | Switzerland | |
| | | | Turkey | |
| | | | United Kingdom | |

*Source:* United States (2005).

still be done, as all countries within Europe should enact laws and develop trafficking plans to combat forced labor exploitation.

## Adherence to Human Rights Standards

Trafficking in human beings is both a cause and a consequence of human rights violations (European Commission 2004, p. 137). A successful antitrafficking response should empower victims and promote the rights of at-risk individuals and victims. Nevertheless, most national antitrafficking responses have tackled trafficking as a law-and-order problem. The victim is not viewed as a holder of rights but rather as an instrument of the state that can enable an effective prosecution. This denies victims the opportunity to restore their basic dignity, contributes to their stigmatization in source and destination countries, discourages interaction with law enforcement and social protection agencies to promote their rights, and following detection, places them in danger of being retrafficked. These actions deny victims their basic rights guaranteed through international human rights standards and exacerbate a victim's vulnerabilities (European Commission 2004, p. 139).

The remaining sections of this chapter consider how European countries comply with major human rights norms in two respects: (1) victim protection measures, and particularly provision of reflection periods and residence permits, and (2) compensation for victims of trafficking.

### Victim Protection Measures

The Palermo Protocol includes provisions for victim protection and assistance, but treaty negotiations only produced vague, nonbinding guidelines. Since the adoption of the Palermo Protocol, numerous countries have adopted schemes to provide victims with the means to remain in the country following detection. These schemes generally include two measures. First, victims are granted a reflection period, which provides the victims with a specified period of time to consider their options, to overcome the trauma of their exploitation, and to decrease fears of immediate arrest and deportation into situations that are or could be potentially dangerous for the victim and his or her family. Second, following the reflection period, and depending on the country, victims are given an opportunity to apply for a temporary residence permit that normally lasts for six months. Although the protocol does not limit application of these protection measures to victims of sexual exploitation, most countries in Europe until recently had only provided protections to victims of sexual exploitation.

The European Union, in 2004, adopted Council Directive 2004/81/EC, which obligated all EU countries, by August 6, 2006, to provide a reflection period and residence permit to victims of trafficking under limited circumstances.

According to the directive, a reflection period, whose length can be determined under national law, should be provided to all victims of trafficking. Thereafter, EU member countries should grant a residence permit depending upon criteria developed by the country, which could include the opportunity for the victim to assist in investigative and judicial proceedings, whether the victim has shown a clear intent to cooperate, and whether the victim has severed all ties with his or her exploiters. It should be noted that these requirements are not dispositive. Article 4 of the directive holds that member states may adopt or maintain more favorable provisions for trafficked persons; therefore, victims of trafficking can be granted a residence permit solely based upon the danger they would face if they were deported to their home country.[24]

In addition, the Council of Europe, under the Convention on Action Against Trafficking in Human Beings, would require states, if they ratified the convention, to provide a reflection period of thirty days to victims of trafficking and thereafter to issue a renewable residence permit to victims of trafficking if "the competent authority considers that their stay is necessary owing to their personal situation" or "the competent authority considers that their stay is necessary for the purpose of their co-operation with the competent authorities in investigation or criminal proceedings" (Articles 13 and 14). This establishes a regional standard that supports delinking the grant of a residence permit from an agreement to cooperate.

An often-cited example is Italy, where the granting of a residence permit is not always conditioned upon a victim's agreement to testify. Under Italian law, an "Article 18 permit," as it is commonly known, can be given under two circumstances, either for agreeing to cooperate with authorities to pursue criminal charges against traffickers, or to migrants in situations of abuse or severe exploitation where their safety is threatened.[25] In either situation, migrants must be willing to participate in a social assistance and inclusion program provided through social organizations and funded by the Italian government. The chief of police for the particular district in which the victim resides grants a residence permit. A permit is granted in the course of an investigation, during an admission or request in court, or through a social welfare agency's request. In any situation, the permit is granted with the assent of the public prosecutor, either by acting on his proposal or as a result of a favorable opinion on his part.

In practice, the Article 18 permit, according to previous reports, "may be obtained by making a simple statement to the police which reports that the crime has occurred, not only by making a full, sworn statement" (Anti-Slavery International 2002, p. 141). A residence permit may be renewed after six months if the victim is in the midst of pursuing criminal charges against the trafficker, or if he or she is employed or enrolled in an education program at the end of the residence permit period (p. 140). Other revisions to the criminal code in 2003 introduced additional measures to support victims of trafficking in Italy. Under Law No. 228 (2003), entitled "Action Against Trafficking in Human Beings," two new funds have been established to support victims following detection and grant of a residence permit. Under Article 12 of the law, a fund has been established to create more assistance and social integration programs for victims, and under Article 13, a special program with a funding grant of 2.5 million euros was created to provide immediate victim assistance, including immediate support and living grants, protected housing, and health assistance.[26] This was the result, according to On the Road, an NGO based in Italy that provides support to victims, of long negotiations with the Italian government to improve the level of services provided to victims.[27]

The United Kingdom, Ireland, and Denmark are not required to abide by the EU council decision on providing protection to victims of trafficking.[28] The UK in particular expressed fear that it would become a major magnet for irregular migrants seeking to take advantage of a law that protects the human rights of trafficking victims. Although victims of trafficking have successfully applied for asylum under the 1951 Refugee Convention and the European Convention of Human Rights, experience shows that this is only granted in the most exceptional of circumstances. Only very few victims (only women trafficked for sexual exploitation) were afforded protection and assistance under the "Poppy project," provided that they cooperated with the authorities. The UK has signed the Council of Europe convention and considers revision of its protection measures in accordance with the convention.

### Problems with Implementation of Victim Protection Measures

Even when victim protection measures have been adopted, numerous problems have arisen. In particular, the following problems have been noted through prior research and through the observations of social protection agencies that often serve as the first point of contact with victims:

- Police and prosecutors press victims not to use the reflection period they are legally entitled to or are reluctant to grant residence permits to qualified victims. In Italy, police and prosecutors have linked grant of the residence permit to willingness to testify, even if not compelled under the law.
- Overzealous application of immigration laws and use of bilateral agreements exclude victims from mandatory reflection periods and residence permits.
- The severity of exploitation a person must suffer to qualify for a residence permit may disqualify victims of labor exploitation.

Numerous reports from nongovernmental organizations have found that police and prosecutors often pressure trafficking victims to file charges before full use of a reflection period. In Belgium, nongovernmental organizations have reported that the procedure to grant a reflection period is "rarely applied." Instead, upon referral to shelters, victims are asked to make declarations and are immediately granted three-month residence permits in lieu of first providing a reflection period of forty-five days.[29] In Italy, grants of residence permits should be provided under limited circumstances even when the individual does not agree to cooperate with investigations or a prosecution of a trafficker (known as the social cooperation route). This is often not practiced in reality, however, though it depends more on the region of the country and its tendency to adhere to national laws and practices.

In 2002 Anti-Slavery International reported that where the police have developed a relationship of mutual trust with nongovernmental organizations, Article 18 permits, in accordance with the law, are granted solely upon the advice provided by nongovernmental organizations. In other regions, however, the police will not grant a permit without a victim's sworn statement and the start of an investigation by a prosecutor (Anti-Slavery International 2002). This pattern appears to have continued. According to NGO sources, the chief of police, who under Italian law is empowered to grant a residence permit, is usually reluctant to grant a residence permit without cooperation from the victim. Normally police chiefs prefer a full report about the trafficker and submission of a report to the prosecutor's office that assures the police that there is sufficient evidence to start a prosecution.[30] This is partly due to the unwillingness of social protection agencies and nongovernmental organizations to assert their right to make requests for victims to be issued a residence permit. Instead of making an assertion, the social protection organizations wait for the prosecutor's opinion before asking for a permit, thereby negating their right under Article 18 to request residence permits.[31]

Many victims of trafficking are not even given the opportunity to submit evidence for the purpose of filing criminal charges and seeking protection through residence permits. As discussed more thoroughly below, overzealous application of immigration laws often results in deportation of victims of trafficking. Thus, in spite of laws that protect and provide victims with the opportunity to seek redress, victims are denied all basic human rights in many destination countries following detection. This violates state obligations to provide protection and assistance to victims of trafficking and to provide them with an opportunity to seek various forms of redress under national legal processes.

Finally, victims of forced labor exploitation may not qualify for residence permits because the exploitation or abuse they suffered does not meet the minimum threshold designated by the relevant laws that require protection to be granted. In Italy, Article 18 states that residence permits may be issued to "victims of abuse or serious exploitation and whenever the safety of the said foreign citizen has been seen to be endangered."[32] Legal advocates for victims have noted that prosecutors and police rarely grant a residence permit to victims of economic exploitation. Since the legislation does not define how serious the exploitation must be and to what extent a person must be "endangered," authorities are unsure as to when victims actually have suffered sufficient abuse or exploitation or are in sufficient danger to qualify for a residence permit.[33]

Generally, law enforcement officials do not interpret Article 18 to justify granting victims of economic exploitation a residence permit.[34] Furthermore, funds for implementation of programs to protect victims of exploitation have been allocated solely to victims of sexual exploitation.[35] Although victims of sexual exploitation are much more likely to have suffered serious abuse and exploitation, a lack of protection or opportunity for victims of labor exploitation to remain in destination countries and file charges violates their basic human right to redress and makes it exceedingly difficult to secure convictions against traffickers. As with the failure to implement other laws that should serve as an effective deterrent against trafficking in persons, a failure to grant protection and assistance to victims of forced labor exploitation discourages victims of such exploitation from interacting with law enforcement personnel. This also contributes to a climate of impunity among traffickers.

Victims of labor exploitation in the United States may face similar problems, although there is little empirical evidence on the issue. The United States provides protection, assistance, and a residence permit to victims of trafficking, but only in exchange for an agreement to cooperate with the authorities. Furthermore, it only provides these benefits to victims of a "severe form of trafficking."[36] Since the victims must prove that they have suffered severe abuse, it appears that federal officials have often not granted certification and residence permits (known in the United States as a T visa) to victims of trafficking because federal and state officials interpret the TVPA as excluding most trafficking victims from protection (Free the Slaves 2004).

One important measure that could rectify some of the shortcomings discussed above would be to diversify the types of government officials within the destination country who could grant victims reflection periods and residence permits. First, nongovernmental organizations already play a role in identifying victims of trafficking in a number of European countries, including Italy and Belgium. Nongovernmental organizations could be given greater influence and decisionmaking ability to provide reflection periods and residence permits to trafficking victims in the process.

A second measure would empower multiple government agencies to issue residence permits. Lobbying groups in the United States have requested the federal government to allow the Department of Labor, within an interagency scheme, to issue residence permits to victims of trafficking (Free the Slaves 2004). In particular, this may be necessary because in many cases where victims have come forward and offered to cooperate, the federal authorities have still chosen not to go forward with the case, thus making the victim deportable under the law. In these cases, the Department of Labor, which may have an interest in pursuing charges against an employer, would be able to confer a residence permit for a victim to file charges through the Labor Department.

One reason why a labor ministry may be inclined (when a prosecutor is not) to pursue charges is that evidentiary standards and burdens of proof to punish employers for labor exploitation are far easier to satisfy. Many prosecutions for forced labor trafficking have been dropped across Europe for lack of evidence or lack of interest in moving forward with the case. One Belgian NGO, Payoke, stated that in 11 cases of labor exploitation that they followed, more than half of the cases were dropped by the prosecutor for a variety of reasons, including a lack of evidence or an inability to identify the trafficker.[37]

## Conclusions

Overall, this chapter argues that penal laws are often as ambiguous as the Trafficking Protocol about what exactly constitutes the "abuse of vulnerability" as a mode of coercion, and that this makes it difficult to punish traffickers. Other sources of ambiguity also make law enforcement difficult. Thus, in the future it will be important to define *abuse of vulnerability* precisely in the penal code as a mode of coercion and to include specific examples of vulnerability as nonexclusive evidence of the vulnerability of victims while still permitting the courts to recognize and punish unanticipated vulnerabilities that may be taken advantage of. There should also be a move toward criminalizing specific acts often employed by traffickers to coerce individuals, including seizure of identity documents or debt bondage.

At the same time, countries should provide maximum protection to victims of trafficking, as obligated under international human rights law, by providing all victims of trafficking for forced labor exploitation a reflection period of three months upon detection and a residence permit thereafter for any victim who has an identifiable need to remain in the destination country and regardless of whether or not the victim agrees to cooperate with either the investigation or prosecution of the crime of trafficking. Oversight mechanisms should also be imposed to ensure that victims are not pressured into foregoing their reflection period in order to immediately cooperate with authorities. Currently, as we have seen, some countries only provide residence permits to individuals who have suffered "serious forms" of exploitation, which can exclude many victims of forced labor exploitation. It is time to change the perception that forced labor victims are less deserving of protection than victims of sexual exploitation.

## Notes

This chapter is based on Malpani (2006). Anne Pawletta and Gabriella Albertini conducted interviews in their work for the ILO Special Action Programme to Combat Forced Labour (SAP-FL) and provided support for this research.

1. See US Department of State (2008) for figures on prosecutions and convictions.

2. See Council of Europe Convention on Action Against Trafficking in Human Beings and its Explanatory Report, Council of Europe Treaty Series No. 197, available at www.coe.int/trafficking.

3. Council of Europe Convention on Action Against Trafficking in Human Beings, Article 4(a).

4. See *Report of the Ad Hoc Committee on the Elaboration of a Convention Against Transnational Organized Crime* on the work of its first to eleventh sessions: "Interpretive Notes for the Official Records (*Travaux Práparatoires*) of the Negotiation of the UN Convention Against Transnational Organized Crime and the Protocols Thereto," A/55/383/Add.1, 55th Session, Agenda item 105, Article 3(a), Paragraph 63.

5. See Council Framework Decision of July 19, 2002, on combating trafficking in human beings, 2002/629/JHA, Article 1(c).

6. See *Affaire Siliadin v. France,* European Court of Human Rights, Requête No. 73316/01 (2005).

7. Ibid., p. 34, para. 134.

8. Ibid.

9. Ibid, p. 6, paras. 37–40.

10. Ibid, p. 35.

11. Ibid.

12. See German Penal Code, Section 233.

13. Personal communication with Norbert Cyrus, University of Oldenburg, member of the Interdisciplinary Centre for Education and Communication in Migratory Processes (IBKM) (interview by Anne Pawletta).

14. Interview with Holger Bernsee, senior officer, State Office of Criminal Investigations, November 14, 2005 (interview conducted by Anne Pawletta).

15. Law No. 228, Article 600, August 11, 2003.

16. Tribunal correctional de Liège, December 22, 2004 (unpublished opinion).

17. Victims of Trafficking and Violence Protection Act of 2000, Public Law 106-386, Section 112.

18. See Council of Europe Convention on Action Against Trafficking in Human Beings and its Explanatory Report, Council of Europe Treaty Series No. 197, available at www.coe.int/trafficking.

19. See German Penal Code, Section 231.

20. See 433, Belgian Penal Code, Section 433, Law of August 10, 2005: "Loi modifiant diverses dispositions en vue de renforcer la lutte contre la traite et le traffic des êtres humains et contre les pratiques des marchands de sommeil."

21. Interview with Yxes Segaert-Vanden Bussche, Belgian prosecutor, October 23, 2005 (interview by Rohit Malpani).

22. Poland recently reported its first conviction of a trafficker for exploiting labor within Poland. A Vietnamese employer recruited a Vietnamese male to work in Poland. He smuggled the male into Poland for a bond of US$3,000. During the victim's employment in Poland, he was housed in an apartment for which he was also charged while working only for pocket money. Thereafter he was sold to a second employer who made the victim pay off the fee for his sale. Following detection, the traffickers were imprisoned for at least three years. This information is based on communication from the Ministry of Justice of Poland at the National Workshop on Combating Trafficking in Persons for Forced Labor Purposes, November 21–22, 2005, Legionowo, Poland.

23. See Council Framework Decision of July 19, 2002, on combating trafficking in human beings, *Official Journal of the European Communities,* L 203/1.

24. Article 4 states: "This Directive shall not prevent Member States from adopting or maintaining more favorable provisions for the persons [victims] covered by this Directive."

25. See Law on Immigration, Decreto Legislativo July 25, 1998, n. 286, Article 18 (translated excerpts). Available at http://www.legislationline.org/.

26. See Legge 11, August 2003, No. 228, "Misure contro la tratta di persone," published in *Gazetta Ufficiale,* No. 195, August 23, 2003, Article 12 and Article 13.

27. Personal communication with Marco Bufo, November 11, 2005 (interview conducted by Gabriella Albertini).

28. See Council Directive 2004/81/EC of April 29, 2004, Article 21.

29. Personal communication with Patricia Le Cocq, Centre pour l'égalité des chances et la lutte contre le racisme, October 28, 2005.

30. Communication with Marco Bufo, November 11, 2005 (interview conducted by Gabriella Albertini).

31. Communication with Gran Andrea Ronchi, November 9, 2005 (interview conducted by Gabriella Albertini).

32. See Law on Immigation, Decreto Legislativo, July 25, 1998, n. 286, Article 18 (translated excerpts). Available at http://www.legislationline.org/.

33. Personal communication with Marco Bufo, November 11, 2005 (interview conducted by Gabriella Albertini).

34. Personal communication with Gran Andrea Ronchi, November 9, 2005 (interview conducted by Gabriella Albertini).

35. Communication with Judge Maria Grazia Giammarinaro, October 27, 2005 (interview conducted by Gabriella Albertini). The Minister of Equal Opportunity has reserved funds only for use by victims of sexual exploitation. Judges have complained to the minister that prosecutions of traffickers for the purpose of labor exploitation are compromised, but to no avail.

36. Trafficking Victims Protection Act, Section 103.

37. Communication by the author with Payoke, November 4, 2005.

# 8

## Empowering Communities: Lessons from Tamil Nadu, India

*Isabelle Guérin, Caroline O'Reilly, Marc Roesch,*
*Maria Sathya, and G. Venkatasubramanian*

Millions of workers—men, women, and children—are bonded to their employers in South Asia, working for low or no wages because they are struggling to repay an outstanding debt. The ILO estimates that of the minimum of 12.3 million victims of forced labor globally, 9.49 million are in the Asia-Pacific region, with a high (though unknown) proportion trapped in bonded labor (International Labour Organization 2005). These people tend to come from the poorest and least educated segments of the population, from low castes and religious minorities. Debt bondage is particularly widespread in agriculture but is prevalent also in mining, rice mills, brick kilns, carpets, textiles, domestic work, and other sectors of the informal economy.

In this chapter, we highlight the importance of empowering communities through microfinance-led strategies in order to prevent negative spirals and help people stay free from bonded labor. Our study is based on the findings of an independent impact assessment of an ILO technical cooperation project called Prevention and Elimination of Bonded Labour in South Asia (PEBLISA). This assessment, undertaken in 2006 by the French Institute of Pondicherry,[1] covered the project's chapter in Tamil Nadu, India, but provides insights that are likely to be valid and applicable for other locations.[2] The project was active in Tamil Nadu between early 2003 and mid-2006, after which external financial support ended, and the NGOs continued field activities as far as their own resources would allow.

Our focus here on the microfinance-led, community-based interventions should not be taken in any way, however, to downplay the importance of other measures. Moreover, we argue that although community-based actions are fully legitimate to improve the lot of people vulnerable to bondage, they make sense only if integrated into a broader set of actions that address the underlying structural factors. Here, other measures supported by the ILO include, inter alia, strengthening the enforcement machinery for the Bonded Labour System (Abolition) Act of 1976, awareness-raising of employers in bonded labor–prone sectors about their rights and obligations toward workers, supporting trade unions to integrate bonded labor within their membership and program priorities, undertaking research and documentation, offering policy advice to the state administration, and networking with NGOs and other partners to advocate the cause of bonded laborers and to share knowledge and good practice.

Our conviction, borne out by our own experience and that of other researchers and practitioners, is that a comprehensive approach that addresses the multiple dimensions of bondage is indispensable. Governments, employers, and trade unions all have their roles to play—government, in enforcing labor rights and pursuing effective development and poverty reduction policies; employers, through providing decent work opportunities; and workers, by fulfilling their potential through freely chosen and productive participation in the labor market. The broad parameters of what needs to be put in place are quite clear. But the devil, of course, lies in the details. This chapter is based on the lessons drawn in the course of our experience in Tiruvallur District of Tamil Nadu, where microfinance-led approaches were successful in reducing vulnerability and promoting social empowerment but had very limited impact on job creation. This demonstrates clearly the need for a global approach to promote employment that respects workers' rights and shows that community-based action alone cannot solve the bonded labor problem.

## Learning from Experience

### Bonded Labor in India

Bonded labor arises through a complex of interlinked issues. Immediate "triggers," such as health emergencies, religious ceremonies, dowries, food shortages, or sudden loss of a job or an income earner, may oblige an impoverished worker to seek a loan or advance from an employer or labor agent. But underlying structural factors in South Asia can transform an inherently unequal but nonetheless transparent economic transaction into a mechanism of social subordination and control. Discrimination and social exclusion, based on religion, ethnicity, or caste; illiteracy and lack of access to information; employer monopolies on local financial and labor markets; and the dominance of social elites can all conspire to subjugate the interests of one section of the community to those of another. Bondage is a deliberate strategy on the part of employers to ensure a cheap and docile labor force, a strategy that is likely to evolve according to market fluctuations and technological change.[3] "Vulnerability," defined as the limited ability of individuals and households to deal with risk, tends to push people into bondage. Although it is bad for all workers, women and children are its worst victims—"bondage within bondage" being a prevalent phenomenon (Breman 1996, 2007). Women and children not only represent a large proportion of the labor force but also remain largely invisible.

In India, despite the long-standing legal prohibition of bonded labor (Bonded Labour System [Abolition] Act, promulgated in 1976 and amended in 1985), the practice is still widespread. So-called neobondage mechanisms have largely replaced the traditional forms of long-term attachment of labor servants in feudal agricultural systems (Breman 1996). Neobondage exhibits some striking differences from the bondage of the past. The arrangement tends to be time-bound to a season or fixed period, not indefinite as in the past; the credit-labor contract is exclusively economic, lacking any element of the former social protection provided by the landlord; the contract is most often concluded through a labor intermediary; and migrant laborers are particularly affected (Breman 2007; Breman, Guerin, and Prakash 2009; Lerche 2007; National Commission for Enterprises in the Unorganized Sector 2007; Srivastava 2005).

Although the wage advance is undoubtedly a means of profit extraction by the employer, it can also put a degree of power in the worker's hands. He or she can use it as a means of bargaining between competing employers, and eventually the worker can walk away when a better opportunity arises (see, for example, de Neve [1999] for an analysis of the contradictions inherent in the giving and receiving of advances in the power-loom industry in Tamil Nadu). A wage advance can provide some degree of security, albeit at a very low level, in an environment in which contract enforcement is weak, unemployment rife, and social protection nonexistent.

The persistence and emergence of new forms of bondage are closely related to the increasing precariousness and informalization of labor markets (in India, around 90 percent of the labor force is in the "unorganized" sector) and to massive seasonal labor migration. In a context of chronic underemployment and irregular employment in both agriculture and nonfarm sectors, the bargaining power of workers is zero, and they have little choice but to accept such forms of exploitation.

## The ILO Strategy

With the main aim of preventing bonded labor, the ILO designed the PEBLISA technical cooperation project strategy in 2002. Three main types of community-based intervention were identified:

1. *Social empowerment* to help vulnerable community members understand and be able to claim their rights, to help them to organize and federate savings and credit groups (SCGs), and to raise awareness about critical issues such as gender equality, health, and hygiene, reducing

household "unsustainable" expenses, and gaining access to government schemes;

2. *Provision of basic services* such as health care, adult literacy, and non-formal education for children who had dropped out of school to work by the project itself in locations where government services were lacking; and

3. *Economic empowerment,* including skills training, support for income-generating activities, and microfinance services, to help households to diversify and increase their income and hence decrease their dependence on their employer.

Microfinance was considered to be a key intervention for two main reasons. First, since debt bondage occurs because of the loan or advance provided by the employer, the basic premise was that alternative sources of credit, plus savings opportunities, would reduce the employer's monopoly on the local financial market. Credit-supported income-generating activities could also enable poor families to diversify their income sources and thus break the employer's monopoly in the local labor market. Second, for unorganized workers in the informal economy, microfinance serves as a convening forum and "door opener." Savings and credit provide an incentive for workers to meet together, and these groups then offer a vehicle to deliver other services, information, and activities (Daru, Churchill, and Beemsterboer 2005).

Another element in the ILO strategy was to implement some project activities through local NGOs.[4] Although for the most part the relationship was a happy one, some tensions inevitably arose. The role of the NGO fieldworkers had an air of a "mission impossible"—the demands of the project on them were considerably higher than under a more normal scenario. Fieldworkers had complex roles to fulfill, and local people had enormous expectations of them. A major advantage of the project lay in the ability of field staff to respond and adapt to clients' needs and priorities.

Overall, 75 villages were targeted by the project in five blocks of Tiruvallur District.[5] These villages can be categorized into three groups depending on the nature of job opportunities available: those focusing exclusively on "reliable" agriculture (with assured water availability), in which strong dependence on landowners continues to exist that may in some cases be characterized as a "mild" form of bondage; those with a declining agricultural sector, where people increasingly seek nonfarm jobs or farmwork elsewhere and actively seek employer advances that act as a guarantee of employment (however exploitative); and periurban villages where people juggle different work opportunities in a highly competitive environment but are least vulnerable to bondage and most able to adapt to changing labor market conditions. It is in the first and second categories that vulnerability to bondage is highest, primarily in agriculture (a "mild" form of bondage in the case of attached laborers) and rice mills (severe bondage among the tribal Irular people; see Box 8.1). Brick kilns also have bonded laborers, but these tend to be seasonal migrant workers coming from the southern districts of Tamil Nadu, not the local residents who were targeted by the project in Tiruvallur.

In these villages, the percentage of people who are vulnerable to bonded labor is probably not very high, but targeting only the "most vulnerable" members of the population is simply not practicable, as they are too geographically dispersed.[6] The efficiency of group lending depends in large part on the quality of intragroup relations: previous social ties, based on social but also *spatial* proximity (living in the same street), are key.

---

### Box 8.1 Bonded Labor in Rice Mills—A Severe Form of Bondage

According to a study by the French Institute of Pondicherry (Roesch et al. forthcoming), the conditions faced by bonded laborers in some rice mills (more specifically, the drying unit or *nerkalam* using manual labor and located in Tiruvallur District) represent a severe form of bondage. Whole families are affected, often confined in locked sheds. Men, women, elders, and often children have no other choice than to live according to the relentless pace of rice drying under extreme working conditions. Their social exclusion is almost total, all ties to the external world, their family, and their native village being cut. Debt is the central element of bondage, through which labor is manipulated in a relationship of dependency. On recruitment, the owner grants an initial advance and then uses various strategies to maintain and increase the debt, making it impossible to repay. Laborers are paid on a piece-rate basis, but they have no say in their work schedule or workload. Working hours range from 12 to 16 hours per day, sometimes even more, with no day off. The drying is done on a large concrete area in the heat of the sun, resulting in frequent burns and skin problems. Women (including pregnant women) and elders work intensively. Even though some of the children go to school, many are involved in sun drying or have to clean the drying area before the sun rises. They do not work continuously, but they stand in for their parents when they are tired. Employers therefore claim that it is the parents who are responsible.

The workers come mainly from the tribal Irular community, one of the most vulnerable groups in Tamil Nadu. Traditionally, Irulars lived in the forests and specialized in hunting for rats and snakes; collecting honey, beeswax, and medicinal plants; and digging out tree roots. Like many other similar communities, since the 1950s they have been gradually obliged to move to the plains and take up other occupations. Most face great difficulties in finding jobs and in broader social integration.

## The Impact Assessment

For the ILO, an important aspect of the project was to learn and document lessons about what does and what does not work, based on experimentation and innovation, for preventing debt bondage among a highly vulnerable target group. This necessarily involves "failure" as well as "success" stories. Hence, many surveys and research and assessment studies were implemented over the duration of the project. One such study was the independent impact assessment undertaken in 2006 by the French Institute of Pondicherry.

As the aim of the project was the prevention of bonded labor, the study did not aim to document a reduction in the number of bonded laborers. Rather, it was based on qualitative and quantitative analysis that aimed to capture the combination of economic and social dimensions of vulnerability to debt bondage and to understand the dynamic aspect of impact, that is, the process in operation. Not all positive impacts necessarily result in an absolute improvement in the situation; they may instead stabilize or slow down a negative trend or spiral.

In a first stage, qualitative methods were used to build up an understanding of the project's socioeconomic context. Four aspects were analyzed in detail: the local labor market, the local financial market, the local power structure, and both gender discrimination and caste discrimination. Six representative villages were selected for in-depth qualitative analysis of the activity's impact in its different fields of intervention. A detailed monograph was prepared on each village. Semistructured interviews were held with individual men and women, with key informants and discussion groups at the village level, and with the staff of the NGOs. No claim is made to be statistically representative; rather the aim was to grasp diversity. All in all, around 150 qualitative interviews were held, including 30 in-depth interviews (life histories) for which researchers sometimes met with respondents twice or even three times.

Quantitative analysis was undertaken in a second stage. A baseline survey done in 2004 by the NGOs made it possible to have a longitudinal analysis, comparing the clients' situation in 2004 and 2006. The baseline survey undertaken by the NGOs revealed the basic characteristics of the "target" population. It showed that the villagers concerned work mostly in agriculture, as casual day laborers (coolies), or on leased land. A minority work in fishing, brick kilns, rice mills, embroidery, and other informal activities. Three-quarters work for daily wages; reported annual average household income was 10,000 rupees or about US$240. Three-quarters of the families belong to the Scheduled Castes and 17 percent to the Scheduled Tribes. Two-thirds did not have a community certificate, which is a requirement to access government welfare schemes. Ninety-one percent were Hindu and nearly 9 percent Christian. Twelve percent were migrant families, who had moved for marriage or employment opportunities close to Chennai. Around three-quarters had title deeds for their homes, the majority of which were *kacha* huts. Regarding education status, 42 percent of family members had no education, and 19 percent had primary-level schooling.

In 2006, given constraints on time and the difficulty of gathering reliable income and other data from poor households, the decision was taken together with the NGOs to focus on questions of indebtedness and assets, the two criteria considered key to an assessment of economic empowerment. Four hundred households were chosen randomly in the six villages, and questionnaire-based interviews were conducted by NGO staff. Again, the study does not claim to have covered the entirety of activities or impacts, but a reasoned selection. The rest of this chapter presents some key findings of this qualitative and quantitative assessment.

## Selected Impacts: Empirical Evidence and Analysis

### A Significant Reduction in Vulnerability: Household Debts and Assets

As explained above, we focused our quantitative analysis on two key indicators of household economic status: indebtedness and assets. The overall picture that emerged was, first, that as a result of the ILO microfinance-led strategy, households had increased their debts but had improved the "quality" of the debt; and second, they had increased their assets, leading to a reduction in vulnerability. Indebtedness, particularly to employers, is of course a particular concern of the project. At the same time, microfinance also raises some questions: would it not be considered perverse for a project that aims to reduce vulnerability to debt bondage to increase the debt burden of its clients by offering them credit?

In this respect, it is important to underline at the outset that chronic indebtedness is a fact of life for the people in Tamil Nadu; credit is their means to cover the mismatch between their low, irregular income and essential expenses that cannot be deferred. All the families targeted by the project are permanently indebted,[7] in different, mainly informal, ways, including advances from employers (see Box 8.2). Families juggle permanently with a multiplicity of credit sources, depending on their needs and what is available. It is not uncommon for a high-interest loan to be repaid by another loan at a lower rate, or simply by another loan taken out when the first creditor claims his or her due.

By contrast, cash savings are almost nonexistent: families struggle to make ends meet, let alone save, given their insufficient and irregular incomes. The most widespread forms of savings are in gold, which is easily converted into cash when the need arises, and through *chit* funds used to finance specific events, to invest, or even to repay debts. Being constantly under pressure to spend by the family and wider social circle, women in particular seek out ways that will

## Box 8.2  Advances from Employers

In regard to advances from employers, great variation exists in terms of price (interest rate), duration, and mode of repayment. Repayment in the form of daily labor is still frequent and sometimes involves an arrangement without pay for a certain period (sometimes fixed in the beginning, sometimes not). The borrower does not necessarily work full-time but has to be available whenever his creditor needs him. Sometimes the repayment is mixed: part monetary, part in the form of working days (calculated either at the going casual labor rate or a discounted rate, the difference corresponding to the cost of the loan). Whatever the conditions of the loan, two elements seem to recur frequently: (1) the debtor—or someone from his family—is at the disposal of the creditor; he can work elsewhere but has to be available on the day that the creditor needs him; and (2) there is no clear "contract."

It is difficult to assess the cost of this type of loan objectively. Quite often, the concerned individuals themselves do not know the exact conditions, including how much has been repaid (as they keep no accounts). Furthermore, it is difficult to distinguish the "cost" from all the connections linking the family of the creditor and the debtor. For example, certain "advantageous" loan conditions are in fact a means of compensating for a delay in wage payment by the creditor-employer. Finally, it should be noted that a number of families who have access to this form of loan consider it a privilege: it is sometimes the only way for them to obtain such an amount; they prefer to offer their labor as security rather than their house or land; and finally it is also a means of staying "connected" with a potential employer. This last point is probably key: the link between the labor and credit markets is undoubtedly a source of servitude, but in a context of large-scale unemployment, the population perceives it also as an advantage.

*force* them to save. But more generally, there is a tendency among people to prefer to see their money circulate, rather than its being "immobilized" and not put to use. They are more used to managing their household expenses through credit than through savings.

The project aimed at reducing people's vulnerability to bonded labor by improving their situation in terms of indebtedness and assets. Women's SCGs established under PEBLISA offered four main types of financial products and services: (1) weekly (sometimes monthly) savings mobilization with amounts that are uniform and fixed by the group itself (most of the time, 10 rupees per week); (2) individual voluntary savings, in a locked "dump box" kept at home; (3) internal loans coming from the group's collected savings (on average 5,000 to 6,000 rupees per year); and (4) external loans from various sources: banks, project funds, governmental schemes.[8] What were the results of these schemes?

With respect to debts, total household indebtedness increased over the two-year period, by 19 percent among the clients of one of the NGOs and by 50 percent among the clients of the other (which had better access to bank loans). But the internal structure of the debt showed significant changes. Both bank loans and internal SCG loans increased substantially, representing the main source of increased debt, whereas the share and amount of moneylender debt decreased in parallel (in part, repaid by the "project" loans).

As the number of financial opportunities increased—6 or 7 different sources of credit as against 3 or 4 before the project—this enabled households to choose those best adapted to their needs and to combine various sources of credit. But as project loans (in their amount, time of availability, and duration) rarely match exactly the demand, people still have to juggle with multiple sources. As the amounts are limited to 5,000 rupees for SCG and 10,000 rupees for bank loans, whenever larger sums are needed, moneylenders or other sources (relatives, pawnbrokers, employers) continue to be sought out. One of the other advantages of informal sources, even given their higher cost, is their flexibility: the repayment schedule is the result of a negotiation process between lender and borrower and can evolve over time if the client has trouble repaying. Frequency of interest payments is also quite flexible, as is the date of repayment of the capital, usually expected as a lump sum. By contrast, "normal" bank and SCG loans tend to have fixed terms and repayment schedules, even though efforts were made in the project to adjust these to borrowers' repayment possibilities and to find an appropriate balance between flexibility and repayment discipline.

The individual voluntary "dump box" savings perhaps deserve a special mention. It represents an adaptation of a traditional practice of keeping savings in a clay pot at home, which had to be broken to access the cash. The locked metal "dump box," which is opened each week so as to hand over the savings at the SCG meeting, balances liquidity and security; money can be conveniently deposited each day (and by any household member) and easily accessed. The product was positively received in all villages, particularly in the early stages of the project, when it was seen to increase household savings by as much as 200 percent over previous weekly savings. Subsequently, the amounts dropped off, but it was still a valued addition to the range of products on offer. Interviews reveal that clients see the savings primarily as a way to get a loan from the SCG, rather than as savings in a true sense (to use in an emergency or to buy a particular item). This is still a positive result, reducing the pressure on women to borrow in order to meet their SCG contributions, something which is often seen in other projects.

Turning to household assets, these have increased in value over the two-year period for clients of both NGOs, by 33 percent and 73 percent respectively. Televisions, cows, gold jewelry and coins, and bicycles are the most commonly held assets. In value terms, gold represents the main form of assets (60 percent of the total value) and the main source of increase, in large part owing to an increase in the gold price (by 60 percent from 2004 to 2006) and less because of an increase in the weight of gold assets per household. The increase in assets is not correlated with household indebtedness; households have not necessarily borrowed in order to purchase assets (although clearly in some cases, like cows, they do). And fewer than 10 percent have sold assets in order to reduce their debt. So we can conclude that for most clients the increase in assets translates into a reduction in vulnerability. An analysis of the debt/asset ratio at household level again shows considerable variation between households but with a significant proportion (40 percent and 63 percent for the two NGOs) improving their situation—moving from a negative to a positive ratio (i.e., asset value is greater than outstanding debts). Unfortunately, for a minority (14 percent and 9 percent) the situation worsened.

As we have seen, the positive "asset" results hinge largely on the increase in gold value in recent years. Whether such a trend will continue in the future is a moot point and calls into question the sustainability and robustness of this impact. In general, gold appears to be a key element in the household's financial strategy, representing a major part of total assets (50 percent and 64 percent of total value for the two NGOs).[9] A large portion of loans is partly or entirely used to buy gold, as an "intermediate good" that can subsequently be pledged to obtain cash to finance other needs. There are various reasons why people buy gold. It is secure, can be easily converted into cash when needs arise, and is also a means of accessing additional loans through pledging.

When the clients are offered a loan through the project, they might not have an immediate need for cash at that time but know that they may have such a need in the future, when credit might no longer be available. So they take the loan and buy assets (especially gold) for future use; it thus becomes a form of "forced savings." In order to repay the debt incurred, they must develop strategies to increase income in the short term, for example, through increasing their own paid labor and that of family elders, seasonal migration, or reduced consumption. Gold is also acquired through a prepayment system, also a form of savings: regular installments are paid, on completion of which a piece of jewelry is received, its value being that of the installments paid plus the interest due.

Even though the analysis of debt and assets has demonstrated positive average trends, it has also demonstrated that there are wide variations between households in their financial management strategies and outcomes. For some households the impact of the project has been *accumulation*. These households were able to juggle different activities and take risks. They enjoy the support of kin and social capital to cope with crises if they arise. A possibility of accumulation exists, and the project has assisted in this process. Project impact is usually more social (reduction of unsustainable expenses, education of children, empowerment of women) than economic or financial. These are not the "bottom poor," but it is unavoidable that such households should form part of the client group, given the geographic dispersal of the poorest. For other households the impact has been stabilization. For these households, PEBLISA assisted them in breaking out of a preexisting vicious cycle of debt, slowing or reversing a downward spiral.

Results for other households were less positive. *At-risk households with preexisting vulnerability* are households that are highly vulnerable owing to suffering successive shocks (such as large health-related expenses or crop or livestock failure). For some of these households, the situation has somewhat improved with project assistance. For a minority, the project may have had a perverse impact by encouraging the clients to take on additional risks that they could ill afford.

Overall, the vulnerability of a household often depends on a combination of factors, among which we can distinguish those relating to the household's profile and those related to the main risks they face. For the household profile, we found that the financial situation (debt burden and composition, and the ratio with assets), the economic situation (income amount, diversity, and regularity), the human and social capital (income-earning members; support from relatives, friends, or employers), and psychological factors (previous experience with debt, ability to plan, geographical horizons) are important in influencing individual outcomes. The main sources of risk and uncertainty are those related to health, loss of a job, life-cycle expenses, and risky investments.

### Social Empowerment:
### Gender Equality and Men's Role

A main objective of PEBLISA was to promote gender equality at the household level as one way to promote better financial management, and more generally to promote women's empowerment in social and community life. In-depth interviews and observation with women and men reveal positive effects of the project, but these are necessarily slow and quite limited so far, taking into account the weight of hierarchies and existing unfavorable social norms for women. The main positive impacts are seen in terms of *awareness* (for women but also for men) and in terms of *decisionmaking*. To appreciate fully the significance of the changes observed, it is important to understand the extent and nature of control over women in the "normal" Indian context (see Box 8.3).

Regarding awareness, it is apparent that women have benefited in many ways through their participation and exposure through PEBLISA. They speak of having acquired a sense of boldness, self-confidence, and ability to manage; an awareness that it is possible to conduct activities other than agriculture; an enhanced exposure to the outside world and ability to move beyond the confines of the house and village; and a recognition that women can demand their

**Box 8.3  The Situation of the Women: Control and Social Pressure**

The Indian woman, whatever the context (except perhaps in certain tribes), as-
sumes to a great extent the responsibility for the *social prestige* of the family,
the social group, or even of the community through food preparation, religious
rituals, and sexuality. *Grosso modo,* restrictions on women, are more marked
in the higher castes; some women do not hesitate to say that they are "better
off" because they are low caste. Among the Scheduled Castes (SC), the legitimacy of women's involvement in public affairs has undoubtedly been reinforced by the political strengthening of the SC, which is particularly marked
in Tiruvallur District. Nonetheless, female behavior within the PEBLISA clien-
tele remains closely controlled. The concern about women's relations with men
outside the family is used to justify restrictions on women's mobility. The small-
est trip necessarily raises suspicion: a woman is allowed to go out only if she
intends to avoid any male contact. Frequently the outing is only allowed in the
presence of a trustworthy person, guaranteeing respect for the rules. On her return she is often questioned on every move and person encountered. This suspicion is permanent and omnipresent and plays a large part in discussions and
internal family conflicts, many women being constantly obliged to justify
themselves. A woman who does not follow the rules of purity is immediately
branded as a prostitute.

Inside the family, female behavior has to conform to modesty and discretion,
and obedience to the husband and the in-laws is the rule. Young women endure
much more control than the older ones. "Gossips" are much criticized, in the
family circle as well as outside. On the other hand, a man is expected to control
his wife and to submit himself to the opinion of his parents, rather than his wife.
As a sign of their submission, women should not mention the names of their husbands and should use the "second person" form of address, remain standing when
they serve them, and so on. Men and women both insist on female morality, questions of which are at the core of discussions in the villages. For their part, men
are judged in part on their capacity to "control" their wives. Alcohol consumption is also an element of male virility. Any "deviant" behavior by his wife therefore puts a man's own pride and status in question. Women do not hesitate to
mock the men who are weak, impotent, or submissive to their wives.

At the level of the local community, women are sometimes the first to
judge and accuse each other of not respecting "morality." It is, in fact, an easy
and effective argument used to punish women for a completely unrelated matter, to seek revenge for some action, or to settle jealousy problems. Finally, we
must emphasize the disastrous consequences of a bad reputation: in a context
of strong endogamy, the reputation of the women conditions, in part, the future marriage prospects of other family members.

rights, including within their own family (even if with some difficulty), and that contact with men is not necessarily a source of impurity and moral degeneration. Many women, mainly leaders of SCGs, now interact directly with male government officials, bankers, and others in authority, a situation that was previously unheard of. Such direct access for low castes, and particularly for low-caste *women,* reduces transaction costs and increases their sense of personal pride and capability as opposed to the feeling of dependence resulting from the use of intermediaries.

Women also participate much more actively in decisionmaking in areas usually devoted to men (such as financial management, marriage, family functions), and for their part, men increasingly engage in areas usually devoted to women (education and health care of the children, family planning).

Financial management is a source of permanent tension and conflict between men and women but also between women and their in-laws. When there is no consensus on how resources should be spent, the pooling system goes hand in hand with individual hidden practices by women (*chit* funds, informal loans, savings box, or gold coins at home) to fulfill their own needs (to buy jewelry, saris, sweets for the children) and to curtail the excessive expenses of their husbands. Men enjoy much greater freedom to spend as they please, keeping aside part of their income for private use or secretly borrowing large amounts of money without the knowledge of their wives.

The PEBLISA project has had some tangible impacts on household financial management. Among the women who previously had no say in financial decisions, some are now recognized as full-fledged household members entitled to take part in such decisionmaking. Others were initially used as "puppets": they had been sent to the SCG by their husbands or their mothers-in-law but were expected to do exactly what they had been told (how much to save, how much to borrow, etc.). Even in such cases, there were some positive developments, with women increasingly asserting their own wishes.

For those women who were already involved in the household financial management, we observed two main impacts. First, managing scarce resources is a real challenge and a permanent source of stress (in case of shortfalls, they are likely to be blamed). An additional source of cash from SCG loans could ease the daily pressure they face. Second, financial transactions tend to become more transparent within the household, largely as a result of men's involvement in men's groups. Some men have realized that it is better to avoid individual decisions that might threaten the balance in the household budget. Women could also use the project loans as a bargaining chip, offering to share the loan on condition that their husbands stop their secret borrowing.

But of course women's empowerment is neither a fast nor a linear process, as recognized by one project client: "Before PEBLISA, I was in a dark room without windows; now, I can see the light of the outside world because I have some windows, but they are still very narrow and don't let me go out."

It is a risky process that implies numerous conflicts and compromises along the way: "The SCG solves some problems, but it creates others," in the words of another SCG member. This is normal and inevitable and not a sign of failure; any multidimensional empowerment process can be expected to have setbacks along the way, which themselves indicate that a real change in power relations is occurring. It is necessary, however, to be aware of these risks, to monitor them continuously, and to attempt to mitigate them as far as possible.

Tensions and conflicts arise at different levels. Within the household, women SCG members can be criticized by both their husbands and in-laws for a variety of reasons: their increased mobility, spending less time on household tasks, and discussing "private" matters in public. The SCG can become a scapegoat used by husbands to blame their wives whenever something goes wrong. Tensions arise also between group members, relating, for example, to repayment problems or to the selection of who will benefit from loans. Internal conflicts can beset the women themselves when they feel torn between their family and group obligations, between the culture of confidence promoted by the project and the submission expected by the community, and between the expectations of the group and those of their husbands.

The situation of the women's group leaders deserves particular note. Their role is an ambiguous one—undoubtedly entailing advantages, but necessarily accompanied by difficulties. Being a leader is rarely a consequence of a deliberate personal choice: most of the leaders become so gradually, encouraged by their peers and the NGO staff because of their dynamism, charisma, reputation, confidence, and skills. For many women, being a leader is a source of pleasure, satisfaction, pride, and social recognition. At the same time, the intensity of responsibilities is a burden. They are torn between the members' claims, the conditions imposed by the NGO, and criticism by their husbands and in-laws and by group members. There are several cases of leaders who resigned, having been forced by their in-laws or because they could not cope with the continual criticism; there are many more, however, who have flourished in their newfound role.

To sum up, again we must emphasize the diversity of women's situations, conditioned in part by their age (women of reproductive age are considered "impure" and most vulnerable), in part by the degree of conservatism in the individual village, in part by women's own personalities and life experiences. The project has enlarged the frame within which women can bargain and negotiate their own position at the level of the household as well as at the level of the community. It helps to give an official character to some practices that were previously done in secret. At the same time, participation in SCGs is a question of compromise: to be allowed to participate, some women must accept additional responsibilities, imposed either by the husbands and the in-laws or self-imposed. And, of course, the diversity of male behavior must also be mentioned. Although some men refuse outright to modify any aspect of their lives, others encourage their wives, giving them active support in their economic projects or leadership role.

## Collective Action and Political Empowerment

PEBLISA promoted collective action in pursuit of specific aims (improved services, conflict resolution, etc.) but also as an end in itself (so as to enhance clients' long-term capacity to claim their rights and build social capital). Collective action took place in two-thirds of the villages targeted (52 villages out of 75), where usually two or three actions have been taken simultaneously. Actions targeted the establishment or maintenance of basic amenities and common goods, such as streetlights, drinking water, or toilets; gaining access to government facilities or schemes, such as ration cards, caste certificates, or house loans; and fighting illegal activities and discrimination, such as sand extraction, wage inequality, and intercaste conflicts.

The main impact consisted of better access to public amenities and schemes, without necessarily improving the functioning of those services (such as schools or hospitals)—which is only to be expected, given PEBLISA's focus on empowering community members to claim their rights. With project support, clients have started to develop the skills (technical and social) needed to better access public services, a process that is normally time-consuming and costly. On the other hand, the project did directly improve the functioning of a number of common facilities at the village level, especially drinking water, streetlights, and roads. This was achieved through a combination of better access to information, bargaining with authorities, and monitoring to ensure better quality, for example of construction materials used in houses or roads. The strength of the SCGs for this type of collective action was greatly enhanced by their federation at various levels—within individual villages into *grama sangam*– or *panchayat*-level federations, and again at the union level. Success depends in large part on the ability of the groups to convince local leaders of their legitimacy in the local political arena.

In some cases (14 percent of all the collective actions undertaken), the women, sometimes with men's support, successfully challenged certain forms of discrimination. One example was the bargaining for higher daily wages from local landowners in Pennalpurpet village, in which the upper caste is extremely dominant; the higher wages then spread to neighboring villages. In another village, Mettupalayam, the SCGs succeeded in bringing a stop to long-standing illegal quarrying of sand at the margins of the village, which was threatening village land and homes alike. A final example is that of the village of Bangarampet, in which the women's SCG was supported to lobby the *gram panchayat* for the release of their menfolk from bondage in a local rice mill. Nineteen workers were released and have since set up their own rice mill, with government and project support. This kind of action is less common than taking up the issue of basic amenities for a very simple reason: it is much more difficult to succeed insofar as it challenges local power structures and therefore necessarily encounters resistance and opposition from local elites.

The success of collective action varies from one village to the next. Several factors can explain such differences: the nature of the services to be claimed or the problems to be solved (some are intrinsically easier to tackle than others); SCG influence at the village level, linked to the local power structure, whether more or less concentrated, more or less conservative; the presence and attitude of "men's support groups" (to which we return below); group dynamism, influenced heavily by the leader; and the support provided by the NGO staff, who play a key and extremely complex role.

Men's support groups were an innovation introduced by the project in its second phase, in response to the realization that in order to be successful, the project needed the "buy-in" and support of male community members. Thus far, the focus had been almost exclusively on women in the community-based interventions. The objectives were twofold: (1) to improve gender relations and strengthen collective action at the community level; and (2) to promote individual savings by men, particularly "contractual" savings directed at a specific purpose such as house construction or marriage. Members were recruited on a voluntary basis among the husbands (or sons or fathers) of SCG members. Some notable positive results have been observed: a heightened awareness of gender inequalities, reduced suspicions and criticisms of SCG activities and women's mobility, better intrahousehold cooperation for savings and loan repayments, and men's support for collective action and strengthened solidarity at community level. In general, men start to appreciate better what the SCG is all about and feel better informed and involved. Some villages have reported a reduction in men's alcohol consumption and domestic violence.

But it is clear that many challenges remain, and NGO staff report that it is often an uphill struggle to sustain the groups; indeed, some MSGs have been discontinued. For example, the men are less ready than women to listen to others and to each other and their leaders, they attach less importance to the group meetings, and members are often absent either because they are migrant laborers or because they are not prepared to sacrifice part of their evenings for attending meetings. There is a permanent expectation from men that they too should receive loans and a greater degree of support from NGO staff; some perceive participation in men's groups as a sign of "weakness"; and there can be discrepancies between men's public affirmation of support for women's activities and their private opposition to them. The very notion of a "men's support group" runs counter to male identity in a patriarchal society, in which women are supposed to follow and obey men.

*Limited Impact on Household Income
and Employment*

One of the project's objectives was to develop income-generating activities through the promotion of livelihood opportunities, vocational skills training, and market studies and linkages. This implied both reinforcing existing household economic activities (animal husbandry, milk production, and marketing) and introducing new activities.

In practice, income diversification was a real challenge, however, and most project loans (around 80 percent) were used for so-called nonproductive purposes that do not directly generate income. This proportion did not change significantly over the project lifetime, though there was a slight increase in "productive" loans in the final year, to 25 percent. Among "nonproductive" purposes, loan repayment (26 percent), medical expenses (19 percent), and purchase of household items (14 percent) were most common in 2006. Such loans are of course still valuable to the household's well-being—not only do they improve daily life, but they can also generate income *indirectly* through reducing the cost of debt servicing (by substituting debt on "good" terms for debt on "bad" terms) and increasing labor productivity (by improving health status). Expenses of social ceremonies, frequently blamed for bondage, also have their positive role to play, by enhancing a family's social capital through gift and countergift exchanges. But as such loans do not generate the cash required for their reimbursement, they should be treated with caution, especially among the poorest. It is usually said that microcredit is initially used for "nonproductive" purposes, and only later, once households' vulnerability has been reduced, are they able to invest "productively."

We have seen above that most households depend on agriculture for a living, but many are involved out of necessity in nonfarm activities to supplement their income. Even though work as a coolie is low paid and irregular, it has two main advantages: first, wages are fixed and known in advance and, when paid on a piece rate, daily wages can be increased by working fast; and second, the work lasts generally from 7 a.m. to 2 or 3 p.m., allowing time for additional household activities or tending animals or land, once the "regular" working day is over. For most people, it is very difficult to imagine doing anything other than agricultural coolie work: the obstacle is as much psychological and social (a lack of confidence in their ability to do something else, coupled with a personal identity rooted in agricultural "values") as technical or financial. Self-employment is rare, the main reason being an aversion to assuming any additional risk, given most households' heavy indebtedness and financial precariousness. In most cases, diversification out of agriculture happens only when there is simply no alternative; and this is easier when the village is close to a main road or to urban centers.

Nonetheless, a minority of project clients were able to start a small business in the nonfarm sector, including petty shops, tailoring, embroidery, and fish selling. But many occupations observed in 2004 had discontinued by 2006, demonstrating the fragility of such enterprises. For example, petty shops, the most popular business, were analyzed in detail. They consist of stalls located at home or in a small cabin that sell small quantities of essential items such as oil, rice, matches, cigarettes, and soap. Profit margins were on average 5 percent, meaning a daily net income of 5–15 rupees. The most common causes of failure were difficulty in recovering credit offered to customers and excessive competition in a saturated market.

Some project loans were used for investment in agriculture on leased land. The PEBLISA loan can substitute for other less favorable loans taken from cooperatives, seed suppliers, or landowners and can dramatically improve enterprise profitability. Crop production remains highly risky, however, especially for small farmers, and losses are rather frequent. Other clients prefer to invest in livestock, mainly cows, followed by goats. But here again, a close analysis of the profitability of breeding activities shows that, for cows, four or five years are needed to generate an income and, as people themselves say, "the profit is the calf." For goats, the activity becomes profitable after three years. In the short term, earnings do not offset the costs incurred; other sources of income are needed to repay the loan, which has to be subsidized or rescheduled.

Depending on a combination of factors particular to the household (such as previous experience in animal breeding, access to markets, milk price, availability of "free" family labor, crop residues for feed, and so on), livestock can variously be a good source of income, a second income, only an asset, or a source of indebtedness and decapitalization. We assessed that, for most PEBLISA households, livestock were "only" an asset and some had to borrow further in order to repay SCG or bank loans. But such results should not shock, given the poverty of the client group, and similar findings reported from elsewhere.[10] Asset formation is itself a positive result, as it can increase household security. Neither is profitability the only objective for women: they value the milk they can give their children, the social prestige of ownership, and the prospect of selling a male calf in the future (if indeed they succeed in keeping the animals alive). Yet the need for caution when offering livestock loans to poor households is clear if perverse impacts are to be avoided.

In terms of job creation, then, the lesson is that it is simply illusory to expect many poor people to transform themselves into microentrepreneurs or to expect microfinance to solve underemployment, one of the root causes of bondage. Apart from individual resistance to self-employment in the nonfarm sector, the hierarchical and monopolistic functioning of local product markets, combined with their limited size, makes it impossible for microfinance to generate jobs on any significant scale.

## Conclusion

The ILO PEBLISA project has generated some valuable lessons about what works, and does not work, at the community level in preventing people from falling into debt traps from which they cannot escape. In short, microfinance-led strategies *do* indeed have a role to play in reducing vulnerability to bondage but must be "handled with care." In Tamil Nadu, they have contributed to reducing people's overall vulnerability by improving the quality of household debt, increasing the value of assets (even though this is partly owing to the increase in gold value over the project period), and promoting empowerment at different levels: individual, gender, collective, and political.

The chapter also illustrates the complexity of implementing effective interventions for the benefit of people vulnerable to falling into bonded labor. It shows in particular the limitations of microcredit in terms of job creation. This is not due to shortcomings in the microfinance service provision itself but rather because the credit is too often used to finance activities that are unprofitable or uncompetitive or for which there is insufficient market demand. Unanticipated negative impacts were also encountered for the 10 percent of the clients who ended up being more vulnerable than at the start of the project.

Some quite specific recommendations for future interventions can be made on the basis of the assessment. Regarding economic empowerment, there is a need for even greater flexibility in project loans (terms of disbursal and repayment) to limit the need for clients to resort to "bad debt" (moneylender loans with excessive or cumulative interest rates, interlinked contracts, and implicit obligations fixed by employers); specific savings products based on gold might be introduced; training and marketing support could be intensified for nonfarm occupations, based specifically on local socioeconomic opportunities; and additional efforts could be made to strengthen risk management, for example, through crop and cattle insurance and by providing clients with fuller information on the "downsides" of taking loans for income-generating activities. Though costly, it might also be possible to devise a system to categorize households in terms of their profile (human and physical assets) and exposure to risk and uncertainty (marriage, migration, investment) and to tailor financial products to suit their respective circumstances.

On the social empowerment front, certainly more time is needed for initial gains to become firmly embedded. Some suggestions for the future are to monitor tensions and conflicts (at group, household, community levels) and seek ways to proactively address or reduce them; to involve in-laws as well as men in awareness-raising programs; to take into account and compensate for the costs of group leadership; to increase men's participation in economic activities (including loans) while guarding against the risk of their "hijacking" project benefits; to improve the articulation with local authorities and leaders, who may already or soon start to feel threatened by the rise of the SCGs; and last, but by no means least, to find ways to better reward NGO and project staff for the invaluable and difficult role they play.

Broader challenges of course remain for the government of India and for the ILO. Conditions in Tiruvallur represent a minute fraction only of the bigger Indian, and indeed South Asian, context in all its diversity and complexity. Given their very limited impact in terms of job creation, actions described in this chapter must be combined with broader action to promote labor standards and jobs through a "high road" development strategy (based on enhancing productivity, wages, and demand), together with employment generation in rural areas through such measures as land reform, infrastructure development, and industrial decentralization.[11] This is in contrast to the "low road" (low wages–low productivity–poor technology) strategy into which much of Indian industry is seemingly currently locked (Srivastava 2007).

A recent report of the National Commission for Enterprises in the Unorganised Sector (2007) indeed calls for a "holistic approach" that combines comprehensive legislation for regulation of minimum conditions of work in the unorganized sector (both agricultural and nonagricultural) with measures to improve the situation of marginal and small farmers, stimulate the growth of the nonfarm sector, and expand job creation and employability. Let us hope these recommendations are heeded. But such actions necessarily need time to take effect. In the meantime, reducing the vulnerability of the poor, through the types of interventions tested by PEBLISA, becomes all the more important.

## Notes

Isabelle Guérin, Marc Roesch, and G. Venkatasubramanian are researchers from the French Institute of Pondichéry, of the French Ministry of Foreign Affairs. The center conducts research, training, and advisory activities in South and Southeast Asia (see www.ifpindia.org).

1. The impact assessment was funded by a grant from the Fonds Fiduciaire of the French Ministry of Foreign Affairs. The final report of the impact assessment will appear as a working paper of the ILO Declaration Programme (Roesch et al. forthcoming).

2. PEBLISA (Nepal, India, and Pakistan chapters) was subject to an overall final evaluation and impact assessment in early 2006. For a summary of main findings, see Premchander et al. (2006). The study by the French Institute of Pondichéry was conducted over a longer time frame and provided more detailed quantitative and qualitative data and analysis than the other impact studies.

3. See, for instance, Engelshoven (1999) for the Surat diamond industry, De Neve (2005) for the weaving sector.

4. In Tiruvallur District, the NGOs were Integrated Rural Community Development Society (IRCDS) and Madras Social Service Society (MSSS).

5. The blocks are Poondi, Kadambathur, and Tiruvallur (covered by IRCDS) and Villivakkam and Ellapuram (covered by MSSS). The project beneficiary households numbered 2,320 within "model clusters" receiving intensive support from the NGOs, and an additional 850 households in "mainstream" areas receiving normal levels of NGO support.

6. In an earlier phase, PEBLISA attempted the development of a Vulnerability to Debt Bondage Index, to identify and then target the most vulnerable households. In practice, the tool/methodology in its initial form proved too unwieldy and complex to apply.

7. According to data from the National Sample Survey Organisation, Tamil Nadu is one of the states in which farmers are the most indebted in India: the rate is 74.5 percent as opposed to 48.6 percent for all of India (National Sample Survey Organisation 2005, quoted in Rath 2005).

8. Microinsurance products were also provided but were not covered in the impact assessment.

9. It is interesting to note that this finding of the impact assessment was at odds with the perception of the NGO implementing partners, who did not consider gold to be a significant part of household savings strategies.

10. See, for example, BLESS (2006).

11. As suggested by Mahajan (2007), if we are to consider economic growth, microfinance must become part of livelihood finance—a framework that includes financial services, agriculture, business development services, and institutional development.

# 9

# Improving Forced Labor Statistics

## Patrick Belser and Michaelle de Cock

This final chapter argues that better statistics are a necessary support for good policy decisions. In effect, this is the whole purpose of statistics. Introductory textbooks typically define statistics as "a way to take numbers and convert them into useful information so that good decisions can be made" (Donnelly 2004, p. 4). Studies on the history of statistics also point out that the development of the science of statistics was motivated primarily by practical considerations, to be used as "an aid in decision making" (Tabak 2005). Although decisions are almost always based on incomplete information, statistics can serve to reduce existing levels of uncertainty as well as to limit subjective bias in policymaking. To quote Abraham (2005, p. 3), without accurate information, policymakers are "flying blind—or at least peering through thick fog."

In our chapter we distinguish between the two usual types of statistics: descriptive statistics of administrative or criminal databases and inferential statistics based on probability theory. The former refers to the art of summarizing and displaying data from administrative sources, such as official crime data or labor inspection data. The second type typically uses a sample of data to make claims about the overall problem—not just about "the tip of the iceberg" recorded in administrative databases. This chapter claims that we urgently need more of both types of statistics. It also highlights some good existing practices and discusses some possible avenues for the future.

The first section of the chapter presents in some detail the experience of the Netherlands in collecting data from a number of different sources and discusses what has been learned from this experience. We highlight the need to replicate this experience in other countries, with a particular effort to obtain better data on the trafficking for labor exploitation. We argue that this will require a clarification in existing definitions of forced labor and human trafficking through the identification of appropriate operational indicators. The second part of our chapter reviews existing global estimates and also proposed ways to produce statistically robust national estimates.


## Country-level Statistics on Reported Cases

### Good Practices

One of the most comprehensive quantitative country-level analyses on trafficking is published every year by the bureau of the Dutch National Rapporteur (BNRM), who was appointed in April 2000 to report to the Dutch government on trafficking in human beings in the country. The BNRM does not run a unique and centralized database of victims of trafficking in the Netherlands. Instead it collects data from various stakeholders, including the Dutch Foundation Against Trafficking in Women (which coordinates the provision of shelters to victims), the police registration system, police investigation files, applications for temporary visas, and the Public Prosecution Service (PPS) office.

The resulting summary statistics published annually by the BNRM provide useful information on the origin, gender, age, and other characteristics of victims. They indicate, for example, that about half of the reported victims of sex trafficking are from Central and Eastern Europe (mainly Bulgaria, Romania, Russia, and Ukraine) and another fourth from Africa (especially Nigeria). The data also show that the victims are almost exclusively female and that about 15 percent are below the age of 18.[1]

These data on victims are collected from three main sources. The first and central element of the network is the STV (Stichting Tegen Vrouwenhandel, or Dutch Foundation Against Trafficking in Women). STV is a decentralized, government-funded organization with 15 regional or local networks covering all areas of the country. It is responsible for finding trafficking victims a place in a shelter and for registering them in a database. Victims are usually referred to STV by the police, reception centers, private individuals, institutions for refugees and asylum seekers, and youth welfare organizations. Periodically, the STV provides an Excel file to the BNRM with aggregate data (i.e., without names and personal identities of victims) on the number of victims, grouped by sex, age, and place of origin.

The second data source is the police victim tracing system. Altogether, 25 regional police forces cover the country. When a person enters in contact with a police station, police officials use a list of indicators as an instrument to help identify victims. Information given by the potential victim is translated into an indicator, which scores a certain number of points. Any person with a score greater than a given threshold is treated as a possible victim of trafficking and is referred to STV. For example, a combination of "Sleeping the night at the workplace" and "Somebody else arranged the journey or the visa" places the women in the status of "possible victim of trafficking."

A third source of information on victims is the so-called B-9 regulation. The B-9 regulation (section B-9 of the Aliens Act Implementation Guidelines) allows foreigners who are possible victims or witnesses of human trafficking to remain temporarily in the Netherlands during the investigation and prosecution, thus remaining available to the police and the PPS. Victims who decide to report the offense after their three-month reflection period benefit from reception and accommodation facilities, medical and legal assistance, and provisions relating to maintenance. These victims are then registered by the Aliens Administrative System and the Immigration and Naturalisation Service (IND). The BNRM has access to the IND files, with detailed information on all the registered persons.

In addition to identified victims, the statistical analysis of the BNRM provides useful information about offenders. Statistics show that 25 to 55 cases are investigated every year and that the police arrest annually between 100 and 200 suspects. Contrary to some stereotypes, not all traffickers are male foreigners belonging to mafia-type organizations. Although 75 percent of all cases involve cross-border trafficking, no fewer than 40 percent are Dutch nationals, including owners of sex establishments, and 25 percent of suspects are actually women. Only half of the cases involve large criminal networks, and the other half involve a maximum of five persons. In two-thirds of the cases, victims were forced to hand over all their incomes to these traffickers.

The information on traffickers is collected from the police investigations that are completed and sent to the Public Prosecution Office. From the police, the BNRM obtains information about the number of investigations that are completed and referred to the PPS during a particular year. Police officials provide both qualitative and quantitative information on modalities of recruitment, means of coercion, number of suspects in each investigation, nationality of suspects, and travel routes.

The PPS also provides data on traffickers. Each year, the BNRM receives a file that contains information from all the Public Prosecution Services offices in the country. The BNRM then extracts the subfile related to human trafficking. Criminal cases against individual suspects may involve several criminal offenses. The analysis of the data provides the BNRM with information on the number of suspects and on their sociodemographic characteristics, the settlement for most serious crimes, the sentences imposed, and the appeals that are lodged.

Despite the fact that the BNRM cannot link the various databases it receives—and hence is not in a position to know if the same victim appears in the different files—this system provides a unique example of good practice.

Simple criminal statistics also exist in other countries—and remain extremely useful even if no attempt is made to complement such data with information from other sources. The German police, for example, issues a yearly report on human trafficking, the *Lagebild Menschenhandel,* that provides data on the number of investigations and the number of registered victims as well as the number of registered suspects. The report also documents the forms of coercion that are used. Thus, according to the Bundeskriminalamt (2003) report, among the victims of trafficking into forced sexual exploitation, about one-third had agreed to work in prostitution before being exploited, half claim to have been deceived into prostitution, and 10 percent report having been forced through physical violence. Overall, half of the victims reported violence while they were exploited, and threats against families were the most frequently reported form of coercion.

The Brazilian Ministry of Labour and Employment similarly collects data on the number and characteristics of people in "slave labor" conditions who are liberated by labor inspection services. These data can be used to monitor the trend in the number of rescued workers. Figure 9.1 shows how this number increased from fewer than 500 liberated workers in the mid-1990s to 2,000 and more liberated workers in more recent years. Chapter 1 in this book relies extensively on the database from these labor inspection services, illustrating how much precious information can be squeezed out of such data for the purpose of developing or adjusting policy responses.

**Figure 9.1  Number of Liberated "Slave Workers" per Year in Brazil**

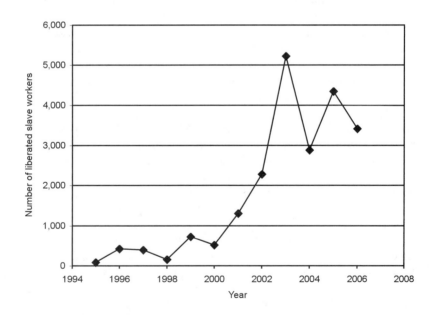

*Source:* Sakamoto (2005).

Reported cases can also be aggregated at the global level. The United States, for example, collects interesting data on the global progress of law enforcement responses. The 2007 *Trafficking in Persons Report* explains that the US Trafficking Victims Protection Reauthorization Act (TVPRA) of 2005 required that foreign governments (the so-called Tier 1 countries) provide the Department of State with data on trafficking investigations, prosecutions, convictions, and sentences in order to be considered in full compliance with the US minimum standard for the elimination of trafficking. The data received by the United States show that the number of convictions in the world has barely increased, from 2,815 in 2003 to 3,160 in 2006 (United States 2007, p. 36). This is a disappointing result.

### Expanding Current Efforts

To date, good practices in the area of data collection remain scarce. National statistics on forced labor or human trafficking are only collected in a handful of countries. The US *Trafficking in Persons Report* regularly points out that many governments in both developed and developing countries fail to provide updated, centralized law enforcement statistics, making it impossible to determine whether or not there was improvement in antitrafficking efforts. Furthermore, even when countries *do* centralize data, statistics often remain exclusively focused on trafficking for sexual exploitation—leaving cases of labor exploitation in the shadow. The data on identified victims thus suffer from partial coverage. In some developing countries, reliable data are completely missing.

There are a number of efforts to close these gaps in data collection. The EU Action Plan against trafficking calls on Europol to develop common guidelines for the collection of data in all EU member states, covering both trafficking for sexual exploitation and trafficking for labor exploitation. At the same time, the International Centre for Migration Policy Development (ICMPD) has been providing support for data collection and information management to enhance antitrafficking responses in the countries of southeastern Europe, in coordination with other initiatives and programs related to data collection in the region. The International Organization for Migration (IOM) also collects data in this region through its victim assistance program.

There is a need, however, to scale up these efforts for better and more comprehensive data collection at the national level and to diversify the sources of the data. A recent expert group from the European Commission highlighted the fact that human trafficking "requires efforts that go beyond the collation of existing national crime statistics" and proposed that member states should also collect data "from relevant NGO's and labour inspectorates, supplemented by open source information (media reports, academic studies)" (European Commission 2007, p. 1).

In fact, official statistics have not kept pace with the recent growth in media reports on the various forms of forced labor and human trafficking. Indeed, press reports have increased dramatically in recent years, as a result of the growing awareness in all parts of the world. Exploring the content of nine leading newspapers or news agencies representing the main regions of the world,[2] we observed that during the 2004–2007 period, reporting increased by about 300 percent (see Figure 9.2).

Labor inspection services, trade unions, and NGOs could be a rich source of data. Many of these institutions—and many of the researchers working with them—are still little aware of forced labor or human trafficking, however. There is also a demand on the part of these institutions for a clear set of operational indicators to help them recognize actual cases of forced labor. Without clear indicators, labor inspectors and others run the risk of not recognizing forced labor when they see it or—conversely—of seeing forced labor where it does not exist.

### Clarifying Definitions

This brings us to the last issue we wish to highlight in this section, namely the need for clear definitions. The 1930 ILO Convention (No. 29) defines forced

**Figure 9.2  Percentage Increase in Press Reports of Forced Labor**

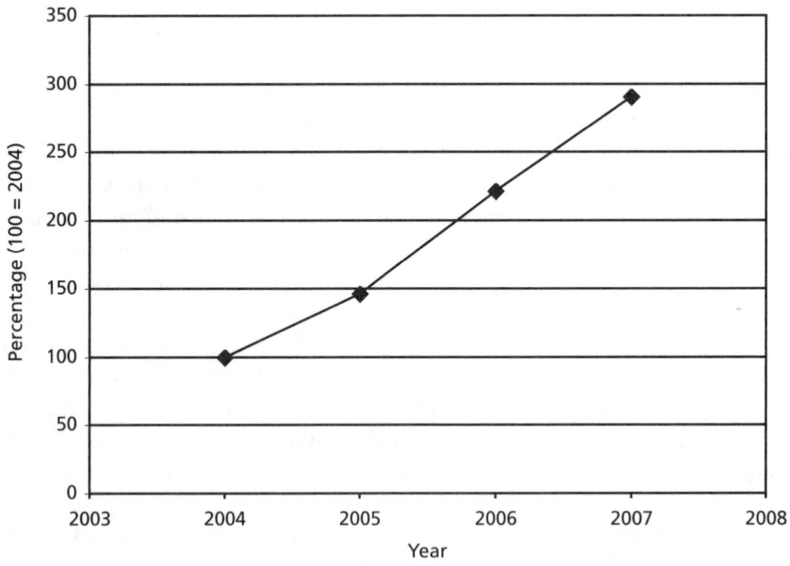

*Source:* Sakamoto (2005).

or compulsory labor as "all work or service which is exacted from any person under the menace of any penalty and for which the said person has not offered himself voluntarily" (Art. 2.1). Hence, forced labor is not just equivalent to low wages or poor working conditions. The above definition in fact highlights two essential elements: the "menace of penalty" and the "involuntariness." Accordingly, a situation can qualify as forced labor when people are subjected to psychological or physical coercion (the menace of a penalty) in order to perform some work or service that they would otherwise not have freely chosen (the involuntariness).

In practice, however, coercion can take many different forms—some of which are more easily observable than others. In the worst cases, victims are locked up, and their physical movements are restricted. Some people may be in slavery-like situations, attached with chains. In the modern world, however, bonds are usually invisible and the forms of coercion are more subtle—as we have seen throughout this book. They include the menace of violence or death, threats toward the victim's family, the confiscation of identity documents, the threat of denunciation to immigration authorities, or even the menace of supernatural retaliation. In many cases, the initial consent of the victim is obtained through fraud or deception, and victims only find out later—when they discover the true nature of the activity or the conditions in which it is performed— that they are not free to withdraw their labor. Debt bondage also occupies a prominent place in modern forced labor, with people being forced to work in order to pay back a manipulated debt or a fraudulent wage advance.

In light of these complications, a recent ILO (2005b) publication suggested that the following six elements point to a forced labor or a trafficking situation: (1) physical or sexual violence, (2) restriction of movement of the worker, (3) requiring work in order to pay back a debt, (4) withholding wages or refusing to pay the worker at all, (5) retention of passports and identity documents, and (6) threat of denunciation to immigration authorities. These, however, remain very general indicators, and researchers—particularly statisticians—will continue to have difficulties with the application of the concept of forced labor. Where, for example, does forced labor start and stop in the sex industry? At what particular moment do poor working conditions and labor exploitation in the Amazon region turn into forced labor? At what point can a person of slave descent in West Africa be considered to be free from forced labor? And what about child labor: can any child labor be considered as "voluntary" at all?[3]

Another difficult area relates to the difference between forced labor and human trafficking. According to the UN Protocol to Prevent, Suppress, and Punish Trafficking in Persons, Especially Women and Children (generally known as the Palermo Protocol), which was adopted in 2000, human trafficking is the "recruitment, transportation, transfer, harbouring or receipt of persons, . . . for the purpose of exploitation." And "exploitation shall include, as a minimum, the exploitation of the prostitution of others or other forms of sexual exploitation, forced labour or services, slavery or practices similar to slavery, or the removal of organs."

This definition leaves much open room for interpretation, and sometimes confusion, particularly with regard to the question of whether movement is necessarily a part of this definition. Another question is whether the concept of trafficking only relates to cross-border trafficking by organized crime (since the Palermo Protocol is attached to a UN convention against transnational organized crime) or whether it can also be usefully applied to domestic problems.

For statistical purposes, the ILO considers that trafficking includes all cases of forced labor or services that involve (1) the geographic movement of victims from one place of origin to a distinct place of exploitation, either across or within national borders; and (2) the recruitment of victims by an intermediary who transports or transfers victims to the place of destination.

Although somewhat arbitrary, this approach has the merit of creating a clear distinction between trafficking and forced labor and characterizes trafficking related to work or services as a subset of the broader problem of forced labor (see Figure 9.3; see also the Foreword by Roger Plant). More work will be needed in the future, however, to develop a consensus among researchers and practitioners as to the boundaries between the two concepts.

In any event, there is a need to develop consensus on a list of operational indicators that can point toward a situation of forced labor or human trafficking and also on the combination of indicators that are necessary to characterize a situation as forced labor or trafficking, at least for the purpose of data collection. In the case of trafficking, for example, operational indicators are

**Figure 9.3  The Intersection Between Forced Labor and Trafficking**

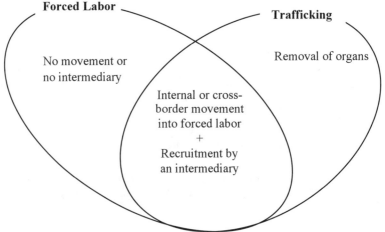

needed because key terms used in the Palermo Protocol definition of trafficking require further elaboration. In particular, there are questions as to what should be understood by terms such as *coercion, deception, fraud, abuse of power or of a position of vulnerability, control over another person,* and *exploitation.* Without further clarification there is a risk that interpretations may continue to diverge widely from one country to another or even within countries, from one researcher or practitioner to the other. To some people, these definitional issues that affect the quality and quantity of statistics may seem purely academic—since what really matters is that the suffering of *all* the victims can be stopped. In practice, however, they are not. An article in the *Washington Post* (Markon 2007), for example, pointed out that although more than US$150 million had been spent on a "war on human trafficking," the US government had only found 1,362 victims since the year 2000. The article then quoted a criminologist who concluded that the problem of trafficking "is being blown out of proportion," implying that the antitrafficking effort should perhaps be scaled down. This is possible indeed. Another possibility, however, is that these numbers are low because they rely exclusively on criminal statistics, reflect a focus of law enforcement on the sex industry, and result from a lack of awareness and clear operational indicators that would help labor inspection services, trade unions, NGOs, and others to detect and report more cases.

## Global and National Estimates

We now turn to global estimates. Global estimates serve a different purpose than the national statistics described in the preceding section. Whereas national statistics support national policies, global estimates underpin global responses and global awareness. They should guide multilateral and bilateral agencies in identifying priorities and in designing appropriate technical cooperation programs, with judicious geographic and thematic distributions. Where are the highest cross-national trafficking flows? What is the most frequent form of forced labor in Asia or Latin America? Are victims mostly women, children, or men? All these questions and others are crucial in the design of appropriate responses. In addition, global numbers can underpin empirically based global awareness-raising and resource-mobilization campaigns.

The ILO has estimated that there are at least 12.3 million people who are subjected to various forms of forced labor worldwide. Of these, 2.4 million have been trafficked, both across borders and internally (ILO 2005a, pp. 12–14). The US government has estimated that every year 600,000 to 800,000 people are trafficked across borders (see United States Government Accountability Office 2006, p. 12). Finally, Kevin Bales, an expert in modern slavery, estimated that 27 million people are victims of modern "slavery" (Bales 2000, p. 8). Taken together, these numbers suggest a range of 600,000 to 2.4 million trafficked victims, out of a total of 12.3 to 27 million people in forced labor.

To produce their estimates, both the US government and the ILO have gone beyond criminal statistics and have collected reports from open sources that included information on the number of victims. Overall, the US government collected 1,594 trafficking reports for the period 2000 and 2001, and the ILO collected more than 5,000 forced labor and trafficking reports for the period 1995–2004 (Kutnick, Belser, and Danailova-Trainor 2005). Both organizations distinguished between reported "cases" (or "incidents") and "aggregate estimates." Reported cases can be defined as individual incidents that occurred at one moment in time in a specific geographic area with victims who were (or could have been) identified. Aggregate estimates are estimates that claim to include both reported and unreported numbers.

The methodologies to produce global estimates differed, however, between the two organizations. The US government used a procedure called Markov chain Monte Carlo (MCMC) simulation, and the ILO made an extrapolation based on a methodology known as "capture-recapture." Although the US government has never published a detailed account of its methodology, such a detailed account can be found in an ILO working paper (Kutnick, Belser, and Danailova-Trainor 2005). The ILO has published a report that contains all the details of its methodology (see Belser, de Cock, and Mehran 2005). In theory both methodologies should give reasonably accurate results, since they are based on the mathematical theory of probabilities. In practice, however, they both suffer from the same main weakness: the relatively poor quality of the underlying data. This has been highlighted in a report by the US Government Accountability Office (GAO) to the House of Representatives (see United States Government Accountability Office 2006). The problem, of course, is that no better data are currently available. So the choice at the present stage really is between tentative estimates and no estimates at all. As we have already pointed out, the ILO methodology is in the public domain and available for anyone to improve or criticize.

In the remainder of this chapter, we first argue that despite their underlying weaknesses, and also despite apparent differences, existing global estimates are in fact rather conservative and also remarkably consistent. Here we include not only the two institutional estimates by the ILO and the US government but also the global estimate by antislavery activist Kevin Bales. We then argue that there is only one way to solve the legitimate doubts about the accuracy of existing estimates, namely, to produce better country-level estimates that can then be aggregated into a more solid global estimate.

## Trafficking Figures

We first discuss the trafficking figures. Although there is a relatively large gap between the two existing figures, this is not altogether surprising. Indeed, the ILO figure includes both internal and international trafficking, whereas the US government includes exclusively international trafficking. Taking into account internal trafficking in populated countries such as India or China, it would not seem implausible that the inclusion of internal trafficking would more than double the US government number. Also it has to be pointed out that US government figures describe an annual flow of trafficked people, whereas the ILO describes a stock of people in forced labor. If trafficked victims are exploited on average during one year in the place of destination, however, then flow and stock figures should be identical.

Both the US government and the ILO have also separated trafficking for sexual exploitation. The US government found that 80 percent of victims are female and that 66 percent of victims are trafficked for sexual exploitation (see US Government Accountability Office 2006, p. 12). This means that every year there are about 400,000 to 525,000 victims of cross-border sex trafficking. The ILO, by contrast, found that the total number of victims of both cross-border and internal sex trafficking is somewhere between 1 million and 1.7 million (Belser 2005, p. 6).

How do these figures compare with what we know about the magnitude of prostitution in general? There exist no official statistics on overall prostitution, and nonofficial estimates vary rather dramatically. The estimated number of women in the sex industry in Cambodia, for example, varies between 15,000 and 100,000 (Derks 2005, p. 123). This clearly creates some difficulty in assessing the extent of prostitution worldwide. But we tried anyway. Collecting all country estimates we could find and computing the averages for the 45 countries on which we could find data, we came up with a picture that looks like the one in Figure 9.4. We see that the incidence of prostitution consistently lies below 0.5 percent of the population, except for two outliers, and more than 85 percent of the country estimates are below 0.35 percent of the population.

**Figure 9.4  Share of Population in Prostitution**

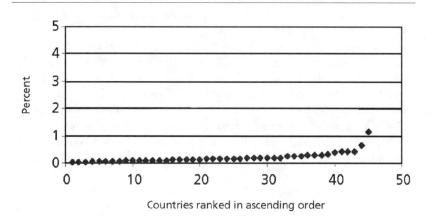

Countries ranked in ascending order

In Switzerland, for example, prostitution estimates appear to vary between 11,500 and 23,000. These figures suggest that between one and three in every 1,000 inhabitants are in prostitution. Looking at cities and regions in more detail, we observe—not surprisingly—that the share of prostitution per inhabitants is typically higher in the cities than in the rural areas. In cities there are typically 3 to 6 persons in prostitution in every 1,000 inhabitants, whereas in rural areas the ratio goes down to less than 1 in every 1,000 inhabitants. Although these numbers are not necessarily representative, they are in line with most other estimates for European countries.

Estimates also exist for developing countries. In their analysis on the number of "sex workers" in Cambodia, Steinfatt, Baker, and Beesey (2002), for example, used an original geographic mapping technique to enumerate major "sex work venues" in Phnom Penh, with multiple interviews at each venue to establish the total numbers. Combined with a sample of smaller venues, the authors estimated that, as of June 2002, there were a total of 5,250 sex workers in Phnom Penh. Based on these findings, and on complementary work in rural areas, the author extrapolated that there were 18,256 sex workers in Cambodia. Other estimates are somewhat higher, with a (much-criticized) maximum estimate of 80,000 people, quoted in various sources. If we compute the average of all the available figures, we find an estimate of 42,000 sex workers in Cambodia. This represents an average figure of 0.3 percent of Cambodia's total population of 14 million, in between a minimum of 0.13 percent and a maximum of 0.57 percent.

So how many people are in prostitution worldwide? We have calculated our own guesstimate by adding up all available country estimates. If there were several estimates for one country, as in the case of Cambodia, we have computed the average. We have then computed regional estimates as shown in Table 9.1. In the first column we have computed regional estimates by multiplying the region's total population by the *median* of country estimates, and in the second column we have multiplied the region's total population by the *average* of country estimates. We have then computed a global estimate by aggregation of regional estimates.

With this method we find that worldwide there are between 13 and 15 million people—mostly women—in prostitution. There is some regional variation, with the lowest share in industrial countries and the highest in Asia and Latin America. Overall, however, the share of prostitution varies within the relatively narrow range of 0.15 to 0.44 percent of the population. The estimates shown in Table 9.1 must, of course, be interpreted with caution. Not all country studies that were used to compute these estimates are based on sound or even transparent methodologies. Some are probably just "guesstimates." Thus the estimate is really only indicative.

Our guesstimate implies that—if all numbers were accurate—the US government figures of cross-border trafficking would represent 2.5 to 3.0 percent

**Table 9.1 Total Prostitution, Estimated Totals**

|  | Estimated Prostitution Based on Country Median (incidence in % of population) | | Estimated Prostitution Based on Country Averages (incidence in % of population) | |
| --- | --- | --- | --- | --- |
| Industrial | 1,306,000 | (0.15) | 1,285,000 | (0.14) |
| Transition | 695,000 | (0.17) | 784,000 | (0.19) |
| Asia | 9,072,000 | (0.29) | 9,114,000 | (0.29) |
| Sub-Saharan Africa | 892,000 | (0.16) | 905,000 | (0.16) |
| Latin America | 1,300,000 | (0.26) | 2,183,000 | (0.44) |
| Middle East and North Africa | 440,000 | (0.17) | 628,000 | (0.24) |
| World | 13,716,000 | (0.22) | 14,885,000 | (0.24) |

of the global prostitution figure, whereas the ILO figure would suggest that cross-border and internal trafficking represents between 8 and 11 percent of all prostitution in the world. Although some commentators may find the numbers of trafficking victims "overblown" in light of the number of detected victims (see earlier discussion), when looked at in proportion to overall prostitution they do not seem implausibly high to us. In fact, they are probably on the conservative side when compared to estimates available from case studies in the sex industry (see, for example, the study on Thailand in Lim [1998] or the Cambodia study by Steinfatt, Baker, and Beesey [2002]).

Another element in support of the view that current estimates are conservative is the large amounts of profits that are up for grabs for traffickers. Indeed, we know that most of the time human trafficking and particularly sexual exploitation are motivated by profits. According to one estimate, trafficking into sexual exploitation generates US$27.8 billion in annual profits for traffickers (Belser 2005). This may seem very high, but taken together with the ILO estimated number of victims, it represents between US$1,400 and US$2,200 in annual profits per victim—which seems rather conservative. And even though the monthly figures may be lower in developing countries, these are often *much* higher in rich industrial countries where customers sometimes pay up to US$100 or more for sexual services.

Whole groups of people benefit from this modern slave trade. Profits are used to pay criminals in all parts of the chain of exploitation: the recruiters who act in the place of origin of the victims, the intermediaries involved in transportation and supervision, and the final exploiter who puts the victims to work—generally a pimp or a brothel owner. Trafficking victims are exploited day after day, month after month, sometimes for several years, with no or little wages. They produce services and products whose value is captured by the traffickers.

*Forced Labor and "Slavery"*

We now also turn briefly to forced labor and "slavery" figures. We have already indicated that the ILO puts the overall figure at a minimum of 12.3 million, and Bales estimates 27 million. This may seem like a large difference. At the same time, both numbers are—as they should logically be—lower than less extreme and more widely known labor market problems or challenges. The ILO estimated, for example, the number of jobless people in the world at 192 million (International Labour Organization 2006b), the number of international migrants at about 175 million (International Labour Organization 2004), and the number of child laborers at around 217 million (International Labour Organization 2006c, p. 6). This implies that the number of unemployed persons, the number of migrants, and the number of working children are each about 15 times higher than the number of people held in modern slavery. This appears a plausible ratio. Any forced labor estimates that would run into the hundreds of millions of victims would be surprisingly high in light of these other figures.

Table 9.2 shows that the difference between the two global estimates by the ILO and Bales arises to a large extent because of different estimates for Asia. The difference there is perhaps due to different estimation methodology. Indeed, although the ILO used reported cases, Bales's method involved the aggregation of country estimates from secondary sources validated by country experts. But most likely, the difference is due to the large uncertainty about the true magnitude of forced labor in just one country, namely India—where the number of people in bonded labor remains a controversial subject. Country estimates in India vary between a few thousand victims (according to official figures) and several million victims (according to various NGOs).

**Table 9.2  Forced Labor/"Slavery" Figures by Region**

|                          | ILO        | Bales      |
|--------------------------|------------|------------|
| Industrialized countries | 360,000    | 348,000    |
| Transition countries     | 210,000    | 92,500     |
| Latin America            | 1,320,000  | 381,900    |
| Sub-Saharan Africa       | 660,000    | 591,500    |
| Arab states              | 260,000    | 74,500     |
| Asia (including India)   | 9,490,000  | 26,402,000 |
| India                    | —          | 22,000,000 |
| Total                    | 12,300,000 | 27,890,400 |

*Sources:* ILO (2005a); Bales (2003).
*Note:* Figures for Bales were computed from the higher figures of the country ranges published in Bales (2003).

In the future, the only obvious way to resolve this uncertainty is to conduct a country-wide survey in India. This was last attempted by the Gandhi
Peace Foundation and the National Labour Institute in 1978–1979, shortly
after the enactment of the Bonded Labour System (Abolition) Act in 1976. The
study randomly sampled 1,000 villages in the ten Indian states thought to be
affected by bonded labor—a system of forced labor where agricultural workers
are attached to landowners. In these villages, a total of 5,585 bonded laborers
were identified. This number was then extrapolated to the 450,000 existing villages in the ten states under consideration, leading to an estimated 2.6 million
bonded laborers in India. The government of India has always rejected these
findings on the basis that the methodology was flawed, hence the need for consultations on methodology *before* the implementation of any sensitive survey
on forced labor.

In the meantime, the global estimates also provide information on the relative proportions of different forms of forced labor. This is perhaps as interesting as the absolute value of the estimate. The ILO global estimate has shown,
for example, that about four-fifths of modern forced labor (about 10 million
out of 12.3 million) takes place in the private economy rather than in the state
sector (see Figure 9.5). Most of this exploitation by private agents—which is
the subject of this book—takes place in the illegal or underground economy.

**Figure 9.5  Forced Labor: Economic, State-imposed, and
Sexual Exploitation (%)**

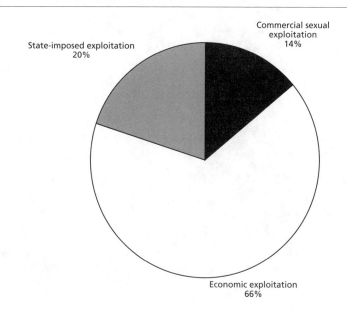

It is also worth noting that "modern slavery" is not exclusively—or even in majority—a problem of sexual exploitation. According to the ILO, there are at least five times more people in labor exploitation than in forced sexual exploitation (ILO 2005b). This, in fact, should not be too surprising, given that the large majority of the world's 3 billion people or so in the labor force work in agriculture, industry, or services, rather than in prostitution. Thus, even if forced labor affects a much smaller proportion in agriculture, domestic services, and construction, the absolute number of victims is likely to be higher than for forced prostitution. An excessive focus on "human trafficking" may in fact distort this picture and lead to a misrepresentation of the proportion of people in forced sexual exploitation relative to those in forced economic exploitation. In Figure 9.6 we show that about one-third of trafficking is for labor exploitation, as opposed to sexual and mixed forms of exploitation. This is unrepresentative of the overall picture of forced labor shown in Figure 9.5, where labor exploitation represents the majority of victims.

Of course, none of the above means that trafficking for sexual exploitation or state-imposed forced labor should fall off the public agenda. Forced prostitution is certainly a crime that deserves special attention in regard to the severity of human suffering inflicted on the victims. And there also remain serious problems in terms of state-imposed forced labor, particularly in Myanmar (formerly Burma), where people have been reported to work involuntarily to clear land mines, transport military material, or construct roads. One benefit of the global estimate is to increase awareness that—contrary to what may have been the case in the past—the bulk of modern slavery is now coercion in the labor market.

**Figure 9.6  Trafficking into Forced Labor: Economic and Sexual Exploitation (%)**

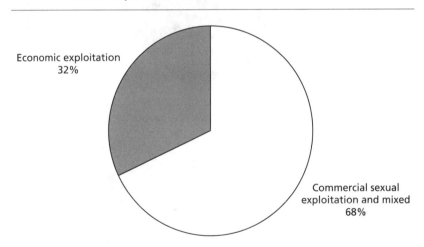

## National Estimates

As we have already indicated, the margins of error of any future global esti-mate will probably only be substantially reduced if it can rely on solid national estimates.[4] Indeed, the best method to derive global estimates of a phenome-non is usually to aggregate corresponding national estimates into regional and then global figures. This, at least, has been the approach taken by the ILO since the 1970s for deriving global estimates and projections of the economi-cally active population and more recently for calculating global and regional estimates of unemployment and of child labor (see Belser, de Cock, and Meh-ran 2005).

But robust national estimates would not only be useful for the purpose of computing global estimates. They would be even more useful at the national level to design and allocate appropriate resources to combat the problem, and especially to establish benchmarks for monitoring progress over time. Coun-tries such as Brazil or Pakistan were highlighted in the 2005 *Global Report* of the ILO as good examples of countries that have put in place strong policies against "slave labor" and "bonded labor," respectively. Unfortunately, because of the absence of any reliable country estimates, there are so far no indications of the positive impact that these policies have had on the overall number of people in forced labor.

In the case of Brazil, the same number of 25,000 victims of "slave labor" in the Amazon region has now been quoted for nearly a decade. In Niger, a widely quoted figure was produced by one NGO, which may have overesti-mated the magnitude of forced labor. In both cases, it would be much better if official institutions would produce their own figures, which they and their partners will trust and which they can use to monitor trends. In the area of human trafficking, there is a similar need to determine whether the low num-ber of identified victims (discussed in the preceding section) reflects a low number of actual victims or whether it represents a very small tip of a much larger iceberg.

Of course, technically country estimates represent one of the most serious challenges on the current research agenda. Estimating forced labor and human trafficking in a given area or country is difficult under the best of circum-stances. As discussed in Berk (2007), the methodological challenges include two major problems. The first one is how best to obtain a representative sample that can be used for extrapolation. The second one is how best to obtain accu-rate information from the people who are sampled. We address both questions in the remainder of this chapter.

### Probability Sampling

To be able to generalize results from a sample to a larger population of interest (such as, say, from a sample of returned migrants to all returned migrants in a country), we know that two key conditions must be met: (1) the sample must be obtained through so-called probability sampling, in which every member of the population has a known nonzero probability of being selected; and (2) the sample must be large enough so that the margins of error of the final estimates can be reasonably low (the larger the sample, the smaller the risks that the characteristics of the sample are different from the characteristics of the larger population). If these conditions are not met, chances are that our sample will be biased and will be unrepresentative of the larger population. That is, sampling errors will be large. In such cases, results obtained from the sample cannot be generalized to the larger population of interest.

In the simplest cases, probability sampling can be obtained through simple random sampling by means of devices such as "random number tables," which will help to randomly select, say, 1 person out 2,000 in a telephone book. These simple techniques will not work when people in forced labor are hidden or clustered. In such cases, simple random sampling is likely to miss all victims and wrongly conclude that there is no forced labor. Here we would need to rely on sampling techniques that have recently been developed to estimate elusive and hard-to-detect populations, such as the homeless or drug addicts.

It is worth pointing out, however, that people who are in forced labor or who have been trafficked are not necessarily hidden or hard to detect. In fact many are not. In India or Pakistan, people in bonded labor openly work in fields and other legitimate economic sectors such as construction. In Niger, people in slavery-like situations, who work long hours as domestics or agricultural workers in exchange for food, are not particularly hidden. In the Gulf countries, migrant workers typically gather in clubs on weekends where they can easily be interviewed. Finally, indigenous peoples working in debt bondage on farms in Bolivia and Paraguay certainly live in remote places but are not impossible to reach. These are only a few examples.

In addition, it is certainly true that trafficked migrants can be clustered or very difficult to detect in places of destination. After their exploitation ends, they often return to their countries of origin, however, where they can be surveyed much more easily. In all such cases, it seems in fact possible to use samples from standard surveys and generalize the results.

### Obtaining Reliable Information

Perhaps more problematic is how to obtain reliable information from the persons who are surveyed. Returned migrants may be particularly reluctant to admit having been trafficked, especially into forced prostitution. For statistical purposes, however, this problem may be overcome by asking indirect questions. These questions should aim at detecting the existence or not of the three dimensions that typically come into play in cases of forced labor, namely "deception," "coercion," and "exploitation."

If asked the right questions in a sensitive way, pilot experience suggests, people are often willing to provide information. This at least is the conclusion from a pilot test in one Eastern European country, in which labor migration is considered as a main socioeconomic problem and which is also known as a place of origin for the international trafficking of people into sexual and labor exploitation. In collaboration with the national statistical office of this country, we developed some questions designed to identify former trafficking victims among current or returned migrants in the context of a larger labor force survey. Questions related to deceptive recruitment, coercion, and exploitation were asked of 1,005 respondents: of these, 750 were members of households with at least one migrant worker currently abroad, and 255 were returned migrants.

We asked a number of questions designed to indicate whether returned migrants had been deceived. Deception usually happens at the phase of recruitment, when a worker is promised a job and later finds out that the job is different or discovers that he has to perform some tasks that were not part of the initial agreement. Such deception conflicts with the principle of "voluntariness": a worker would perhaps not have consented to the job offer if properly and fully informed. Taking the example of forced prostitution, deception can cover at least two different situations: (1) cases where a woman is promised a job that does not exist and is then forced into prostitution, or (2) situations where forced prostitution occurs in addition to the normal tasks (of a domestic worker, a dancer, or any other job); this may happen after several weeks or months on the job. In both cases, the woman had not offered herself voluntarily for prostitution. Of course, the use of deception to obtain a person's consent is not limited to prostitution but also applies to other sectors of activity.

We also asked questions about whether returned migrants were coerced. For practical purposes, the concept of "coercion" regroups all the means used by an employer or a recruiter to force someone to work against his or her will or to prevent him or her from leaving. These means may be psychological or physical. It is not only people who are physically locked up who are prevented from leaving an employer. Retention of salary can be used as a means of coercion, as the person who has already worked for weeks or months and is waiting for his or her salary will not leave before having received the wages that are due. Confiscation of identity papers is another such means.

Finally, we asked whether—and why—returned migrants ever felt exploited. "Exploitation" can be characterized by such things as excessive hours of work, a low salary, or hazardous conditions of work. The sector of activity in which exploitation takes place is not taken into account in the definition, as it can be any activity in the primary, secondary, or tertiary economic sector. Special attention must be given to prostitution (or related activities), where the risk of exploitation is particularly high. One can note that the indicators of decent work (social security, conditions of work, etc.) are not explicitly introduced in this research, although it may be interesting in the future to have a global approach for measuring the whole range of working situations, from forced labor to decent work.

We show some of the results in Table 9.3. On deception and involuntariness, the results show that more than 20 percent of the sampled returned migrants received either a lower salary than agreed upon or had working conditions that were worse than agreed upon. At the other end of the spectrum, 15 percent

**Table 9.3  Forced Labor Indicators**

|  | Family of Migrant | | Returned Migrant | |
|---|---|---|---|---|
|  | Yes | No | Yes | No |
| *Deception* |  |  |  |  |
| Job was different | 75 | 427 | 38 | 189 |
| Transferred to other employer |  |  |  |  |
| without consent | 20 | 518 | 16 | 211 |
| Obliged to work day and night | 35 | 483 | 8 | 216 |
| Working conditions were worse | 80 | 415 | 60 | 166 |
| Salary was lower | 143 | 376 | 71 | 155 |
| Location of workplace |  |  |  |  |
| was different | 43 | 452 | 29 | 197 |
| *Means of coercion* |  |  |  |  |
| Physical sexual violence | 7 | 570 | 3 | 224 |
| Nonpayment of wages or |  |  |  |  |
| salary withheld | 64 | 492 | 31 | 196 |
| Denied contact with family | 3 | 613 | 5 | 221 |
| Threats against person | 10 | 552 | 6 | 218 |
| Threats against family | 0 | 607 | 1 | 223 |
| Physically confined | 1 | 577 | 7 | 219 |
| Identity papers confiscated | 17 | 562 | 17 | 209 |
| Threats of deportation |  |  |  |  |
| or immigration | 16 | 532 | 13 | 210 |
| Loans or advance imposed |  |  |  |  |
| or falsified | 3 | 521 | 3 | 222 |
| *Forms of exploitation* |  |  |  |  |
| Low salary | 196 | 321 | 89 | 136 |
| Delayed payment | 169 | 366 | 67 | 160 |
| Excessive working hours/days | 110 | 378 | 56 | 167 |
| Violence from employer | 14 | 504 | 10 | 215 |
| Violence from colleagues | 10 | 518 | 10 | 216 |
| Violence from customers, clients | 12 | 487 | 16 | 205 |
| Hazardous work without protection | 71 | 394 | 54 | 168 |

reported that the job was different than the one agreed upon, 11 percent reported that the geographic location of the employment was different than the one agreed upon, and, finally, 3 percent were unexpectedly "obliged to work day and night." People were then asked whether the "employer or recruiter ever used means of coercion to force [them] to work or prevent [them] from leaving the job." Results show that a few returned migrants reported physical violence (1 percent), manipulated debts (1 percent), threats (2 percent), or physical confinement (3 percent). A larger proportion reported threats of denunciation to immigration authorities (5 percent), confiscation of identity documents (7 percent), and nonpayment or retention of wages (12 percent).

And when people were also asked if they ever felt exploited and for what reasons, about 35 percent said they felt exploited because of low wages, slightly more than 20 percent felt exploited because of excessive working hours or hazardous work without protection, and 4 to 6 percent felt exploited through physical violence. We emphasize again that the questionnaire was not applied to a representative sample and that the exercise was designed mainly to find out whether returned migrants were willing to speak out or not. The results are not representative.

But the results clearly show that people are willing to speak. One remaining challenge then is to combine people's answers and decide who should be counted as in forced labor and who should not. At one end of the spectrum, people who report all three problems—deception, coercion, and exploitation—are clear cases of forced labor. At the other end, people who report exploitation without any deception or coercion cannot be counted as being in forced labor. In between these cases, however, there are some gray areas, including, for example, people who have been deceived and exploited without reporting coercion (people tricked into exploitative jobs abroad and who chose to stay anyway, perhaps to avoid humiliation back home). But here again, these dilemmas do not seem unsolvable.

Thus, although estimating the scale of forced labor or trafficking at the country level is a difficult technical task, we do believe that it is actually feasible. And it will be particularly useful as a benchmark to monitor actual trends (and not just trends in the number of cases detected by the police or others). It would also allow a statistically robust analysis of the variables associated with forced labor, including the characteristics of victims, their sector of activity, or the geographic location of their exploitation. Ultimately, it would also contribute to solving the debate between those who believe that trafficking is one of the most important modern challenges to human rights and those who think that the problem is "overblown."

## Conclusion

In this chapter we have argued that improving forced labor and trafficking statistics is both important for policymaking and feasible. At one level, countries should follow the example of the Netherlands and a few others in setting up a data collection system from various sources. Sources should be as broad as possible and include not only criminal statistics but instead rely on a multiplicity of sources, including police registration systems, police investigation files, applications for temporary visa, public prosecution service offices, NGOs, trade unions, labor inspection services, and others. This would provide a more realistic picture than the limited statistics currently available at the country level.

At a second level, countries should also attempt to produce robust national estimates of the number of people in forced labor and trafficking based on scientific statistical methods. This is difficult but far from impossible. Currently, there only exist guesstimates that vary dramatically from one source to another and that seem to reflect subjective beliefs rather than empirical facts. Robust country estimates are the only way to monitor actual trends and the results of policies and to solve the debate generated by the low number of recorded cases. A by-product of national estimates will also be the possibility of improving global estimates. As long as no reliable national estimates exist, there cannot be more than tentative global estimates.

Although we do agree with the argument often heard that "one victim is one too many," we strongly disagree with the notion that statistics are not needed. Some antitrafficking advocates sometimes appear to think that quantitative analytical or policy tools somehow devalue the human drama of forced labor and human trafficking. We believe, on the contrary, that qualitative and quantitative approaches are complementary and that the failure to produce good statistics ultimately does the victims a dramatic disservice.

### Notes

1. This figure is calculated on the basis of all cases from the 2001–2005 reports in which age is known.

2. These are *allAfrica* (sub-Saharan Africa), *Gulf News* (United Arab Emirates), *O Globo* (Brazil), *El Comercio* (Peru), *Dawn* (Pakistan), *Hindu* (India), *Moscow Times* (Russia), *Le Monde* (France), and *New York Times* (United States).

3. For statistical purposes, child labor is considered by the ILO to amount to forced labor when the coercion is applied by someone other than the parents or when a child's work is the direct result of the parents' being in forced labor.

4. Country-level estimates differ, of course, from the country-level statistics that we discussed earlier, since the former should include both reported and unreported victims. Trafficking statistics or other "slave labor" statistics from labor inspection services only refer to reported cases and hence represent the visible "tip of the iceberg." That is, they refer to the number of known offenses, out of an unknown sum total of crimes committed (Walklate 2005). As was also highlighted by Bales (2000), the number of unknown cases is often referred to as the "dark figure of crime."

# References

Abba Souleymane, S. 1990. "La chefferie traditionnelle en question," *Politique Afri-caine,* no. 38, pp. 51–60.

Abdelkader, G. 2004. *Étude sur le dénombrement des victimes de l'esclavage au Niger.* Niamey: Anti-Slavery International and Timidria.

Abraham, K. G. 2005. "What we don't know could hurt us: Some reflections on the measurement of economic activity," *Journal of Economic Perspectives,* vol. 19, no. 3, pp. 3–18.

Adamou, A. 1979. *Agadez et sa région,* Etudes Nigériennes, No. 44. Niamey: IRSH.

Adji, S. 1991. *Logiques socio-communautaires et loyautés politiques en Afrique: Essai d'analyse de la construction de l'état au Niger,* doctorate thesis. Bordeaux: Université de Bordeaux.

———. 1997. *L'offre et la demande: Promotion de la démocratie et défense des droits de la personne humaine.* Niamey: Étude/ACDI.

———. 2002a. "Globalization and union strategies in Niger." In A. V. Jose, ed., *Organized labour in the 20th century.* Geneva: ILO, pp. 347–372.

———. 2002b. "Ethnicité, culture, et politique au Niger," *Alternative,* no. 277 (September).

Agrodev/Asian Development Bank. 2000. *Sindh rural development project: Social assessment report.* Islamabad.

Alavi, H. 1987. "Introduction to sociology of the developing societies." In Teodor Shanin, ed., *Peasants and peasant societies,* 2nd ed. Oxford: Blackwell, pp. 185–196.

Álvarez, A. J. 2003. "El bosque prohibido," *Mi Tierra–Iquitps,* September 15.

Amselle, J.-L.; M'bokolo, E. 1996. *Au cœur de l'ethnie.* Paris: La Découverte.

Anderson, B.; O'Connell Davidson, J. 2003. *Is trafficking in human beings demand driven? A multi-country pilot study.* Geneva: IOM.

Andrees, B. 2006. "Combating criminal activities in the recruitment of migrant workers." In C. Kuptsch, ed., *Merchants of labour.* Geneva: ILO/IILS, pp. 175–183.

———. 2008. *Forced labour and trafficking in Europe: How people are trapped in, live through, and come out,* Declaration Working Paper No. 57. Geneva: ILO.

———; van der Linden, M.N.J. 2005. "Designing trafficking research from a labour market perspective: The ILO experience." In International Organization for Migration,

*Data and research on human trafficking: A global survey* (Special Issue of *International Migration,* vol. 43, no. 1/2). Geneva: IOM.

Anggraeni, D. 2006. *Dreamseekers: Indonesian women as domestic workers in Asia.* Jakarta: ILO.

Anti-Slavery International. 2002. *Human traffic, human rights: Redefining victim protection.* London.

Arif, G. M. 2004. *Bonded labour in agriculture: A rapid assessment in Punjab and North West Frontier Province, Pakistan.* Islamabad: ILO.

Arrowsmith, J. 2006. *Temporary agency work in an enlarged European Union.* Dublin: European Foundation for the Improvement of Living and Working Conditions.

Asian Development Bank [ADB]. 2002. *Combating trafficking of women and children in South Asia,* RETA 5948 REG. Manila.

Assies, W. 2002. "From rubber estate to simple commodity production: Agrarian struggles in the northern Bolivian Amazon," *Journal of Peasant Studies,* vol. 29, nos. 3/4, pp. 83–130.

Averia, C. A. 2006. "Private recruitment agencies in the era of globalization: Challenges and responses—The case of the Philippines." In C. Kuptsch, ed., *Merchants of labour.* Geneva: ILO/IILS, pp. 47–52.

Bales, K. 2000. *Disposable people.* Berkeley: University of California Press.

———. 2003. "International labor standards: Quality of information and measures of progress in combating forced labor," *Comparative Labor Law and Policy Journal,* vol. 24, no. 2, pp. 321–364.

Baroin, C. 1982. "Organisation territoriale, organisation sociale," *Journal des Africanistes,* vol. 52, no. 1/2, pp. 223–224.

———. 1985. *Anarchie et cohésion sociale chez les Toubou. Les Daza—Keserda du Niger.* Cambridge: Cambridge University Press; Paris: Éditions de la Maison des Sciences de l'Homme.

Barrientos, S. 2007. *Global production systems and decent work,* Policy Integration Department Working Paper No. 77. Geneva: ILO.

Basu, K. 1986. "One kind of power." *Oxford Economic Papers,* vol. 38, no. 2, pp. 259–282.

Bedoya Garland, E. 1993. *Bonded Labour in Peru,* PhD diss. Binghamton: SUNY.

———; Bedoya Silva-Santisteban, A. 2005a. *El trabajo forzoso en la extracción de la madera en la Amazonía Peruana,* Declaration Working Paper No. 40. Geneva: ILO.

———. 2005b. *Enganche y servidumbre por deudas en Bolivia,* Declaration Working Paper No. 41. Geneva: ILO.

———. 2005c. *Servidumbre por deudas y marginación en el chaco de Paraguay,* Declaration Working Paper No. 45. Geneva: ILO.

Belser, P. 2005. *Forced labour and human trafficking: Estimating the profits,* Declaration Working Paper No. 42. Geneva: ILO.

———; Albracht, G.; Degrand-Guillaud, M.; and Kuntz, H. No date. "Enforcing labour standards in the global economy: Is the number of labour inspectors sufficient?" Geneva: ILO.

———; de Cock, M.; Mehran, F. 2005. *ILO minimum estimate of forced labour in the world.* Geneva: ILO.

Berg, J.; Ernst, C.; Auer, P. 2006. *Meeting the employment challenge: Argentina, Brazil, and Mexico in the global economy.* Boulder: Lynne Rienner.

———; Kucera, D. 2008. "Introduction." In J. Berg and D. Kucera, eds., *In defence of labour market institutions: Cultivating justice in the developing world.* Geneva: ILO, pp. 1–31.

Berk, R. 2007. *Some thoughts on estimating the size of hidden populations: The special case of forced labor,* unpublished ILO paper.

Bernus, E. 1981. *Touaregs Nigériens: Unité culturelle et diversité régionale d'un peuple pasteur,* Office de la Recherche Scientifique et Technique d'Outre Mer No. 94. Paris.

Bhaduri, A. 1973. "A study in agricultural backwardness under semi-feudalism." *The Economic Journal,* vol. 83, no. 329, pp. 120–137.

Bianchi, G.; Popper, M.; Luksik, I. 2007. *Between demand and supply: A regional analysis of the supply and demand for sex services and trafficking in Hungary, Poland, Slovakia, and Slovenia.* Budapest: IOM.

BLESS. 2006. *Emergency, community-based reconstruction of shelter, sanitation, and livelihood for tsunami-affected operations in south India,* Social audit report. AFED/DFID.

Bojanic Helbingen, A. J. 2001. *Balance is beautiful: Assessing sustainable development in the rain forests of the Bolivian Amazon,* PROMAB Scientific Series No. 4. Utrecht: PROMAB.

Bollé, P. 1998. "Supervising labour standards and human rights: The case of forced labour in Myanmar," *International Labour Review,* vol. 137, no. 3, pp. 391–409.

Bonte, P.; Echard N. 1976. "Conception du passé chez les Hausa et les Touaregs Kel Gress de l'Ader," *Cahiers d'Études Africaines,* vol. 16, nos. 1–2, pp. 237–296.

Botte, R. 1999. "Riimaybe, Haratin, Iklani: Les damnés de la terre, le développement et la démocratie." In A. Bourgeot, ed., *Horizons nomades en Afrique sahélienne.* Paris: Karthala.

Bourdieu, P. 1979. *La distinction, critique sociale du jugement.* Paris: Minuit.

Bourgeot, A. 1990. "Identité touarègue: De l'aristocratie à la révolution," *Études Rurales,* No. 46. Paris: CNRS.

Brass, T. 1986. "Unfree labour and capitalist restructuring in the agrarian sector: Peru and India," *Journal of Peasant Studies,* vol. 14, no. 1.

———. 1999. *Towards a comparative political economy of unfree labour: Case studies and debates.* London: Routledge.

———; van der Linden, M. 1997. *Free and unfree labour: The debate continues.* New York: Peter Lang.

Breman, J. 1996. *Footloose labour: Working in the Indian informal economy.* Cambridge: Cambridge University Press.

———. 1999. "The study of industrial labour in post-colonial India—The formal sector: An introductory review." In J. P. Parry, J. Breman, and K. Kapadia, eds., *The worlds of Indian industrial labour.* New Delhi: Sage Publications, pp. 407–431.

———. 2007. *Labour bondage in West India: From past to present.* Delhi: Oxford University Press.

———; Guérin, I.; Prakash, A. 2009. *India's unfree workforce: Of bondage old and new.* New Delhi: Oxford University Press.

———; Lieten, K. 2002. "A pro-poor development project in rural Pakistan: An academic analysis and a non-intervention," *Journal of Agrarian Change,* vol. 2, no. 3, pp. 331–355.

Bundeskriminalamt. 2003. *Lagebild Menschenhandel.* Germany. Available at http://www.bka.de/lageberichte/mh/2003/mh2003.pdf.

Bureau d'Études [BEST]. 2001. *Le travail des enfants domestiques à Maradi et Niamey.* Niamey.

Cadet, J.-R. 1998. *Restavec: From Haitian slave child to middle-class American.* Austin: University of Texas Press.

Canuto, A.; Luz, C. R.; Afonso, J. B., eds. 2003. *Conflitos no campo—Brasil 2003.* Goiânia: CPT Nacional.

Card, D.; Krueger, A. B. 1995. *Myth and measurement: The new economics of the minimum wage.* Princeton, NJ: Princeton University Press.

Cardoso, F. H. 1971. *Política e desenvolvimento em sociedades dependentes—Ideologias do empresariado industrial Argentino e Brasileiro.* Rio de Janeiro: Zahar Editores.

———; Faletto, E. 1973. *Dependência e desenvolvimento na América Latina.* Rio de Janeiro: Zahar Editores.

Carling, J. 2006. *Migration, human smuggling, and trafficking from Nigeria to Europe.* Geneva: IOM.

Castoriadis C. 1975. *L'institution imaginaire de la société.* Paris: Seuil.

Castro, de, A. B. 1984. "As mãos e os pés do senhor de engenho: Dinâmica do escravismo colonial." In P. S. Pinheiro, ed., *Trabalho escravo, economia, e sociedade.* Rio de Janeiro: Paz e Terra.

Charlick, R. B. 1991. *Niger: Personal rule and survival in the Sahel.* Boulder, CO: Westview Press.

Chase-Sardi, M.; Brun, A.; Enciso, M. A. 1990. *Situación sociocultural, económica, jurídico-política actual de las comunidades indígenas en el Paraguay.* Asunción: Centro Interdisciplinario de Derecho Social y Economía Política, Universidad Católica.

Chebel, M. 2007. *L'esclavage en terre d'Islam.* Paris: Fayard.

Cheick Boureima, D. 2001. *L'esclavage et les pratiques analogues: Le point de vue de l'Islam.* Niamey, unpublished.

Chevalier, J. M. 1982. *Civilization and the stolen gift: Capital, kin, and cult in eastern Peru.* Toronto: University of Toronto Press.

Cissé Souleymane, M. 2002. *Pratiques esclavagistes en Afrique, quelle implication sur le développement social? Le cas du Niger,* Mémoire. Geneva: IUED.

Cohen, L. E.; Felson, M. 1979. "Social change and crime rate trends: A routine activity approach." *American Sociological Review,* vol. 44, pp. 588–607.

Cohen, R. 1987. *New helots: Migrants in the international division of labour.* Aldershot, Hants, England: Gower.

Comite Contre L'Esclavage Moderne [CCEM]. 2005. *Enseignements et observations sur la législation française actuelle face à la répression de la servitude.* Paris.

Council of Europe. 2005. Convention on action against trafficking in human beings and its explanatory report, Council of Europe Treaty Series No. 197. Available at www.coe.int.

———. 2006. *The situation of migrant workers in temporary employment agencies,* Report of the Committee on Migration, Refugees, and Population, Doc. 11130. Brussels: Council of Europe.

Danailova-Trainor, G.; Belser, P. 2006. *Globalization and the illicit market for human trafficking: An empirical analysis of supply and demand,* Declaration Working Paper No. 53. Geneva: ILO.

Daru, P.; Churchill, C.; Beemsterboer, E. 2005. "The prevention of debt bondage with microfinance-led services," *The European Journal of Development Research,* vol. 17, no. 1, pp. 132–154.

Dean, B. 1995. "Múltiples régimenes de valor: Intercambio desigual y la circulación de bienes intercambiables de Fibra de Palmera entre los Urarina," *Amazonía Peruana,* vol. 13, no. 25, pp. 75–118.

De Cock, M. 2007. *Directions for national and international data collection on forced labour,* Declaration Working Paper No. 30. Geneva: ILO.

De Neve, G. 1999 "Asking for and giving baki: Neo bondage or the interplay of bondage and resistance in the Tamil Nadu power-loom industry." In J. P. Parry, J. Breman, and K. Kapadia, eds., *The worlds of Indian industrial labour.* New Delhi: Sage Publications.

—. 2005. *The everyday politics of labour: Working lives in India's informal economy.* New Delhi: Social Sciences Press.

Derks, A. 2005. *Khmer women on the move: Migration and urban experiences in Cambodia.* Amsterdam: Dutch University Press.

Donnelly, R. A., Jr. 2004. *The complete idiot's guide to statistics.* New York: Alpha.

Eltis, D. 2001. "The volume and structure of the transatlantic slave trade: A reassessment," *The William and Mary Quarterly,* vol. 58, no. 1, pp. 17–46.

Engelshoven, M. 1999. "Diamonds and Patels: A report on the diamond industry of Surat," *Contributions to Indian Sociology,* vol. 33, nos. 1–2, pp. 353–377.

Ercelawn, A.; Nauman, N. 2001. *Bonded labour in Pakistan.* Geneva: ILO.

Ernst, C. 2007. "Recent dynamics in Brazil's labour market," Economic and Labour Market Paper 2007/10, ILO. Geneva.

Ethical Trading Initiative [ETI]. 2006. *The ETI code of labour practice: Do workers really benefit?* Sussex: Institute of Development Studies.

European Commission. 2004. *Report of the experts group on trafficking in human beings.* Brussels: Directorate-General Justice, Freedom, and Security.

—. 2007. *Report of the sub-group on the policy needs of data on trafficking in human beings (THB) to the expert group meeting of 03 December 2007,* JLS/D2/RT/at D(2007)16526. Brussels: Directorate-General Justice, Freedom, and Security.

Europol. 2005. *Legislation on Trafficking in Human Beings,* Annex III. The Hague.

—. 2003. *Trafficking of human beings: A Europol perspective.* The Hague.

Figueira, R. R. 2004. *Pisando fora da própria sombra: A escravidão por dívida no Brasil contemporâneo.* Rio de Janeiro: Civilização Brasileira.

Finley, M. I. 1991. *Escravidão antiga e moderna.* Rio de Janeiro: Graal.

Fiorentini, G.; Peltzman, S. 1995. *The economics of organized crime.* Cambridge: Cambridge University Press.

Fogel, R.; Engerman, S. L. 1974. *Time on the cross.* New York: W. W. Norton.

Free the Slaves; Human Rights Center at the University of California at Berkeley. 2004. *Hidden slaves: Forced labor in the United States.* Washington, DC, and Berkeley, CA.

Fuglestad, F. 1983. *A history of Niger, 1850–1960.* Cambridge: Cambridge University Press.

Furtado, C. 1966. *Subdesenvolvimento e estagnação na América Latina.* Rio de Janeiro: Civilização Brasileira.

Gado, B. 1980. *Le Zarmataray: Contribution à l'histoire des populations d'entre Niger et Dallol Mawri,* Études Nigériennes, No. 45. Niamey: IRSH.

Gao, Y.; Poisson, V. 2005. *Le trafic et l'exploitation des immigrants Chinois en France.* Geneva: ILO.

Gazdar, H. 1999. *Review of Pakistan poverty data,* Monograph Series No. 9. Islamabad: Sustainable Development Policy Institute.

—; Khan, A.; Khan, T. 2002. *Land tenure, rural livelihoods, and institutional innovation,* mimeo. Collective for Social Science Research. London, DFID.

Genicot, G. 2002. "Bonded labor and serfdom: A paradox of voluntary choice," *Journal of Development Economics,* vol. 67, pp. 101–127.

Gorender, J. 1978. *O escravismo colonial.* São Paulo: Editora Ática.

—. 1991. *A escravidão reabilitada.* São Paulo: Editora Ática.

Gray, A. 1997. "Freedom and territory: Slavery in the Peruvian Amazon." In International Work Group for Indigenous Affairs, *Enslaved peoples in the 1990s.* Copenhagen: Anti-Slavery International.

Guérin, I.; Palier, J., eds. 2005. *Microfinance challenges: Empowerment or disempowerment of the poor?* Pondichéry: French Institute of Pondichéry.

———; Venkatasubramanian, G.; Churchill, C. 2005. "Bonded labour, social capital, and microfinance: Lessons from two case studies," *Indian Journal of Labour Economics,* vol. 48, no. 3, pp. 521–536.

Hall, G.; Patrinos, H. A., eds. 2006. *Indigenous peoples, poverty, and human development in Latin America.* London: Palgrave Macmillan.

Hamani, D. 1975. *Le Sultanat Touareg de l'Ayar: Au carrefour du Soudan et de la Berbérie,* Études Nigériennes, No. 38. Niamey: IRSH.

———. 1994. "Une gigantesque falsification de l'histoire." In *Éléments de réponse au Programme cadre de la "Résistance Armée," Niyya,* vol. 4, Niamey, pp. 5–8.

———. 2001. *L'esclavage au Niger: Histoire et survivance,* unpublished paper.

Hamit, A. 1997. *La piste du commerce transsaharien: Tripoli–Lac Tchad.* Paris: Université Paris VIII.

Hart, K. 1973. "Informal income opportunities and urban employment in Ghana," *Journal of Modern African Studies,* vol. 11, no. 1, pp. 61–89.

Hassane, A. 2002. "Mariage précoce: Un fléau social au Niger." *Alternative,* vol. 270.

Henkemans, A. 2001. *Tranquilidad and hardship in the forest: Livelihood and perceptions of Camba forest dwellers in the northern Bolivian Amazon,* PROMAB Scientific Series 5. Riberalta, Bolivia: PROMAB.

Howard, N.; Lalani, M. 2008. "Editorial introduction: The politics of human trafficking," *St. Anthony's International Review,* vol. 4, no. 1, pp. 5–15.

Hussein, M., et al. 2004. *Bonded labour in agriculture: A rapid assessment in Sindh and Balochistan, Pakistan.* Islamabad: ILO.

İçduygu, A., Köser Akçapar. 2004. *Labour outcome of irregular migration and human trafficking in Turkey: Forced labour or not?* Working Paper. Geneva: ILO.

ICMPD. 2006. *Guidelines for the development and implementation of a comprehensive national anti-trafficking response.* Vienna.

———. 2007. *Listening to victims: Experiences of identification, return, and assistance in South-Eastern Europe.* Vienna.

Idrissa, K. 1980. *Guerres et sociétés, les populations du Niger occidental au XIXème siècle et leurs réactions face à la colonisation, 1896–1906,* Études Nigériennes, No. 46. Niamey: IRSH.

———, ed. 2001. *Le Niger: Etat et démocratie.* Paris: L'Harmattan.

International Labour Organization [ILO]. 2001. *Stopping forced labour: Global report under the follow-up to the ILO Declaration on Fundamental Principles and Rights at Work,* Report of the Director-General, International Labour Conference, 89th session, Geneva.

———. 2002a. *Human trafficking from Albania, Moldova, Romania, and Ukraine for labour and sexual exploitation: Methodology guidelines for the rapid assessment survey.* Geneva.

———. 2002b. *Combating child labour: A handbook for labour inspectors.* Geneva.

———. 2003. *Individual observation concerning Convention No. 29, Forced Labour, 1930, Niger (ratification: 1961),* Report of the Committee of Experts on the Application of Conventions and Recommendations. Geneva.

———. 2004. *Towards a fair deal for migrant workers in the global economy,* Report VI, International Labour Conference, 92nd session, Geneva.

———. 2005a. *A global alliance against forced labour: Global report under the follow-up to the ILO Declaration on Fundamental Principles and Rights at Work,* Report of the Director-General, International Labour Conference, 93rd session, Geneva.

————. 2005b. *Human trafficking and forced labour exploitation: Guidance for legislation and law enforcement.* Geneva.

————. 2006a. *Labour inspection,* Report III (Part 1B), International Labour Conference, 95th session, Geneva.

————. 2006b. *Global employment trends.* Geneva.

————. 2006c. *The end of child labour: Within reach.* Global report under the follow-up to the ILO Declaration on Fundamental Principles and Rights at Work 2006. Geneva: ILO.

————. 2007a. *Eradication of forced labour,* Report III (Part 1B), International Labour Conference, 96th session, Geneva.

————. 2007b. *Guide to private employment agencies: Regulation, monitoring, and enforcement.* Geneva.

————. 2008. *In search of decent work: Migrant workers' rights: A manual for trade unionists.* Geneva.

International Organization for Migration [IOM]. 2005. *Data and research on human trafficking: A global survey.* Geneva.

————. 2007. *Trafficking in human beings and the 2006 World Cup in Germany,* MRS No. 29. Geneva.

Iskander, N. 2000. "Immigrant workers in an irregular situation: The case of the garment industry in Paris and its suburbs." In OECD (ed.), *Combating the illegal employment of foreign workers.* Paris: OECD.

Jatoba, V. 2002. *Labour inspection within a modernized labour administration.* Lima: ILO.

Juhasz, J. 2005. *Forced labour and trafficking into labour exploitation in Hungary,* unpublished.

Jureidini, R.; Moukarbel, N. 2004. "Female Sri Lankan domestic workers in Lebanon: A case of 'contract slavery'?" *Journal of Ethnic and Migration Studies,* vol. 30, no. 4, pp. 581–607.

Kadi Oumani, M. 2005. *Un tabou brisé: L'esclavage en Afrique.* Paris: L'Harmattan.

Kapadia, K. 1999. "Gender ideologies and the formation of rural industrial classes in South India today." In J. P. Parry, J. Breman, and K. Kapadia, eds., *The worlds of Indian industrial labour.* New Delhi: Sage Publications, pp. 329–352.

Kidd, S. W. 1994. *Los indígenas Enxet: Condiciones laborales.* Asunción: Centro de Documentación y Estudios.

Kiryan, T.; van der Linden, M. 2005. *Trafficking of migrant workers from Ukraine: Issues of labour and sexual exploitation.* Geneva: ILO.

Kloosterboer, W. 1960. *Involuntary labour since the abolition of slavery: A survey of compulsory labour throughout the world.* Leiden: E. J. Brill.

Knight, A. 1988. "Debt bondage in Latin America." In L. Archer, ed., *Slavery and other forms of unfree labour.* London: Routledge.

Knorringa, P. 1996. *Economics of collaboration: Indian shoemakers between market and hierarchy.* New Delhi: Sage Publications.

————. 1999. "Artisan labour in the Agra footwear industry: Continued informality and changing threats." In J. P. Parry, J. Breman, and K. Kapadia, eds., *The worlds of Indian industrial labour.* New Delhi: Sage Publications.

Korvinus, A. 2005. *Trafficking in human beings: Supplementary figures,* Fourth Report of the Dutch National Rapporteur. The Hague: NRM.

Kuptsch, C., ed. 2006. *Merchants of labour.* Geneva: ILO/IILS.

Kutnick, B.; Belser, P.; Danailova-Trainor, G. 2005. *Methodologies for global and national estimation of human trafficking victims: Current and future approaches,* Declaration Working Paper No. 29. Geneva: ILO.

Kwong, P. 1997. *Forbidden workers: Illegal Chinese immigrants and American labor.* New York: New Press.

Le Breton, B. 2002. *Vidas roubadas: A escravidão moderna na Amazônia Brasileira.* Goiânia: Edições Loyola.

Lerche J. 2007. "A global alliance against forced labour? Unfree labour, neo-liberal globalization, and the International Labour Organization," *Journal of Agrarian Studies,* vol. 7, no. 4, pp. 425–452.

Lim, L. L. 1998. *The sex sector: The economic and social bases of prostitution in Southeast Asia.* Geneva: ILO.

Limanowska, B. 2005. *Trafficking in human beings in South Eastern Europe.* Focus on Prevention, UNICEF/UNOHCHR/OSCE-ODIHR. Published by UNDP.

Lins, J.; Stepan, A. 1999. *A Transição e consolidação da democracia—A experiência do sul da Europa e da América do Sul.* São Paulo: Paz e Terra.

Lovejoy, P. E. 2000. *Transformations in slavery: A history of slavery in Africa,* 2nd ed. Cambridge: Cambridge University Press.

Mahajan, V. 2007. "From microcredit to livelihood finance." In T. Dichter and M. Harper, eds., *What's wrong with microfinance?* London: Practical Action Publishing, pp. 242–249.

Maikorema, Z. 1985. *Contribution à l'histoire des populations du sud-est Nigérien: Le cas du Manga XVIème–XIXème siècles,* Études Nigériennes, No. 53. Niamey: IRSH.

Malpani, R. 2006. *Legal aspects of forced labour and trafficking in Europe,* Declaration Working Paper No. 48. Geneva: ILO.

Margulis, S. 2003. *Causas do desmatamento na Amazônia Brasileira.* Brazilia: World Bank.

Markon, J. 2007. "Human trafficking evokes outrage, little evidence," *Washington Post,* September 23.

Martin, P. 2006. "Regulating private recruiters: The core issues." In C. Kuptsch, ed., *Merchants of labour.* Geneva: ILO/IILS, pp. 13–26.

Meillassoux, C., ed. 1986. *Anthropologie de l'esclavage.* Paris: Presses Universitaires de France.

Millet, D. 2002. "L'échec des politiques d'ajustement au Niger," *Alternative,* no. 275.

Naqvi, N.; Wemhöner, F. 1995. "Power, coercion, and games landlords play," *Journal of Development Economics,* vol. 47, no. 2, pp. 191–205.

National Commission for Enterprises in the Unorganised Sector [NCEUS]. 2007. *Report on conditions of work and promotion of livelihoods in the unorganised sector.* New Delhi.

National Labor Committee. 2006. "U.S.-Jordan Free Trade Agreement descends into human trafficking & involuntary servitude." New York.

National Sample Survey Organisation [NSSO]. 2005. *Indebtedness of farmer households, NSS 59th Round, Jan.–Dec. 2003,* Report No. 498(59/33/1). New Delhi.

Neumayer, E.; de Soysa, I. 2007. "Globalisation, women's economic rights, and forced labour," *The World Economy,* vol. 30, no. 10, pp. 1510–1535.

Nicolas, G. 1975. *Dynamique sociale et appréhension du monde au sein d'une société Haoussa.* Paris: Institut d'Ethnologie.

Nikolic-Ristanoviç, V., et al. 2004. "Trafficking in people in Serbia," *Temida,* vol. 8, no. 4, pp. 5–14.

O'Connell Davidson, J. 2006. "Will the real sex slave please stand up?" *Feminist Review,* vol. 83, no. 1, pp. 4–22.

Organization for Economic Cooperation and Development [OECD]. 1996. *Trade, employment, and labour standards: A study of core worker's rights and international trade.* Paris.

OECD, IMF, ILO, and CIS STAT. 2002. *Measuring the non-observed economy: A handbook.* Paris: OECD.

Olivier de Sardan, J.-P. 1969. *Les voleurs d'hommes: Notes sur l'histoire des Kurtey,* Études Nigériennes, No. 9. Niamey: IRSH.

———. 1984. *Les sociétés songhay-zarma: Chefs, guerriers, esclaves, paysans.* Paris: Éditions Karthala.

Oumarou, M. 2001. *Défis et opportunités pour la Déclaration au Niger,* Declaration Working Paper No. 4. Geneva: ILO.

Pacheco, P. 1994. *Determinantes y tendencias del mercado de trabajo de temporada en la empresa agricola de Santa Cruz,* internal document. Santa Cruz: CEDLA.

Pakistan. 2003. *Accelerating economic growth and reducing poverty: The road ahead,* Poverty Reduction Strategy Paper. Islamabad.

Patnaik, U. 1983. "On the evolution of the class of agricultural labourers in India," *Social Scientist,* vol. 11, no. 7, pp. 3–24.

Pereira, S.; Vasconcelos, J. 2008. *Combating human trafficking and forced labour: Case studies and responses from Portugal.* Geneva: ILO.

Pieke, F., et al. 2004. *Transnational Chinese: Fujianese migrants in Europe.* Stanford, CA: Stanford University Press.

Pina-Guerassimoff, C., et al. 2002. *La circulation migratoire de quelques nouveaux migrants Chinois en France.* Paris: Documentation Française.

Platform for International Co-operation on Undocumented Migrants [PICUM]. 2005. *Ten ways to protect undocumented migrant workers.* Brussels.

Platteau, J.-P. 1995. "An Indian model of aristocratic patronage," *Oxford Economic Papers,* vol. 47, no. 4, pp. 636–662.

Potts, L. 1990. *World labour market: A history of migration.* London: Zed Books.

Premchander, S., et al. 2006. *From bondage to freedom: ILO PEBLISA's experience in South Asia.* New Delhi: ILO.

Quivy, R.; Van Campenhoudt, L. 1995. *Méthodologie de la recherche en sciences sociales.* Paris: Dunod.

Rangel, V., ed. 1993. *Direito e relações internacionais.* São Paulo: Editora Revista dos Tribunais.

Rath, N. 2005. "Revival of cooperatives," *Economic and Political Weekly,* vol. 40, no. 43, pp. 4582–4584.

Ray, D. 1998. *Development economics.* Princeton, NJ: Princeton University Press.

Raynaut C.; Abba S. 1990. "Trente ans d'indépendance: Repères et tendances," *Politique Africaine,* no. 38, pp. 3–30.

Renshaw, J. 1996. *Los indígenas del Chaco Paraguay: Economía y sociedad.* Asunción: Editora Intercontinental.

Roesch, M.; Venkatasubramanian, G.; Guérin, I. 2009. "Bonded labour in the rice mills: Fate or opportunity?" In J. Breman, I. Guérin, and A. Prakash, eds., *India's unfree workforce: Old and new practices of labour bondage.* New Delhi: Oxford University Press, pp. 284–311.

Roesch, M. et al. Forthcoming. *Impact assessment of PEBLISA in Tamil Nadu,* Declaration Working Paper. Geneva: ILO.

Sakamoto, L. 2005. *Trabalho escravo no Brasil do século XXI.* Brasilia: ILO.

Salifou, A. 1971. *Le Damagaram ou Sultanat de Zinder au XIXème siècle,* Études Nigériennes No. 27. Niamey: IRSH.

———. 1993. *La question Touarègue au Niger.* Paris: Karthala.

Santana, E. 1993. *Órfaos da abolição: Tráfico de trabalhadores e trabalho escravo.* Fortaleza: Imprensa Oficial do Ceará.

Santos, R. 1993. *O problema do trabalho forçado no Brasil contemporâneo: Subsídios ao informe da delegação do Governo do Brasil à Conferência Internacional do Trabalho.* Brasília: Ministério do Trabalho.

Sathya, M. 2005. "Bonded labour in Tamil Nadu: A challenge for labour administration." In A. Sivananthiran and C. S. Venkata Ratnam, eds., *Informal economy: The growing challenge for labour administration.* Geneva: ILO; New Delhi: Indian Industrial Relations Association, pp. 185–196.

Scheidel, W. Forthcoming. "The Roman slave supply." In K. Bradley and P. Cartledge, eds., *The Cambridge world history of slavery.* Vol. 1: *The ancient Mediterranean world.* Cambridge: Cambridge University Press.

Sékou, A. R. 2002. *Étude de base du Projet Espoir.* Niamey: Université de Niamey.

Sen, A. 1999. *Development as freedom.* New York: Anchor Books.

Sento-Sé, J. 2000. *Trabalho escravo no Brasil na atualidade.* São Paulo: LTr.

Sevilla-Siero, C. A. 1991. "Economic development through contrived dependence," *Journal of Comparative Economics,* vol. 15, no. 83, pp. 403–420.

Shelley, L. 2003. "Trafficking in women: The business model approach," *The Brown Journal of World Affairs,* vol. 10, no. 1, pp. 119–131.

Sindh Rural Development Project. 2000. *Social assessment report.* Islamabad: Asian Development Bank.

Somavia, J. 2000. *Perspectives on decent work.* Geneva: ILO.

Squire, S.; Suthiwart-Narueput, S. 1997. *The impact of labour market regulations.* Washington, DC: World Bank.

Srinivasan, T. N. 1980. "Bonded labor contracts and incentives to adopt yield-raising innovations in 'semi-feudal' agriculture," *Indian Economic Review,* vol. 14, pp. 165–169.

———. 1989. "On choice among creditors and bonded labor contracts." In P. Bardhan, ed., *The economic theory of agrarian institutions.* Oxford: Clarendon Press.

Srivastava, R. 2007. *Conceptualising continuity and change in emerging forms of labour bondage in India,* paper presented at the International Seminar "Debt bondage: Issues and perspectives," Institute for Human Development/French Institute of Pondichéry/FNV Vakcentrale (Dutch Trade Union), New Delhi, April 19–20.

Srivastava, R. S. 2005. *Bonded labour in India: Its incidence and pattern,* Declaration Working Paper No. 43. Geneva: ILO.

Steinfatt, T.; Baker, S.; Beesey, A. 2002. *Measuring the number of trafficked women in Cambodia: 2002—Part I,* paper presented at the Human Rights Challenge of Globalization in Asia-Pacific-US, Honolulu, November 13–15.

Stiglitz, J. 2002. "Information and the change in the paradigm in economics," *The American Economic Review,* vol. 92, no. 3, pp. 460–501.

Stoian, D. 2000. "Variations and dynamics of extractive economies: The rural-urban nexus of non-timber forest use in the Bolivian Amazon," doctoral diss. Freiburg: Albert-Ludwigs-Universität.

Stoller, P. 1981. "Social interaction and the management of Songhay socio-political change," *Africa,* vol. 51, no. 3, pp. 765–781.

Sutton, A. 1994. *Slavery in Brazil: Link in the chain of modernisation.* London: Anti-Slavery International.

Tabak, J. 2005. *Probability and statistics: The science of uncertainty.* New York: Checkmark Books.

Taylor, J. R. 1977. "Exploitation through contrived dependence." *Journal of Economic Issues,* vol. 11, no. 1, pp. 51–59.

Tchangari, M. 2002. "L'école publique sous ajustement: Le droit à l'éducation remis en cause," *Alternative,* no. 278.

Temporary Labour Working Group. 2004. *New measures to tackle exploitation of temporary workers in the UK agricultural industry.* London.

Thanh-Dam, T. 2006. *Poverty, gender, and human trafficking in sub-Saharan Africa: Rethinking best practices in migration management.* Paris: UNESCO.

Timidria. 2000. *Contexte démocratique et survivance des pratiques esclavagistes au Niger: Quelle stratégie pour l'éradication, Travaux du Séminaire.* Maradi.

Tinker, H. 1974. *A new system of slavery: The export of Indian labour overseas, 1830–1920.* London: Oxford University Press.

Triaud, J.-L. 1982. "L'Islam et l'État au Niger," *Le mois en Afrique,* January 16.

Trivelli, C.; Morales, R. Forthcoming. *Empleo, pobreza, y ascendencia indígena.* Geneva: ILO.

Tyuryukanova, E. 2006. *Forced labour in the Russian Federation today: Irregular migration and trafficking in human beings.* Geneva: ILO.

UNICEF. 1994. *Analyse de la situation des femmes et des enfants au Niger.* Agadez, Niger.

United Kingdom. 2007. *UK action plan on tackling human trafficking.* London: Home Office and Scottish Executive.

United Nations [UN]. 1956. *Supplementary Convention on the Abolition of Slavery, the Slave Trade, and Institutions and Practices Similar to Slavery,* Economic and Social Council Resolution 608 (21). Geneva.

————. 2000. *Protocol to Prevent, Suppress, and Punish Trafficking in Persons, Especially Women and Children, Supplementing the United Nations Convention Against Transnational Organized Crime.* Geneva.

United Nations Development Program [UNDP]. 1999. *Human Development Report: Globalization with a human face.* New York.

————. 2005. *Legislative compendium.* Former Yugoslav Republic of Macedonia. Available at www.anti-trafficking.net.

————. 2006. *Human Development Report: Beyond scarcity: Power, poverty, and the global water crisis.* New York.

United States, Department of State. 2005. *Trafficking in persons report.* Washington, DC.

————. 2007. *Trafficking in persons report.* Washington, DC.

————. 2008. *Trafficking in persons report.* Washington, DC.

United States Government Accountability Office [GAO]. 2006. *Human trafficking: Better data, strategy, and reporting needed to enhance U.S. antitrafficking efforts abroad,* Report to the Chairman, Committee on the Judiciary and the Chairman, Committee on International Relations, House of Representatives. Washington, DC.

————. 2007. *Human trafficking.* Report to congressional requesters. Washington, DC.

United States Agency for International Development [USAID]. 2003. *Trafficking in persons: The USAID strategy for response.* Washington, DC.

von Richthofen, W. 2007. *The role of labour inspectors in combating human trafficking and forced labour in Europe,* unpublished background document to ILO expert meeting, Geneva, December 5–6.

Walklate, S. 2005. *Criminology: The basics.* London: Routledge.

Williams, E. 1944. *Capitalism and slavery.* Chapel Hill: University of North Carolina Press.

Yin, R. K. 2003. *Case study research: Design and methods,* 3rd ed., Applied Social Science Research Methods Series No. 5. London: Sage Publications.

Yun, G.; Poisson, V. 2005. *Le trafic et l'exploitation des immigrants chinois en France.* Geneva: ILO.

Zanardini, J.; Biedermann, W. 2001. *Los indígenas del Paraguay.* Asunción: Centro de Estudios Antropológicos de la Universidad Católica.

# The Contributors

**Saidou Abdoulkarimou** is an independent consultant who lives in Niamey, Niger. He has worked as a coordinator and technical adviser on several development projects, including for the European Commission and the German Ministry of Economic Cooperation and Development (BMZ). He did his postgraduate studies in Senegal and holds a DESS from the Institut National Agronomique de Paris Grignon (INAPG), France.

**Beate Andrees** works as an antitrafficking expert for the ILO Special Action Programme to Combat Forced Labour. Before joining the ILO, she was a lecturer at the Free University Berlin and also worked for the German Parliament and the German Office for Foreign Affairs. She studied political science at the Free University Berlin, with a special focus on migration.

**Alvaro Bedoya** is an associate in a private law firm in Washington, D.C. He currently serves on the board of directors of the Hispanic Bar Association of the District of Columbia and serves as cofounder of the Esperanza Education Fund, a college scholarship program for immigrants in the Washington, D.C., area. He has a B.A. in social studies from Harvard University and in 2007 he graduated from Yale Law School.

**Eduardo Bedoya** is professor at the University UPC and the Universidad del Pacifico in Lima, Peru, and in the environmental program at FLACSO, Ecuador. He has worked extensively as a consultant for the ILO to document forced labor practices in various Latin American countries. He holds a Ph.D. in anthropology from the University of Binghamton in New York.

**Patrick Belser** is an economist with the ILO, working on forced labor and wage policies. Before working at the ILO, he spent time at the World Bank in

Hanoi and at the Swiss State Secretariat for Economic Affairs. He has a Ph.D. in economics from the Institute of Development Studies (IDS) at the University of Sussex and has also studied at Columbia University, New York.

**Michaelle de Cock** is an international consultant who has worked extensively on forced labor and child labor issues. She has worked for various international organizations, including the ILO, the International Organization for Migration (IOM), UNICEF, and the NGO Terre des Hommes. She holds a Ph.D. in mathematics from the University of Paris VI.

**Isabelle Guérin** is a researcher at the French Institute of Pondichéry, of the French Ministry of Foreign Affairs. She is a socioeconomist specializing in interactions among household behavior, vulnerability, and social justice. She has taught in various universities, including in Toulouse and Geneva. She holds a Ph.D. in economics from the Université Lyon II.

**Ali Khan** is assistant professor at the Lahore University of Management Sciences in Pakistan, where he teaches courses on child and bonded labor, the anthropology of development, and applied methods of research. He has worked in Washington, D.C., for the World Bank's South Asia Region. He has an M.Phil. and a Ph.D. in social anthropology from the University of Cambridge.

**Rohit Malpani** is a lawyer and human rights advocate, currently working as a senior campaigns adviser at Oxfam America, an international development and humanitarian agency. Previously, he worked as a consultant for the World Health Organization and with local civil society groups in Thailand and Argentina. He has a doctorate in jurisprudence from the New York University School of Law and started his legal career as an intellectual property attorney with a law firm.

**Caroline O'Reilly** is a senior specialist for the ILO's Special Action Programme to Combat Forced Labour. Before joining the ILO she worked for the UK's Department for International Development (DFID) and as a social scientist at the Natural Resources Institute. She holds an M.Sc. in agricultural economics from Wye College, University of London.

**Roger Plant** is the head of the International Labour Organization's Special Action Programme to Combat Forced Labour. He has been a leading investigator and activist on forced labor and modern slavery for more than thirty years and is the author of several books. He has a B.A., M.A., and D.Phil. from Oxford University and has also held several academic positions.

**Marc Roesch** is an agro-economist at the French Institute of Pondichéry, of the French Ministry of Foreign Affairs. His current specialization is household economy and particularly indebtedness in India. He has worked extensively in Africa and for nine years was in charge of the Training Service of the Centre International de Recherche Agronomique pour le Développement (CIRAD). He holds a Ph.D. in agro-economics from Montpellier University.

**Leonardo Sakamoto** is a journalist, coordinator of the NGO Reporter Brasil, and member of Brazil's National Commission for the Eradication of Slave Labour (CONATRAE). Earlier he taught journalism at the ECA-USP and has received several prizes in journalism. He holds a doctorate in political science from the University of São Paulo.

**Maria Sathya** is the national program manager of the ILO's Project "Reducing Vulnerability to Bondage in India through Promotion of Decent Work." She has previously worked for ActionAid India as program manager. She holds an M.A. in social work from Stella Maris College, Chennai, and another in women's studies from Mother Teresa Women's University, Kodaikanal, Tamil Nadu, India.

**Ali R. Sékou** is program manager of ONG Démocratie 2000, an NGO in Niamey, Niger. Previously, he worked at the Ministry of National Education and at the National Institute for Pedagogical Documentation, Research, and Animation (INDRAP). He holds a master's degree from the University of Ouagadougou, Burkina Faso.

**G. Venkatasubramanian** is a researcher at the French Institute of Pondichéry, of the French Ministry of Foreign Affairs, and conducts research, training, and advisory activities in South and Southeast Asia.

# Index

Abdelkader, Gali, 74
Abduction as recruitment mechanism, 4
Abuse of vulnerability, 130–137, 147
Accumulation of assets, 160–161
Action Plan on Tackling Human
  Trafficking of the United Kingdom,
  111
Action plans, national and regional:
  Africa, 113; European Union, 177;
  Niger, 71, 75; Pakistan, 51, 111–112;
  Ukraine, 112; United Kingdom, 111,
  122; United States, 113
Advance payments. *See* Wage advances
*Affaire Siliadin v. France,* 132
Africa: forced labor/slavery figures,
  186(table); labor inspectors shortfall,
  116(table); national action plan, 113;
  prostitution statistics, 185(table);
  slavery in the Islamic world, 6. *See
  also specific countries*
Aggregate estimates, 182
Agrarian reform: Brazil, 32
Agriculture: bonded labor in rice mills,
  155(box); Boukou, Niger, 83–84;
  Brazil's deforestation, 15; factors
  underlying the demand for exploitable
  migrant workers, 103; Gabou, Niger,
  82–83; main products of farms on
  Brazil's Dirty List, 29(fig.);
  methodology for investigating debt
  bondage in Pakistan, 52–54; Niger's
  crops, 87(nn4,6); Niger's history of
  slavery, 73; nut collection sector,
  37–41, 47; objectives of Latin

American study, 37–39; Pakistan's
  self-cultivating agricultural sector,
  57–58; PEBLISA intervention,
  154–157; *peshgi* in Pakistan's
  sharecropping sector, 63–64; *peshgi*
  leading to debt bondage, 66–67;
  recruitment mechanisms for European
  workers, 93; recruitment systems for
  agricultural workers in Pakistan,
  55–59; UK agriculture and
  horticulture, 121. *See also* Brazil
Albania: classification of transit, source,
  and destination countries, 141(table);
  human trafficking research, 91–92;
  recruitment agencies, 107(n7); ways
  of obtaining job offers abroad, 97(fig.)
Amazon basin, 39–40, 45–46
American continents: history of slavery,
  6
Ancient civilizations, 6
Animal husbandry, Niger, 83, 87(nn4,6)
Anti-Slavery International, 74, 145
Arab population, Niger's, 72–73, 79
Aristocracy, Niger's, 73, 78–79, 85
Article 18 permits (Italy), 143, 145–146
Ashaninka people, 39
Assets as indication of household
  economic status, 157–161
Association of the Southeast Asian
  Nations (ASEAN), 113
Association of Traditional Chiefs in
  Niger (ACTN), 74
Asymmetric information, 3, 35
Attorneys, labor, 117–118

Austria: classification of transit, source, and destination countries, 141(table); penal code, 138

Awareness building, 71, 161–163

Azarori, Niger, 84–86

Bahia state, Brazil, 20(fig.), 21(table), 24

Bales, Kevin, 181–182, 186

Balochistan region, Pakistan, 53, 68, 70(nn2,4)

Banking sector: Brazil's punishment of labor regulation offenders, 17–18

Bargaining power, 3; debt bondage in Latin America, 35; institutions mitigating, 110; Pakistan's *peshgi* system, 68–69; resulting from wage advances, 153; trade unions, 125–126

*Barracas* (jungle estates), 40, 45–46

Begging, 53–54

Belarus: classification of transit, source, and destination countries, 141(table)

Belgium: abuse of vulnerability, 135; classification of transit, source, and destination countries, 141(table); defining forced labor, 140; victim protection measures, 144–147

Benefits, worker, 60

Bhutto, Zulfiqar Ali, 60

Blackmail: withholding of wages, threat of denunciation to the authorities, and debt bondage, 138–139

*Blanqueo de madera* (wood laundering), 39

Bolivia: accessibility of forced laborers, 190; case study findings, 39; documentary evidence of debt bondage, 38–39; duration of debt bondage and nonpayment of wages, 45–46; history of indigenous population's exploitation, 37; income inequality, 49(n2); indigenous population in labor supply, 36; labor inspectors, 117; magnitude of forced labor, 46(table), 47; manipulation of debt, 43; recruitment through wage advances, 41–42

Bonded labor: defining, 51; global estimates on forced labor and slavery figures, 187; persistence of, 7–8; rice mill workers, 155(box); structural factors controlling, 152–153; survival factors, 10–11; transnational trafficking and, 2

Bonded labor, Pakistan: agricultural sector, 55–59; fieldwork and information sources, 54–55; industrial sector, 59–62; recruitment systems for agricultural workers, 55–59

Bonded Labour Research Forum (Pakistan), 52

Bonded Labour System (Abolition) Act (1976), 152, 187

Border protections, 89

Bosnia-Herzegovina: classification of transit, source, and destination countries, 141(table)

Boukou, Niger, 83–84

Boycotts, consumer, 49

Brazil: coercion of Brazilian migrants in Portugal, 100–101; country-level statistics, 176–177; dangers to labor inspectors, 116; debt and nonpayment of wages, 27–28; economic activities, 28–30; geography of slave labor, violence, and deforestation, 20–23; internal trafficking of labor, 10; labor inspection and rescue database, 18–20; living and working conditions, 30–31; main products of farms on the Dirty List, 29(fig.); mobile inspection units, 48–49, 117–118; national estimates on trafficking and exploitation, 189; national policy development, 16–18; policy response and penalties for slave labor, 31–32; recruitment, 23–27; slave labor, violence, and deforestation by region, 21(table); slave labor by state, 20(fig.); state of origin of rescued laborers, 24(fig.); state weakness supporting forced labor, 3; statistics on labor inspection and rescue, 19(table)

B-9 regulation, 175

Brick making, 52–53, 60–61, 70(n2), 155

Britain. *See* United Kingdom

Bulgaria: classification of transit, source, and destination countries, 141(table)

Cambodia: prostitution statistics, 183–184

Capable guardian, lack of, 2–3
Capacity, state. *See* State capacity
*Capitalism and Slavery* (Williams), 6
Capture-recapture methodology, 182
Cardoso, Fernando Henrique, 17
Carpet making, 52–53, 55, 67
Casaldáliga, Pedro, 16
*Castaña* collection, 40
Castes, Pakistan's: Khosa caste, 57;
    Kohli caste, 57; Meghwar caste, 57;
    patron-client relationships in non-
    agricultural sectors, 60; patron-client
    relationships in sharecropping areas,
    56–57; recruitment mechanisms based
    on, 61–62, 64–65; Scheduled Castes,
    156, 162(box); Talpur caste, 57;
    women's situation, 162(box)
*Castigo de madera* (wood punishment),
    44
Casual labor: Pakistan's self-cultivating
    agricultural sector, 58
Catholic Church: denunciation of
    Brazilian slave labor, 16
Cattle ranching: Amazon deforestation,
    22–23; Brazil's Dirty List, 29;
    indigenous population as bonded
    slaves, 40; main products of farms on
    Brazil's Dirty List, 29(fig.);
    occupational risks for laborers,
    30–31
*Causas do desmatamento na Amazônia
    Brasileira* (Causes of Deforestation in
    the Brazilian Amazon; World Bank
    report), 22–23
Chaco region, Paraguay and Bolivia, 37,
    39–40, 44, 46–48, 50(n4)
*Changas* (short-term assignments), 40
Charcoal production, 29(fig.)
Chiefs, Niger's, 78
Child labor: ASEAN Declaration against
    Trafficking in Persons, 113; bonded
    labor in India, 153; bonded labor in
    Pakistan, 67; defining forced labor,
    194(n3); ECOWAS Initial Plan of
    Action against Trafficking in Persons,
    113; history of slavery in Niger,
    73–74, 79; *Hoffman* ruling affecting,
    124; interregional Plan against
    Trafficking in Human Beings,
    113–114; statistical figures on, 186;
    UK Action Plan on Tackling Human

Trafficking, 111. *See also* Women and
    children
China: indentured labor and debt
    bondage, 7
Chinese migrants in Europe, 98, 101,
    104, 108(n8)
Cockle pickers, death of, 104, 121
Coercion, x–xi; "abuse of vulnerability"
    as mode of, 130–137; country-level
    statistics, 176; debt and nonpayment
    of wages in Brazil, 27–28; debt
    bondage in Latin America, 35;
    defining forced labor in terms of, 179;
    extraeconomic forms, xi; forms of
    coercion against migrant workers in
    Europe, 99–102; human trafficking in
    Europe, 90; Niger's descendants of
    slaves, 76; obtaining reliable
    information about, 190–193;
    opportunity cost, 8; *peshgi* leading to
    debt bondage, 66; recruitment
    mechanisms, 5; retention of Brazil's
    bonded labor, 15; unequal bargaining
    power, 3. *See also* Debt bondage;
    Wage manipulation
Colonialism: Niger's history of slavery,
    73; slavery and indentured labor,
    6–7
Comisiones Oberas (Spain), 125–126
Committee of Experts on the
    Applications of Conventions and
    Recommendations (CEACR), 76
Common law, 130
Community-based intervention. *See*
    Prevention and Elimination of Bonded
    Labour in South Asia
Community debt bondage, 40
Company store, 33(n1), 38, 43–44, 47
Compulsory labor following slavery, 7
Consensual exploitation, xi–xii
Construction industry, 2–3, 11, 53, 60,
    68–69, 89, 93, 98, 100, 103–105, 126,
    188, 190
Contractors, labor: debt manipulation,
    42–45; *gatos,* 23–24; subcontracting
    chains and, 41–42
Convention on Action Against
    Trafficking in Human Beings, 113,
    130, 143
Corruption: combating Latin American
    debt bondage, 48–49; recruitment

mechanisms for European labor
markets, 95–96(table)
Cottage industries, 60, 62
Cotton cultivation, 29, 29(fig.)
Council of Europe, 113, 130, 138, 143
Courts, labor, 123–125
Credit markets, debt bondage and, 7–8
Crime: sociology and economics of, 2–3
Criminalization of forced labor: abuse of
vulnerability as mode of coercion,
130–137; adherence to human rights
standards, 142–147; Brazil, 16;
criminalization of prostitution, 9;
defining forced labor, 139–140;
effectiveness of, 12; factors inducing,
2–3; forced labor as failure of labor
market governance, 109–110; no
criminalization of movement, 140;
penal laws in countries transitioning
from source to destination country,
140–142; victim protection measures,
142–147; withholding of wages, threat
of denunciation to the authorities, and
debt bondage, 138–139; wrongful
possession of identity documents,
137–138
Croatia: classification of transit, source,
and destination countries, 141(table)
Cultural factors as: obstacle for labor
inspectors, 117
Cyprus: classification of transit, source,
and destination countries, 141(table)
Czech Republic: classification of transit,
source, and destination countries,
141(table)

Dark figure of crime, 194(n4)
Database compilation: Brazilian labor
inspection and rescue database,
18–20; Brazilian labor profile, 23–24;
country-level statistics, 174–176
Death: poor health of Brazilian laborers,
30
Death threats, 127(n6)
Debt bondage: abuse of vulnerability as
mode of coercion, 137; Asia-Pacific
region forced labor victims, 151;
Brazil, 26; Chinese migrants in
France, 101; debt as recruitment
mechanism, 4, 7–8, 15, 23; defining
forced labor in terms of coercion, 179;

duration of bondage and nonpayment
of wages, 45–46; internal trafficking
of labor, 10; Latin America's history
of indigenous exploitation, 37;
manipulation of debt, 42–45;
microfinance as community-based
intervention strategy, 154;
nonpayment of wages in Brazil,
27–28; number of workers involved
in, 46–48; objectives of Latin
American study, 37–39; Pakistan, 52,
66; policy response, 48–49; as
recruitment mechanism, 4; recruitment
mechanisms in cross-border European
labor exchanges, 96(table); Russian
migrant workers, 99–100; Russian
workers, 99–100; Vietnamese laborers
in Poland, 148(n22); withholding of
wages, threat of denunciation to the
authorities, and debt bondage,
138–139. *See also* Wage advances;
Wage manipulation
Decentralization of Pakistan's labor,
60–62
Deception: as forced labor indicator,
192(table); obtaining reliable
information about, 190–193; as
recruitment mechanism, 1, 4
Decision making. *See* Policy response
Declaration Against Trafficking in
Persons, Particularly Women and
Children, 113
Declaration on Fundamental Principles
and Rights at Work, 74
Defining forced labor, ix–xii; abuse of
vulnerability, 134–135; abuse of
vulnerability as mode of, 131–133;
bonded labor, 51; child labor, 194(n3);
clarifying definitions for improved
data collection and analysis, 178–181;
forced labor and discrimination, 75;
lack of definition impeding action
against, 129; slavery and, 6;
trafficking for forced labor, 139–140
Deforestation, 15, 21–23, 21(table)
Deforestation Arc, Amazonia, 22–23
Demand, labor: factors underlying the
demand for exploitable migrant
workers, 103–106; irregular migration
in Europe, 89; low-skilled labor in
Europe, 93

Denmark: classification of transit, source, and destination countries, 141(table); victim protection measures, 144
Department of Labor, US, 146
Deportation of victims, 145–146
Descriptive statistics, 173
Destination countries for trafficked humans: classification of, 141(table); human trafficking in Europe, 91–92; legislative approaches, 130; penal laws in countries transitioning from source to, 140–142; Portugal, 107(n4)
Detection, risk of, 115
Devaluation of work, 42–44
Development, economic: Brazilian model, 16
Diada people, Niger, 84
Direct recruitment, 4
Dirty List (Brazil), 17–18, 28–29, 29(fig.)
Discrimination: continuum of exploitation and, 109; defining forced labor and, 75; labor inspectors, 117; Latin America's indigenous population, 37, 49–50(n2); migrants in the European labor market, 99; Niger's passive slavery, 74; against Niger's slave descendants, 80–86; social origin determining, 71
Disease, 30
Domestic service: abuse of vulnerability as mode of coercion, 133; bonded labor in Pakistan, 53; economic exploitation, 9; European labor markets, 94; factors underlying the demand for migrant workers, 103; family debt bondage, 42; Latin American statistics, 46; Niger's history of slavery, 73; Pakistan's *peshgi* system, 54, 64–65, 67; Paraguayan cattle ranching, 40; researching bonded labor in Pakistan, 54
Drug use and trafficking, 54, 96(table)
Dual economies: Brazil, 16
Dump box savings, 158–159
Dutch Foundation Against Trafficking in Women, 174
Dutch National Rapporteur (BNRM), 174–176

*The Economist,* ix
ECOWAS Initial Plan of Action Against Trafficking in Persons, 113
Education: community-based intervention, 154; inequality in Niger's slave descendants, 85; profile of Brazilian laborers, 24–25; Tamil Nadu community project, 157
Egypt, ancient, 6
Employers: Brazil's Dirty List, 28–29; Dirty List, 28–29; as motivated offenders of forced labor, 2–5; punishment of labor law offenders, 18. *See also* Recruitment, labor; Wage advances; Wage manipulation
Employment tribunals, 123–125
Empowerment, economic and social, 153–154
Enforcement of labor standards, 3; abuse of vulnerability, 147; combating Latin American debt bondage, 48; death threats as result of, 127(n6); human trafficking in Europe, 89; labor inspection, 115, 119; national action plans, 111–114; Niger's colonial slavery, 73. *See also* Criminalization of forced labor
*Enganche* recruitment mechanism, 40–41, 45, 47, 110
Escape: debt bondage in Brazil, 27–28; Niger's slaves' unwillingness to, 79–80
Espirito Santo, Brazil, 21(table), 28
Estonia: classification of transit, source, and destination countries, 141(table)
Ethical Trading Initiative (ETI), 104, 121
Ethnicity: Niger's history of slavery, 72–73; Pakistan's recruitment, 61–62; Tamil Nadu community project, 156–157
EU Action Plan, 177
EU Council Directive 2004/81/EC, 142–143
EU Council Framework Decision (2002), 141
European Convention of Human Rights, 133, 144
European Court of Human Rights (ECHR), 132–133
European Union (EU): abuse of vulnerability as mode of coercion,

131; adherence to human rights standards, 142–147; defining forced labor, 139–140; expanding data collection efforts, 177; factors underlying the demand for exploitable migrant workers, 103–106; forms of coercion against migrant workers, 99–102; legislation to combat trafficking for forced labor, 130–142; methodology of human trafficking studies, 90–92; national action plan, 111–113; no criminalization of movement, 140; penal laws in countries transitioning from source to destination country, 140–142; recruitment mechanisms for cross-border labor exchanges, 95–96(table); recruitment mechanisms for trafficked humans, 93–99; victim protection measures, 142–147; ways of obtaining job offers abroad, 97(fig.); withholding of wages, threat of denunciation to the authorities, and debt bondage, 138–139; wrongful possession of identity documents, 137–138

Europol, 8–9

Executive Group for the Suppression of Forced Labour (GERTRAF; Brazil), 17

Exploitation, economic and sexual: abuse of vulnerability, 135–136; consensual exploitation, xi–xii; continuum of, 109; debt and nonpayment of wages in Brazil, 27–28; defining forced labor and human trafficking, x–xi, 179–181; defining slavery and forced labor, 6; global estimates on economic, state-imposed, and sexual, 187(fig.), 188; human trafficking in Europe, 89; as objective of trafficking, 8–9; obtaining reliable information about, 190–193; Palermo Protocol, 13(n3); victim protection measures, 145–146

Expropriation of lands, 32

Extortion, 100–102

Factories Act, 119

Factory Act (Pakistan), 61

Family: debt bondage of Chinese migrants in France, 101; Niger's

slavery through inheritance, 79; recruitment mechanisms in cross-border European labor exchanges, 96(table); ways of obtaining job offers abroad, 97(fig.), 98. *See also* Women and children

Family debt bondage: abuse of vulnerability as mode of coercion, 135–136; Latin America, 38, 40, 42; rice mill workers in India, 155(box)

Financial constraints of migrant labor, 94, 98

Finland: classification of transit, source, and destination countries, 141(table)

First Rent Act (1859; India), 70(n5)

Fisheries, 52–53, 65

Formal labor sector, Pakistan's, 60–61

France: abuse of vulnerability as mode of coercion, 132–134; classification of transit, source, and destination countries, 141(table); coercion of Chinese migrants in, 101; dangers to labor inspectors, 116; defining forced labor, 139–140; demand for migrant workers in the garment industry, 103; exploiting Niger's slave population, 73; human trafficking report, 91–92; labor standards, 114

Freedom of movement, restricting: as coercive factor against migrant workers, 102; elements indicating forced labor situations, 179; gangmasters in the United Kingdom, 121; Jordan's QIZ, 119. *See also* Wage advances; Wage manipulation

French Institute of Pondichéry, 156

Gabou, Niger, 82–83

Gandhi Peace Foundation, 187

Gangmasters, 104, 121–122

Gangmasters (Licensing) Act (2005), 104, 121

Gangmasters Licensing Authority (GLA), 121–122

Garcia, Alan, 36

*Gatos* (labor contractors), 23, 25–27

Gender equality, 161–165

Georgia: classification of transit, source, and destination countries, 141(table)

Germany: abuse of vulnerability, 134–135; classification of transit, source, and destination countries, 141(table); country-level statistics, 175–176; defining forced labor, 139; demand for exploitable migrant labor, 105

Glass bangle manufacturing, 53, 65, 70(n3)

*A Global Alliance Against Forced Labour* (ILO global report), viii, 15

Global estimates on forced labor and trafficking, 181–193

*Global Report* (ILO publication), 189

Goianésia, Brazil, 31

Gold as asset, 160

Goods, overvaluation of, 44

Government Accountability Office, US (GAO), 182

Greece: classification of transit, source, and destination countries, 141(table); wage protection, xiii

Greece, ancient, 6

Guarani people, 39–40, 46

*Habilitacion* recruitment mechanism, 40–41, 45

*Habitus,* 79–80

Hausa people, 72–73

Hazardous industries, Pakistan's, 52–53, 60

Health of laborers in Brazil, 30

Historical perspectives: forced labor, 5–9; land-related violence in Brazil, 22

*Hoffman Plastics v. National Labor Relations Board,* 123–124

Honor, payment of debt as, 27

Horso people, 83–84

Household economic status, 157–161

Household financial management, 163–164

Human development index, 72–73

Human rights standards, 142–147

Human trafficking: abuse of vulnerability as a mode of coercion, 130–137; Brazil's internal trafficking of labor, 10; defining forced labor, x–xi, 139–140; economic exploitation as objective of, 8–9; European case studies, 11; factors underlying the demand for exploitable migrant workers, 103–106; forced labor and, 179–181; forms of coercion against migrant workers in Europe, 99–102; global estimates on victims of, 181–182, 188; human rights standards, 142–147; legislation to combat trafficking for forced labor, 130–142; methodology of European studies, 90–92; no criminalization of movement, 140; obtaining reliable information about, 190–191; Palermo Protocol, 13(n3), 129; penal laws in countries transitioning from source to destination country, 140–142; policies against forced labor and trafficking, 110–114; recruitment mechanisms for European workers, 93–99; state weakness supporting, 3; statistical figures on, 182–185; successful migrants and victims of trafficking, 92; victim protection measures, 142–147; vulnerability of workers, 2; withholding of wages, threat of denunciation to the authorities, and debt bondage, 138–139; wrongful possession of identity documents, 137–138. *See also* Palermo Trafficking Protocol

Human Trafficking Centre (UK), 111

Hungary: classification of transit, source, and destination countries, 141(table); human trafficking report, 91–92

Hunting, 31

Identity documents: indications of forced labor, 179, 193; wrongful possession of identity documents, 133, 137–138

ILO Forced Labour Convention, No. 29, ix, 6, 50(n4), 109, 178–179

ILO Forced Labour Convention, No. 105, ix

ILO Protection of Wages Convention No. 95, 13(n1)

Immigration authorities, threat of: abuse of vulnerability, 133, 136–137; indications of forced labor, 179, 193; withholding of wages, threat of denunciation to the authorities, and debt bondage, 138–139; wrongful possession of identity documents, 137–138

Impunity, 109

Indentured labor, 6–7, 13(n2)
India: estimates on victims of trafficking, 186–187; forced labor/slavery figures, 186(table); hidden and open bonded labor, 190; indentured labor and debt bondage, 7–8; labor inspection, 119; legislation against forced labor, xii; structural factors controlling bonded labor, 152–153; tenants' rights, 70(n5); trade unions combating sex trafficking, 126. *See also* Prevention and Elimination of Bonded Labour in South Asia
Indigenous and Tribal People's Convention (1989), 50(n4)
Indigenous population: combating Latin American debt bondage, 49; income inequality in Bolivia and Peru, 49(n2); India's rice mill workers, 155(box); Latin American case study findings, 39; magnitude of Latin American forced labor, 47–48; manipulation of debt, 43–44; recruitment through wage advances, 42; sugar plantations of Bolivia, 40; vulnerability of Latin America's, 36–37
Industrialized countries: forced labor/slavery figures, 186(table); human trafficking, 89; labor inspectors shortfall, 115, 116(table); prostitution statistics, 185(table)
Industrial Revolution, 114
Industrial sector, Pakistan's: low wages and *peshgi* leading to long-term bondage, 67–68; recruitment of Pakistani laborers, 55–56, 59–62
Inferential statistics, 173
Inflation of debt, 42–44
Informal economy: Brazil, 16; demand for exploitable migrant labor, 105; labor inspectors, 116–117; Pakistan, 60–61
Informants, 55
Information: informational constraints of migrant workers, 102; investigating bonded labor in Pakistan, 54–55; labor recruitment, 3–4; obtaining reliable information from migrants, 190–193; recruitment through wage advances, 41; social resources of transborder migrants, 98
Inheritance, slavery through, 79

In-kind payment, 47–48, 64, 71
Inspection, labor: Brazil's database compilation, 18–20; Brazil's labor inspection and worker rescue statistics, 19(table); Brazil's mobile inspection units, 15, 17, 28, 48–49, 117–118; Brazil's slave labor, violence, and deforestation, 21–22; combating Latin American debt bondage, 48–49; inspectors as data source, 178; labor inspectors shortfall, 115–116, 116(table); qualified industrial zones in Jordan, 118–119; strengths and weaknesses, 114–117
Institutions. *See* Labor market governance
Inter-American Court for Human Rights, 124
Intermediaries: manipulation of debt, 43–44; Pakistan, 61–62; recruiting migrant workers in Europe, 94, 98; recruitment mechanisms in cross-border European labor exchanges, 95–96(table); recruitment through wage advances, 41–42; ways of obtaining job offers abroad, 97(fig.), 98
Internal trafficking, 182–183
International Catholic Migration Commission (ICMC), 91
International Centre for Migration Policy Development (ICMPD), 177
International Covenant on Civil and Political Rights, 2
International Labour Organization (ILO): abuse of vulnerability as mode of coercion, 136–137; community-based actions, 151–152; defining forced labor, 139–140; denunciation of Brazilian slave labor, 16; elements indicating forced labor situations, 179; Forced Labour Convention, No. 29, ix, 6, 50(n4), 109, 178–179; Forced Labour Convention, No. 105, ix; global estimates on forced labor, trafficking and slavery, 181–182, 186–188; monitoring abusive recruitment practices, 120; Niger's ratification of the conventions, 73; PEBLISA community-based intervention design, 153–155; Protection of Wages Convention No.

95, 13(n1); trafficking figures, 183–185; withholding of wages, threat of denunciation to the authorities, and debt bondage, 138–139. *See also* Prevention and Elimination of Bonded Labour in South Asia

International Organization for Migration (IOM), 177

Internet: recruiting migrant workers, 94

Interviews: Azarori, Niger, 84–86; discrimination against Niger's slave descendants, 81; European human trafficking, 91; Gabou, Niger, 82–83; investigating bonded labor in Pakistan, 53, 55; Latin American case studies, 38; Niger's nomadic and pastoral regions, 78–79; obtaining reliable information about, 190–191

Involuntariness, 179, 191–193

Ireland: victim protection measures, 144

Irregular migration, 89, 93, 108(n13)

Irular community, Tamil Nadu, India, 155(box)

Islamic world, 6

Israel: classification of transit, source, and destination countries, 141(table)

Italy: abuse of vulnerability, 135; classification of transit, source, and destination countries, 141(table); operational guidelines for labor inspectors, 116; prosecuting labor trafficking, xii–xiii; slavery during the Roman Empire, 6; victim protection measures, 143–144, 146

Jajmani system, 57

*Jamadar* (labor agent), 58

Japan: indentured labor and debt bondage, 7

Java: indentured labor and debt bondage, 7

Job creation, 152

Jordan: qualified industrial zones, 118–119

Kadi Oumani, Moustapha, 74

Kidnapping as recruitment mechanism, 4

Kinship: recruitment based on, 61–62

Kosovo: classification of transit, source, and destination countries, 141(table)

Labor costs, 2

Labor inspection. *See* Inspection, labor

Labor market governance, 2–5; Brazil's labor market inequalities, 16; driving slavery and indentured labor, 7–8; employment tribunals, 123–125; forced labor as failure of, 109–110; holistic perspective of combating forced labor, 126; inspection of qualified industrial zones in Jordan, 118–119; mobile inspection units in Brazil, 117–118; monitoring abusive recruitment practices, 120–126; national action plans, 111; Philippine Overseas Employment Administration, 122–123; recruitment mechanisms, 3–5; strengths and weaknesses of labor inspection, 114–117; trade unions, 125–126; victim protection measures, 123–126

Labor standards, 3, 35, 49, 114. *See also* Enforcement of labor standards

Labour Inspection Convention (No. 81), 114–115

*Lagebild Menschenhandel,* 175–176

Land access and use: land grabbing, 18; Niger's slaves and slave descendants, 80–82, 84; seizure of Brazilian slaveholders' lands, 32

La Strada organization, 91

Latin America: duration of debt bondage and nonpayment of wages, 45–46; forced labor/slavery figures, 186(table); labor inspectors shortfall, 116(table); labor standards, 114; magnitude of forced labor, 46–48, 46(table); manipulation of debt, 42–45; prostitution statistics, 184, 185(table). *See also specific countries*

Latvia: classification of transit, source, and destination countries, 141(table)

League of Nations Slavery Convention (1926), 6

Legal recruitment mechanisms, 95–96(table)

Legislation: to combat trafficking for forced labor, 130–142; empowering labor inspections, 115; against forced labor in Europe, 129. *See also* Policy response

Life events, payment for, 65

Literacy, 49

Lithuania: classification of transit, source, and destination countries, 141(table)

Living conditions: Brazil's debt bondage, 16; Brazil's labor force, 30–31; debt for accommodation, 27

Loans: Pakistan's domestic workers, 64–65; Pakistan's sharecropping sector, 63–64; PEBLISA services, 158. *See also* Debt bondage; *Peshgi;* Wage advances

Logging industry, 39

Low-technology sector, 36, 93. *See also* Agriculture

Luxembourg: classification of transit, source, and destination countries, 141(table)

Macedonia: classification of transit, source, and destination countries, 141(table); wrongful possession of identity documents, 137–138

Maize cultivation, 29(fig.)

Manipulation of debt, 42–45

Maranhão state, Brazil, 20(fig.), 21(table), 24–25

Markov chain Monte Carlo (MCMC) method, 182

Marriage: Niger's slave descendants, 81–85

Mato Grosso state, Brazil, 20(fig.), 21(table), 23

Media: Brazilian awareness of slave labor, 31; increasing coverage of labor and trafficking, 178; independent media combating debt bondage, 49; Niger's slave-liberation hoax, 75; Niger's vibrant media, 72; recruitment mechanisms in cross-border European labor exchanges, 95(table)

Menace of penalty, 179

Mental deficiency, 135

Mestizos, 39

Methodology: bonded labor in Pakistan, 51–55; Brazilian labor inspection and rescue database, 18–20; global estimates on victims of trafficking, 182, 186–188; household economic status, 157–161; human trafficking in Europe, 90–92; Niger study, 75–78; objectives of Latin American study, 37–39; PEBLISA impact assessment, 156–157; probability sampling, 189–190

Mexico: employment tribunals, 124

Microfinance. *See* Prevention and Elimination of Bonded Labour in South Asia

Middle East: labor inspectors shortfall, 116(table); prostitution statistics, 185(table)

Middlemen. *See* Intermediaries

Migrant workers: employment tribunals, 124; irregular migration in Europe, 89; successful migrants and victims of trafficking, 91; trade unions, 126

Military labor, 1

Military rule, 60

Minas Gerais state, Brazil, 20(fig.), 21(table)

Minimum Wage Act, 119

Mining industry, 52–55, 60–61, 67

Ministry of Labour and Employment (Brazil), 117

Mobile Inspection Group (Brazil), 17, 19

Mobile Inspection Unit (MIU; Brazil), 15, 17, 28, 48–49, 117–118

Moldova, 141–142, 141(table); human trafficking research, 92; ways of obtaining job offers abroad, 97(fig.)

Moneylenders, 63–64

Monopolistic control of subsistence goods, 43

Morales, Evo, 36

Morality, 162(box)

Motivated offender, 2, 103

Multiple-case study, 37–39

Murder, 21–22, 28

Myanmar, 188

National Action Plan Against Human Trafficking (UK), 122

National Commission for the Eradication of Slavery (CONATRAE; Brazil), 17

National Institute for Colonization and Agrarian Reform (INCRA; Brazil), 17–18

National Institute for Space Research (INPE; Brazil), 22

National Labor Committee (NLC), 118–119

National Labor Relations Act, 124

National Labour Institute, 187

National policies, 110–114

National Policy and Plan of Action for the Abolition of Bonded Labour and the Rehabilitation of Freed Bonded Labourers (Pakistan), 51, 111–112

Neobondage, 8, 45, 153

Nepalese Transport Workers Union Yatayat Mazadoor Sangh, 126

Netherlands: abuse of vulnerability as mode of coercion, 132; B-9 regulation, 175; classification of transit, source, and destination countries, 141(table); country-level statistical analysis, 174–175

Niger: discrimination against slave descendants in non-nomadic populations, 80–86; history of slavery, 72–73; national estimates on trafficking and exploitation, 189; occupations, wage payments, and working conditions, 80; persistence of slavery in nomadic and pastoral regions, 78–80; population distribution, 72; post-independence slavery legislation, 73–75; research methodology, 75–78

Nomads, 72, 74

Nongovernmental organizations (NGOs), 133; community-based intervention strategies, 154; denunciation of Brazilian slave labor, 16; empowering communities through PEBLISA project, 151, 156–157; human trafficking in Europe, 91; Niger slavery study, 76; victim protection measures, 144–145

Nonpayment of wages: abuse of vulnerability as mode of coercion, 133; Niger, 71; obtaining reliable information about, 191; Pakistan's debt bondage, 68; withholding of wages, threat of denunciation to the authorities, and debt bondage, 138–139. *See also* Wage manipulation

Norway: classification of transit, source, and destination countries, 141(table)

Nut collection sector, 37–41, 47

Occupational risks: Brazil's cattle ranching, 30–31

Oceania: indentured labor and debt bondage, 7

Offenders, statistical information, 175

Opportunity cost, labor's, 8

Organization for Security and Cooperation in Europe (OSCE), 113

Organization of American States (OAS), 28

Organized crime networks, 96(table)

Pakistan, 10–11; agricultural sector recruitment, 55–59; agricultural sector wage manipulation, 63–64; fieldwork and information sources, 54–55; hidden and open bonded labor, 190; industrial sector recruitment, 59–62; labor inspection, 119; low wages and *peshgi* leading to long-term bondage, 67–68; methodology for investigating bonded labor, 51–55; national action plans, 111–112; national estimates on trafficking and exploitation, 189; *peshgi* in the nonagricultural sectors, 64–65; reasons for recourse to *peshgi*s, 65–67; self-cultivating agricultural sector, 57–59; statistics on bonded workers, 69; wage manipulation, 62–68

Palermo Trafficking Protocol: abuse of vulnerability as mode of coercion, 130–137; defining forced labor, 139–140; defining forced labor and human trafficking, 179–181; enactment of, 129; labor inspectors' importance, 115; legislation to combat trafficking for forced labor, 130; victim protection measures, 142–147

Paraguay: case study findings, 39; government response to debt bondage, 36; history of indigenous population's exploitation, 37; ILO forced labor convention, 50(n4); indigenous population in labor supply, 36, 40; lack of labor inspection, 48–49; magnitude of forced labor, 46(table), 47–48; sampling methods, 190

Pará state, Brazil, 20–21, 20(fig.), 21(table), 23–27, 26(fig.), 31

Passive slavery, Niger's, 74

Pastoral Land Commission (CPT; Brazil), 16, 18–19, 22, 117

Patron-client relations, Pakistan, 56–57, 59–60, 63–64

*Patrones* (bosses), 41, 44

Penal codes, 75, 129. *See also*
Criminalization of forced labor;
Penalties against forced labor
employers
Penalties against forced labor employers:
Brazil's criminalization of forced
labor, 16–18, 31–32; legislation to
combat trafficking for forced labor,
130–142; Niger, 75; sanctions against
employers of irregular migrant labor,
108(n13)
Pereira Ferreira, José, 28
Permanent labor: Pakistan's self-
cultivating agricultural sector, 58–59
Peru: case study findings, 39; duration of
debt bondage and nonpayment of
wages, 46; government response to
debt bondage, 36; history of
indigenous population's exploitation,
37; ILO forced labor convention,
50(n4); income inequality, 49(n2);
indigenous population in labor supply,
36; magnitude of forced labor,
46(table); manipulation of debt,
43–44; policy response to debt
bondage, 48; recruitment through
wage advances, 41–42
*Peshgi* (Pakistan's credit payment
system): industrial sector, 61–62; low
wages and *peshgi* leading to long-term
bondage, 67–68; nonagricultural
sectors, 64–65; reasons for recourse
to, 65–67; recruitment in the
agricultural sector, 57; self-cultivated
agricultural sector, 58–59;
sharecropping sector, 63–64; unequal
bargaining power, 110
Peul-Fulani people, 72
Philippine Overseas Employment
Administration (POEA), 122–123
Physical deficiency, 135
Piauí state, Brazil, 24–25
Plan Against Trafficking in Human
Beings, Especially Women and
Children, 113–114
Plan for the Eradication of Slave Labour
(Brazil), 32
Plan on Best Practices, Standards, and
Procedures for Combating and
Preventing Trafficking in Human
Beings, 113
Poison, 30–31

Poland: classification of transit, source,
and destination countries, 141(table);
conviction of traffickers, 148(n22)
Police: country-level statistical analysis,
174–175; support for labor inspectors,
116; victim protection measures,
144–146
Policy dialogue: targeting debt bondage
in Peru and Paraguay, 35–36
Policy response: addressing systemic
global labor problems, xiii; Brazil's
policy development, 16–18;
combating debt bondage through trade
policy, 49; debt bondage in Latin
America, 48–49; importance of good
statistics, 173; to murder of slave
laborers in Brazil, 28; Niger and
Mauritania strengthening policy, 71;
policies against forced labor and
trafficking, 110–114. *See also*
Criminalization of forced labor; Labor
market governance
Polish workers, xii–xiii
Political will, 115
Portugal: classification of transit, source,
and destination countries, 141(table);
coercion of migrant workers,
100–101; demand for exploitable
migrant labor, 105; as source and
destination country, 107(n4)
Poverty and discrimination against
minority groups: abuse of
vulnerability, 131, 135; Niger's slave
descendants, 72, 82–83; recruitment
methods, 4; vulnerability of workers,
2
Poverty reduction programs, 49
Prevention and Elimination of Bonded
Labour in South Asia (PEBLISA),
151; community-based intervention,
154; control and social pressure of
India women, 162(box); impact
assessment, 156–157; impact on
household debts and assets, 157–161;
social empowerment of women,
161–165; strategy of community-
based intervention, 153–155
Preventive policies: Brazil, 32
Prison labor, 1
Private employment agencies, xiii,
93–96(table)
Private underground economy, 1

Probability sampling, 189–190
Profile of Brazilian laborers, 24(fig.), 26;
   Brazil, 23–24
Profits: cattle-ranching in Brazil, 23;
   motivating offenders, 2; sexual
   trafficking figures, 185; wage
   manipulation increasing, 5
Proletarization of workers, 7
Property, seizure of, 32
Prosecuting labor trafficking, xii–xiii,
   129, 177
Prostitution, 2; estimated totals,
   185(table); recruitment methods, 4;
   statistical figures, 183–185,
   183(table). *See also* Sex trafficking
Public Prosecution Service (PPS;
   Netherlands), 174–176
Punjab region, Pakistan, 53, 57–59

Qualified industrial zones (QIZ; Jordan),
   118–119
Quechua people, 40

*Rahaks* (permanent agricultural
   laborers), 58–59
Recognition of forced labor: Brazil's
   policy response, 17
Recruitment, labor: Brazil, 23–24;
   Brazil's debt bondage, 15; Brazil's
   rescued workers by area of
   recruitment, 26(fig.); British
   gangmasters, 121–122; criminalization
   of, 141; defining slavery and forced
   labor, 6; *enganche* system, 40;
   European case studies of trafficking,
   11; European labor market, 107(n7);
   *habilito* in the Amazon basin, 40;
   human trafficking in Europe, 89;
   impact on all forms of forced labor,
   10; indentured labor and debt
   bondage, 7; Latin American
   mechanisms, 40; magnitude of Latin
   American forced labor, 47;
   mechanisms of, 3–5; migrant labor in
   Turkey, 104; monitoring abusive
   recruitment practices, 120–126;
   Niger's lack of, 79–80; obtaining
   reliable information about, 191;
   Pakistan's agricultural sector, 55–59;
   Pakistan's industrial sector, 59–62;
   Pakistan's patron-client relationships,
   57; Pará, Brazil, 25–27; *peshgi* wage

advance system, 62–68; POEA
   monitoring, 122–123; rice mill
   workers, 155(box); wage advances,
   41–42; ways of obtaining job offers
   abroad, 97(fig.)
Reflection period, 144–145, 175
Refugee Convention (1951), 144
Regional action plans, 113–114
Regional policies, 110–114
Regulation of labor, 11–12; British
   gangmasters, 121–122; debt bondage
   in Latin America, 35; human
   trafficking in Europe, 89
Reported cases, 182
Rescued workers, Brazil, 18–20,
   19(table), 21–24, 24(fig.), 25, 26(fig.),
   176
Research methodology. *See*
   Methodology
Residence permits, 142–146
Restriction of freedom of movement. *See*
   Freedom of movement, restricting
Returned migrants, 90
Rice mill workers, 155(box)
Road blockers, Niger's, 77
Roman Empire, 6
Romania: classification of transit,
   source, and destination countries,
   141(table); human trafficking
   research, 92; ways of obtaining job
   offers abroad, 97(fig.)
Rondônia state, Brazil, 21(table), 23
Rural Credit Survey (Pakistan), 69
Russian Federation: classification of
   transit, source, and destination
   countries, 141(table); demand for
   exploitable migrant labor, 105; forms
   of coercion against migrant workers,
   99–100; human trafficking report, 92;
   recruiting migrant workers, 94;
   sanctions against employers of
   irregular migrant labor, 108(n13);
   trade unions favoring regulated
   migration, 126

Safety equipment, 30–31
Sampling methods: snowballing, 91
Sanctions, 115
Santa Cruz department, Bolivia, 40–41
Savings and credit groups (SCGs),
   153–154, 158–159, 163–164
Scheduled Castes (SC), 156, 162(box)

Seasonal labor migration, 105, 153
*Seeris* (permanent agricultural laborers), 58–59
Segregation: Niger's slave descendants, 85
Senate Commission report (Bolivia), 39
Sepidari system, 57
Serbia and Montenegro: classification of transit, source, and destination countries, 141(table)
Serfdom: Niger's slave descendants, 81, 85
Service provision, 154
Sex trafficking: abuse of vulnerability as mode of coercion, 130; coercion debate, 9; country-level statistical analysis, 174–175; global estimates on economic, state-imposed, and, 188; Latin American statistics, 46; obtaining reliable information about, 191; statistical figures, 183–185; suppliers' reaction to the demand for, 103; trade unions combating, 126; vulnerability of workers, 2; wage manipulation increasing profits, 5
Shame as threat, 102
Sharecropping: Niger's slave descendants, 81, 85; Pakistan, 56–57; *peshgi* leading to debt bondage, 66–67; self-cultivation and, 58–59; technology's role in, 7–8
Shipibo people, 39
Short-term debt bondage, 45, 47
Sindh province, Pakistan, 53, 57–59, 63–64, 119
Skin color, Niger's slavery and, 72–73, 79
Slavery: in ancient civilizations, 6; defining, 6; Niger's history of, 71–73; Niger's post-independence slavery legislation, 73–75; Niger's slave descendants, 75–76; prostitution as, 9; West Africa's legacy of, 11
Slovak Republic: classification of transit, source, and destination countries, 141(table)
Slovenia: classification of transit, source, and destination countries, 141(table)
Smuggling, x–xi, 8, 94. *See also* Human trafficking
Snowballing method of sampling, 91–92
Soares da Costa Filho, Daniel, 22

Social capital constraints of migrant labor, 94
Social connections, obtaining jobs through, 97(fig.), 98
Social dialogue, xiii
Social empowerment, 153–154
Social exclusion, 155(box)
Social origin and hierarchy, Niger's, 71, 78–80, 82–84
Social protection agencies, 144
Socioeconomic conditions: abuse of vulnerability as mode of coercion, 131; profile of Brazilian laborers, 24
Sociology of crime, 2
Songhaï-Djerma people, 72, 82
Source countries of human trafficking: classification of, 141(table); European studies, 90; legislation combating trafficking, 130; penal laws in countries transitioning from source to destination country, 140–142; Philippine Overseas Employment Administration, 122–123; Portugal, 107(n4); recruitment industry, 93–94
Soybean cultivation, 29, 29(fig.)
Spain: classification of transit, source, and destination countries, 141(table); employment tribunals for undocumented workers, 124–125; trade unions, 125–126
Special Action Programme to Combat Forced Labour (SAP-FL), vii–viii
State capacity: absence of a "capable guardian," 3, 103; combating Latin American debt bondage, 48; debt bondage in Latin America, 36; trade unions and, 125–126
State-imposed labor, 1, 188
Statistical analysis. *See* Methodology
Statistics and demographics: agricultural sector in Pakistan, 56; Asia-Pacific region forced labor victims, 151; Brazil's labor inspection and worker rescue, 19(table); clarifying labor exploitation definitions, 178–181; current forced labor figures, 1; economic, state-imposed, and sexual exploitation, 187(fig.); expanding data collection efforts, 177–178; forced labor/slavery figures, 186(table); geography of slave labor, violence, and deforestation in Brazil, 20–23;

global and national estimates, 177, 181–193, 194(n4); good practices at the country level, 174–177; importance for improved policymaking, 173; labor inspector shortfall, 115; national estimates on trafficking and exploitation, 189; number of workers involved in debt bondage, 46–48; obtaining reliable information, 190–193; Pakistan's bonded laborers, 69; Pakistan's self-cultivating agricultural sector, 57–58; probability sampling, 189–190; profile of Brazilian laborers, 23–25; recruitment in Pará, Brazil, 25–27; trafficking figures, 182–185

*Stopping Forced Labour* (ILO global report), vii

Subcontracting chains, 41–42, 60–62, 89, 105

Subsistence goods, 38, 42–43, 57

Successful migrants, 91, 98

Sugar industry, 29, 40–41, 47, 58

Suitable target, 2–3, 103

Summit of the Americas, 113

Supply chains, slave labor, 18, 49, 89–90

Supreme Court, US, 123

Sweden: classification of transit, source, and destination countries, 141(table)

Switzerland: classification of transit, source, and destination countries, 141(table); prostitution statistics, 184

Tamil Nadu, India, 151, 155(box), 157–158

Tanneries, 53, 70(n3)

Tarija department, Bolivia, 40

Tchintabaraden, Niger, 78, 80

Temporary Labour Working Group (TLWG), 121

Tenancy Act (1885; India), 70(n5)

Tenancy Acts (Pakistan), 56–57

Tenants' rights, 70(n5)

Textiles and garment sector, 103, 118

Threats as form of coercion, 101–102

Timber industry, 39

Timidria, 74–75, 77

Tiruvallar District, India, 154, 155(box)

Tithe, Niger's, 81

Tocantins state, Brazil, 20(fig.), 21(table), 24–25

Togolese laborer, 132–134

Toubou people, 72

Trade unions: Comisiones Oberas, 125–126; employment tribunals and, 124; labor market governance, 125–126; Nepalese Transport Workers' Yatayat Mazadoor Sangh, 126; Pakistan, 60; reducing Latin American workers' vulnerability, 49; regulating gangmasters in the United Kingdom, 121

Trafficking in Persons Report (US government report), xi, xii, 113

Transit countries for human trafficking: classification of, 141(table); human trafficking in Europe, 91–92; legislation combating trafficking, 130; penal laws in countries transitioning from source to destination country, 140–142

Transition economies: forced labor figures, 186(table); labor inspectors shortfall, 115, 116(table); prostitution figures, 185(table)

Transnational human trafficking. *See* Human trafficking

Transportation: costs for indentured laborers, 23; manipulated transport fees for migrant workers in Europe, 100; as obstacle to Niger study, 77

*Travaux Preparatoires,* 131

Travel agencies, 95(table), 97(fig.), 100

Tuareg people, 72–73, 75, 77, 79, 82–86

Turkey: classification of transit, source, and destination countries, 141(table); demand for exploitable migrant labor, 104; human trafficking report, 91–92

T visa, 146

Ukraine: classification of transit, source, and destination countries, 141(table); human trafficking research, 92; national action plan, 112; recruitment agencies, 107(n7); ways of obtaining job offers abroad, 97(fig.)

Undocumented laborers: employment tribunals, 124

Unemployment benefits: Brazil, 23–24

United Kingdom: classification of transit, source, and destination countries, 141(table); demand for migrant workers in the horticulture

industry, 103–104; labor standards,
114; national action plan, 111;
regulating gangmasters, 121–122
United Nations Convention Against
Transnational Organized Crime, x
United Nations Protocol to Prevent,
Suppress, and Punish Trafficking in
Persons. *See* Palermo Trafficking
Protocol
United States: abuse of vulnerability as
mode of coercion, 136; employment
tribunals, 123–124; global estimates
on forced labor and trafficking,
181–182; global-level data collection,
177; Jordan's textiles sector, 118;
national action plan, 113; prostitution
statistics, 184–185; trafficking figures,
182–183; T visa, 146; victim
protection measures, 144, 146–147;
wrongful possession of identity
documents, 137–138
Universal Declaration of Human Rights,
2
Untouchables, 64
Uranium extraction, 72
Usury, 7–8

Validation of Latin American findings,
39
Victim protection measures: adherence
to human rights standards, 142–147;
employment tribunals, 123–125; role
of labor market institutions, 123–126
Victims of Trafficking and Violence
Prevention Act (TVPA), 136–137, 146
Vieira, Jorge, 127(n6)
Vietnamese laborers, 148(n22)
Vigilance committees, 119
Violence: abuse of vulnerability as mode
of coercion, 137; Brazil's slave labor,
violence, and deforestation by region,
21(table); against Chinese migrants,
98, 101; community debt bondage, 40;
against forced laborers in Brazil,
21–22; indications of forced labor,
193; Latin American debt bondage,
40; against migrant labor in Portugal,
101; obtaining economic rent through,
44–45; *peshgi* leading to debt
bondage, 66; retention of Brazil's
bonded labor, 15

Virtual wage deductions, 43
Vulnerability of workers: "abuse of
vulnerability" as mode of coercion,
130–137; employment tribunals
protecting victims, 123–125; India's
agricultural districts, 154–155; labor
inspection, 117; Latin America's
indigenous population, 36–37; migrant
workers in Europe, 99; PEBLISA
intervention, 156–158; recruitment of
workers in Brazil, 25–27; reducing
Latin American workers' vulnerability,
49; structural factors controlling
bonded labor, 152–153; suitable
target, 2

Wage advances: bargaining power
resulting from, 153; debt bondage in
Latin America, 35, 41–42, 47; debt
bondage in Pakistan, 52; defining
bonded labor, 51; duration of debt
bondage and nonpayment of wages,
45–46; *enganche* system, 40;
manipulation of debt, 43–44;
repayment methods, 158(box). *See
also Peshgi*
Wage manipulation: abuse of
vulnerability, 135–137; bonded labor
in Pakistan, 52; debt and nonpayment
of wages in Brazil, 27–28; identifying
and prosecuting forced labor, xii–xiii;
ILO Protection of Wages Convention
No. 95, 13(n1); impact on all forms of
forced labor, 10; low wages and
*peshgi* leading to long-term bondage,
67–68; migrant workers in Europe, 89,
99–102; neobondage and trafficking,
8; nonpayment of wages, 45–46;
Pakistan's industrial sector, 61;
recruitment mechanisms, 4–5. *See
also Peshgi*
Wages: Niger's slaves, 80; PEBLISA
impact assessment, 156–157
Water, potable, 30–31
Weapons, 28, 44–45
Weddings, 65–66
Williams, Eric, 6
Women and children: control and social
pressure of India's women, 162(box);
domestic work on Paraguayan cattle
ranches, 40; economic and social

empowerment through PEBLISA, 157–165; Latin American workers in debt bondage, 46; Niger's history of slavery, 73; Niger's slaves' duties, 80; Niger study, 77; *peshgi* leading to debt bondage, 67; profile of Latin American bonded laborers, 25, 42; rice mill workers, 155(box); victim protection measures, 144; as victims of "bondage within bondage," 152–153; women as sex traffic offenders, 175. *See also* Domestic service; Sex trafficking

Wood extraction, 39, 42, 44, 47
Work, devaluation of, 43–44

Working conditions: Brazil's debt bondage, 16; Brazil's labor force, 30–31; defining forced labor, 139; employment tribunals redressing, 123; hazardous industries in Pakistan, 53; indications of forced labor, 193; Niger's slaves, 80; rice mill workers, 155(box)

World Bank: deforestation in Brazil, 22–23

World Confederation of Labour (WCL), 50(n4)

Yatayat Mazadoor Sangh union, 126
Youth: Brazil's recruited laborers, 26

# About the Book

Two centuries after the abolition of the transatlantic slave trade, at least 12.3 million people are subjected to modern forms of forced labor—in rich countries, as well as poor ones. The authors of Forced Labor present state-of-the art research on the manifestations of these slavery-like practices, why they continue to survive, and how they can be eliminated. Their conceptually rich analysis, combined with insightful case studies from Asia, Europe, and Latin America, is a major contribution on an issue of pressing global concern.

**Beate Andrees** is an antitrafficking expert in the ILO's Special Action Programme to Combat Forced Labour. **Patrick Belser** is an economist with the ILO, where he works on forced labor and wage issues.